JAMES CRACKNELL won gold rowing medals at the Sydney 2000 Olympics and the Athens 2004 Olympics and holds three world records. He writes regularly for the *Daily Telegraph*. His first book, *James Cracknell's No Gym Health Plan,* was published in April 2006.

BEN FOGLE was made famous by the BBC's *Castaway* programme and is now a TV presenter, his shows include *Country file* and *Animal Park*. His first book, *The Teatime Islands* was published in 2003. His latest book, *Offshore*, was also published in April 2006.

'Read this… It's reassuring to know that there is still adventure to be had in this sanitized world as two very different men fight, play games and nearly lose their lives when their boat capsizes.'

The Times

'Our congratulations go to James Cracknell and Ben Fogle, the world's foremost naked transatlantic rowers, on their victorious arrival after 50 days at sea. The pair have crossed the Atlantic using nothing but the power of their own arms in a boat built from a flat-pack, enduring terrible weather, erratic water supplies and a life-threatening capsize just days from the finishing line.'

Telegraph.co.uk

'They survived appalling weather and a life-threatening capsize but lived to tell the tale with humour and honesty in this sure-fire autumn bestseller.'

John Lewis / Waitrose Magazine

'I'm not sure if these guys are insanely brave or just insane… An epic adve

Andy McNab

JAMES CRACKNELL AND BEN FOGLE

THE CROSSING

CONQUERING THE ATLANTIC IN THE
WORLD'S TOUGHEST ROWING RACE

Atlantic Books
London

First published in Great Britain in hardback in 2006 by Atlantic Books,
an imprint of Grove Atlantic Ltd.

This paperback edition published in Great Britain in 2007 by Atlantic Books.

The authors and publisher would like to thank the following for permission
to quote material from 'Californication'. Words and music by Anthony
Kiedis, Michale Blazary, John Anthony Frusciante & Chad Smith © 1999
Moebetoblame Music.
All rights administered by Warner/Chappell Music Ltd, London W6 8BS.

9 8 7 6 5

A CIP catalogue record for this book is available from the British Library.

ISBN 978 1 84354 512 5

Designed by www.carrstudio.co.uk
Printed and bound by CPI Group (UK) Ltd., Croydon, CR0 4YY

Atlantic Books
An imprint of Grove Atlantic Ltd
Ormond House
26–27 Boswell Street
London WC1N 3JZ

BEN

My gratitude and love to darling Marina,
my beautiful girlfriend, best friend and now my wife.

JAMES

Croyde, thanks for inspiring me to be someone you'll hopefully
be proud of and for not forgetting who your daddy is.
Bev there are too many things for me to thank you for.
I owe you one Beautiful.

Contents

Acknowledgements

We would like to thank the following:

Our sponsors – EDF Energy, MITIE, The Glenlivet, Vodafone and FRL.

Our suppliers – Aquapacs, Adidas, Be-Well, Breitling, Carlisle Bay Hotel, Concept 2, Heatermeals, Leica, Lifeventure, Liquorice, Lucozade Sport, Merrel, Musto, Oakley and SIS.

Our supporters – grateful thanks to Ex+Med and all the staff for the medical training and to the RNLI for their invaluable sea survival course. Ian Roots, Steph Westlake and Rob Hamill, thank you for sharing your Atlantic experiences and giving advice – if only we'd acted on it earlier. We'll also always be indebted to Alexis Girardet and the team at Twofour, Kate Humble, Jonathan Marks, Anna Bruce and all at MTC, Alison Griffin and Hilary Murray.

We would also like to thank everybody who sent messages of support and made donations to Children in Need and Q and Fezza for making that possible.

For helping us to get this book out and into the world thank you to Julian Alexander and Peta Nightingale at LAW. Thank you also to Toby Mundy, Daniel Scott, Clare Pierotti and everyone at Atlantic books for your trust in us, your invaluable support along the way and for helping us publish our dream. To Louisa Joyner and Jonny Butler thank you for not only editing the book but lifting our spirits during the race – except, Jonny, for that one Friday night!

Our competitors – I hope you learnt as much about yourselves as we did. Special thanks to *All Relative* for the help before the start of the race, *Gurkha Spirit* for the Christmas Jaffa Cakes and *Atlantic 4* for being there when it really mattered. Thank you also to all the Woodvale staff for organising and administrating the 2005 Atlantic Rowing Race.

Our families – to Grandma Foster, you will be sorely missed. To Dr Chiara Hunt for applying her medical skills to our sorry bodies in Antigua and to Joyce and Roger Turner for proving all the stereotypes about parents-in-law wrong we're forever thankful. To our Mums for never saying how worried you were or doubting us, to our sisters Louise, Tamara and Emily for coming out, helping us prepare and cheering us on and to our Dads, for maintaining mission control and for teaching us the value of a good spreadsheet, and Grandma Fogle, thanks for all those Canadian summers.

To all the other friends and family members who kept us going over the last six months we're immensely grateful for all your love and friendship. We can't list you all here, but you know who you are.

Prologue

BEN

'Can I have a picture with you?' giggled Martine McCutcheon as she handed her camera to a friend, and flung her arm around James Cracknell's broad shoulders.

'You're amazing,' she added, admiring the gold medals around his neck before disappearing into the crowded room.

I lined up behind Chris Tarrant and Melinda Messenger to congratulate Britain's recent Olympic hero. It was late summer 2004 and I was at a celebrity bash at London Weekend Television. The room was brimming over with reality TV contestants and soap stars falling out of tiny dresses. It was an incongruous place to find an Olympic rower, I thought.

More photos and autographs and then it was my turn.

JAMES

The event was the highly inclusive and not at all prestigious National Celebrity Awards, held a month after the Olympics had ended – a time in an athlete's year when any free champagne is gratefully received. Matthew Pinsent and I were presenting an award to Kelly Holmes for being the 'Sporting Celebrity of the Year' and now I was at the after-show party, where everyone was staring round the room trying to find the most famous person in the room to talk to – or in my case, trying to work out who anybody was. *Big Brother* had passed me by while I was out of the country preparing for the Olympics and besides, the soaps are on at the same time as my wife Bev and I are trying to slam-dunk our beautiful boy

Croyde into bed. I hardly recognized anyone – the A-list stars must have missed the RSVP date.

One programme I had seen was *The Million Dollar Property Experiment,* presented by two guys called Colin and Justin. I was telling them how Bev and I enjoyed the show, but the conversation petered out when they asked me what I did and sport didn't really hit their spot. Luckily, somebody else wandered up and saved us all from an embarrassing silence. It was Ben Fogle – the king of BBC daytime. We had met each other once before at a charity dinner, and he was his usual polite and enthusiastic self. We engaged in a bit of nondescript chit-chat, but that was blown out of the water when he said, 'I'm rowing across the Atlantic next year. Do you want to do it with me?'

BEN

As James stared at me, a small furrow appeared on his brow.

'No,' he replied bluntly.

Wow, he doesn't mince his words, I thought as I scurried off in search of another drink.

JAMES

Having just come off the back of four years' preparation for the Olympics, I had spent a month undoing all the good work I'd done to my body, and the idea of rowing 3,000 miles was the last thing on my mind. I also sensed my wife Bev flinch as Ben asked the question.

If I wanted to be considered for the British team at the 2005 World Championships, I would have to report for training on 1 October. This was two weeks away; mentally I was not in a position to make up my mind about whether I wanted to race at Beijing in 2008, but I was sure that I did not want to begin training so soon. I met with Jürgen Grobler, the British Chief Coach, and told him that I'd like to take a year away from the sport to do other things and come back totally refreshed, mentally and physically.

For me, rowing is the ultimate team sport. In a game of football, rugby or cricket, you can still win even if a member of your team has a shocking day. If that happens in rowing, you will lose. In a four-man boat, everybody has to do their 25 per cent or you're going down, meaning that for every moment of a race, your dreams are in other people's hands, and their dreams are in your hands. As I wasn't sure what my dreams were now that the Olympics were over, I knew that I couldn't be trusted with other people's. If I'm honest I hadn't enjoyed much of the rowing over the previous four years; despite being successful I always felt (probably unfairly) I had to motivate Matthew Pinsent and it had drained me of enthusiasm. I did not want anybody to feel that I was a burden and the one that had to be motivated.

So there it was, I now had a 'year off'. What was I going to do? Being a successful British Olympian is a magical thing and is mirrored by the opportunities that come your way. I had the chance to do more writing for the *Daily Telegraph* and TV work, and to speak in public about our preparation for Athens to businesses and schools.

Great as that diversity of activities was, however, there wasn't anything on the horizon to get my competitive teeth into. All I knew was that I wanted to stay in shape, so that I would be in a position to rejoin the national squad and fight for a place at the 2008 Olympics if that dream reignited within me. So I entered marathons and triathlons, and agreed to paddle across the Channel on a surfboard for charity. That should have been enough, but there was still a nagging question at the back of my mind: 'Do you want to row across the Atlantic with me?'

Being a rower, I was well aware of the Atlantic Rowing Race. Our sport is not that big, and anything with oars is happily included. If I'm honest, my perception of the race was tainted by arrogance on my part, as the winner of the inaugural 1997 race was a world silver-medallist New Zealand oarsman, partnered by a sailor and surf-lifeboat rower. Other British guys and girls that had crossed weren't even in the national team – how hard could it be?

I have always loved the movement of rowing; the way the boat cuts through the water propelled by manpower alone and the freedom that being out on the water gives me. I was beginning to miss that feeling already, but I still wasn't ready to commit to the regime of training three

3

times a day, seven days a week for six weeks, followed by a day off spent travelling to or from a training camp or race. There was, however, a big space in my year off for some sort of competition at the end of 2005, just before I would be forced to make a decision on whether I would don the British Lycra full time again.

I spoke to some of my rowing colleagues about whether they fancied a row across the pond; I didn't receive any enthusiastic responses. I knew that if I entered the race, even though it is billed primarily as an adventure, I would want to win. Would doing it with Ben give me the best chance of winning it? No. On the other hand, there was part of me that thought I might enjoy not being the favourite for once. Having spent much of the last ten years being in the boat that most people in the world wanted to beat, the chance to be an underdog with no pressure was appealing.

I got in contact with Ben.

BEN

I had been thinking about rowing the Atlantic for some time, having heard about the Woodvale Atlantic Race in 2001 when Debra Veal hit the headlines. Hers was an inspirational story: when her husband dropped out of the race after only a few days, she decided to continue on her own and, against all the odds, succeeded in crossing 3,000 miles of ocean by herself. I had been bowled over not only by the fact that it was possible to row across an ocean at all, but that there was even an organized race in which to do so. I was intrigued and, more importantly, tempted. At this stage I should point out that I've never really rowed. I tried it once at school on the River Stour, but was hopelessly uncoordinated and lacking in balance, so naturally I wouldn't have any problems rowing across the Atlantic. Clearly, if I was to do it, I needed someone who knew what they were doing.

I had been hatching this plan for months, therefore, when I turned up at the ITV summer party, but it's fair to say it was somewhat hazy. I was determined that I would take part in the race but I'd given almost no thought to who I would persuade to accompany me. I had considered placing a 'small ad' asking for a 'fellow rower' and running auditions for those who responded. It would have been a sort of 'Rowing Idol' but I didn't feel that I was equipped to judge the winner. As far as more experienced rowers were concerned I knew next to nothing about the 'oarsome foursome'. Like the rest of the UK, I was aware of the prowess of Messrs Redgrave, Foster, Pinsent and Cracknell, but I had no idea which of them I'd most like to spend six weeks alone at sea with.

The first part of my evening at the awards was taken up with committing myself wholeheartedly to the drinks that were being liberally distributed and I'm fairly certain that the alcohol on offer contributed to my later decision to approach James. At the time it had seemed like too good an opportunity to miss: I was sorely in need of a renowned oarsman and there one was, sandwiched between two celebrity decorators, ripe for the picking. Looking back I realize it was a definitively serendipitous moment. If I hadn't approached James then, I'm not sure that I ever would have had the courage to do so. I certainly haven't done anything like it before or since. And my choice was particularly incongruous. Matthew Pinsent was about to announce his retirement and would be looking for new projects to take on. He would have been an obvious candidate. For all I knew James was still an Olympian first and foremost – his gaze unflinchingly focused on Beijing – and my suggestion could well have stuck in his memory purely for its strangeness, like an after-dinner anecdote: 'You'll never guess what Ben Fogle, you know, the TV presenter with the Labrador, asked me to do...' I had no idea that he had, in fact, absorbed my invitation and was considering it as I left him to continue making inroads into ITV's alcohol budget for 2004.

JAMES

After I had persuaded Ben's agent that I was not a stalker, she agreed to forward an email to him. Having thought it over for quite some time, I told her that I was interested in doing the race and asked if I could meet up with Ben to have a chat about it.

Ben is one of the most positive people I've ever met – a quality which was not lost on me when trying to judge my potential rowing partner's likelihood of turning into a suicidal (or worse, homicidal) maniac in the middle of the Atlantic. If he was either of those things, then he was hiding it very well. Don't be fooled by the posh accent, slightly bumbling manner (think Hugh Grant in, well, in any film) and comfortable upbringing at public school: Ben is incredibly competitive and driven by a fierce desire to succeed. Just look at what he's achieved since coming off the *Castaway* island; sure, he gained the initial benefit of being on Britain's first reality show, but he'd done well to make himself a long-term career from it.

I never saw him on the show, as I was in and out of the country preparing for the Sydney Games; he didn't see any of the Sydney Olympics, as he was stuck on an island. That pretty much sums up how much we knew about each other when we agreed to enter the race together.

Ben was going to take part in the race anyway and had somehow scraped together the considerable entry fee and the deposit for a boat – a fact that made the race a very real possibility, rather than an idle conversation. We spoke about the financial cost of the race. Once the race fee, boat, equipment, food and communications had been paid for, it was going to cost about £70,000 – a huge amount of money to find in such a short time. We stood a better chance of getting sponsorship than most, but it would still take work to secure it and we were leaving it very, very late.

On top of the expense of doing the race, of course, I also had to take into account the loss of earnings that would result from being away from home for such a long time. Of all the ways to earn money as a retired professional sportsman, corporate speaking is one of the most profitable. Most companies have their conferences in a key financial quarter and it would be foolish of me to be away from home then. I enjoy the speaking and it is flattering that people are interested and seem to enjoy the inside track on how we prepared for the Olympics. But I find it hard talking about something I've done without having another major goal. The question I least look forward to is 'What are you doing now?' as nothing seems as worthwhile as the answer 'I'm in training for the next Olympics.'

Participating in the race would mean I wouldn't be talking about past achievements. I'd actually be doing something again: rowing across the Atlantic. I knew that, mentally, it would be a good thing for me to aim for, allowing me to make the most of my year away from the sport.

More importantly still, I had family responsibilities, both financially and as a husband and father. We'd just bought a new house that needed a lot of work, and despite her own professional commitments and despite being in the middle of writing a book, Bev had taken on the vast majority of the childcare while I was training for the Olympics. Was it unbelievably selfish of me to go away for six or seven weeks? I tried to console myself that I'd been away a lot more when I was rowing, often for six months of the year; at the end of the day, six weeks wasn't that big a deal... except that I'd be away over Christmas.

I left the meeting telling Ben that I was interested, but that I couldn't justify doing it if we didn't get sponsorship for the race. I had my family commitments, while Ben only had to look after his dog, Inca the Labrador, the 'one luxury item' he was allowed to take with him on *Castaway*. I made sure he knew that it was one luxury item that wouldn't be allowed on the boat.

BEN

About a month after the party, a 'You have mail' message appeared on my desktop. It was from James Cracknell. He explained that he had been thinking about my question, and that in retrospect he would like to retract his 'no' and meet to discuss the idea further. I was thrilled.

We organized to meet at the Hogarth sports club in Chiswick, near James's home. I was nervous about seeing him, and I remember thinking that he looked a lot larger than I had remembered him being at the party, but my faculties were slightly impaired that evening so I dismissed the recollection. James was straight to the point: he explained that he had a son and a wife to support and that he couldn't just leave them for a jolly, but that he was taking a sabbatical from rowing and was essentially free during the race dates, from late November 2005 to January 2006. In short, he was now very much interested.

The problem was that James had recently announced that he was taking a year out from rowing, and he didn't want to confuse issues by revealing his intention to row across the Atlantic, so we agreed to keep it quiet. This conversation left me with rather mixed feelings. I was genuinely excited, not only that James had agreed to be my rowing partner, but that the project was finally off the ground. I was flattered, too, that James had agreed to row with me, a novice. But the fact that we couldn't announce James's decision put me in a difficult position. I had already begun conversations with sponsors and knew that, quite reasonably, they were reluctant to commit without knowing who the second rower was to be. Sponsoring James Cracknell and Ben Fogle was one thing; discovering that you have actually sponsored Ben Fogle and Jimmy Savile would have been quite another. If I was to secure the money we needed I had to be able to tell people exactly who they were giving their cash to. We decided to put the project on hold for a couple of months while I fulfilled filming commitments out in Namibia. We still had over a year to plan the expedition and we planned to meet again the following year.

In January 2005, Woodvale Events, the organization that runs the Atlantic Rowing Race, were showing at the *Daily Telegraph* Travel and Adventure show at Olympia. They would have a boat with them as well as an assortment of ex-ocean rowers, and it seemed the perfect opportunity to publicly announce our participation in the event, but James still felt it was too early. We agreed a compromise and decided that I would announce my intention to row the Atlantic. That way, we could formally start looking for sponsors and if that failed, we still had our secret weapon: James.

A photocall was held. Several dozen photographers came down to the show, but the call failed to generate much press interest. Then, about a week later, I was at a party in London and a diarist from the *Daily Mail* asked me about the race. The penny dropped when I revealed to her that all past competitors had rowed it naked.

'Naked?' she said, in a splutter of champagne.

'I believe so,' I shrugged.

The next day, the paper ran a large story about my intention to row the Atlantic NAKED, and this seemed to capture the public imagination. I was baffled, but the press loved the idea. It seemed crazy that my intention to row 3,000 miles across the Atlantic was of less interest than the prospect of my nakedness, particularly given that the only person who would be able to appreciate my fine physique would be James, but then we British have always had a sniggering, *Carry On* fascination with bottoms and bareness and I was happy to play along with it if it was going to help us pay for the boat.

I was filming for *Countryfile* in the Shetlands at that point and was beginning to have considerable anxieties about how our endeavour was going to pan out. So far all I had from James was a gentleman's agreement – he could, quite reasonably, withdraw at any point. I, however, was already in hock for signing up to the race. There was absolutely no going back for me and if James was unable to take part in the race I had very little time to find another rower. It was crunch time. I rang James to discuss our predicament and was slightly floored that he was incandescent with rage at *me*.

'Why did you tell the BBC about the race without discussing the pitch with me first?' he demanded. He explained that the commissioning editor had asked him about the rowing and told him that the BBC were unlikely to want the documentary. 'You've jeopardized the whole project. If we're going to film it we've got to go about it properly and not put in half-arsed proposals,' said James.

It wasn't a great start to our relationship; we still didn't know each other and already we were stepping on toes. I was astonished by his reaction; he knew I was trying to find a broadcaster for the project as it had been one of his terms for coming on board. I was disappointed, and began to doubt his intentions.

'James, I don't think this is going to work,' I sighed down the phone while sheltering from a bitter Shetland wind, 'I have to get this project under way.' I'd already invested more than £10,000 in race fees and we didn't have a boat or, more to the point, a sponsor. James was still reluctant to announce his involvement, and we were running out of time.

'Mate, I want to do it, we just need to work as a team on this,' he countered. He had a point; if we couldn't communicate at this stage, then it was unlikely we would fare better out in the middle of the Atlantic. We talked through our differences and I explained my financial concerns. James agreed to split the costs we'd met to date. It was a very tangible step in what had up until that stage been a purely theoretical partnership and, for me, it was the moment I felt that we were truly in this together. We arranged to meet up again in London, and put together a strategy that would in principle work for both of us. We had also had our first disagreement, and something told me it wouldn't be the last.

JAMES

It should have been about this time that I expressed to Bev how seriously I was planning to race if we got the sponsorship, rather than saying, 'There's no point in discussing it too much until I know for sure that I'm doing it.'

If I could go back in time there are many aspects of our preparation I would change, and discussing the race in more detail – and earlier – with Bev would be one of them. I should have explained to her all the safety procedures we have to go through, and I should have said that the fact that I wanted to go away for six weeks didn't mean I loved her any less.

In the event, Ben and I dithered and didn't make much use of the first half of the year to plan, which left us in a huge rush to get ready, operating on the Japanese industrial model of Just In Time Management. I learnt a hell of a lot while planning this adventure, but one of the biggest lessons was to be thankful for the easy life of a full-time athlete. Make no mistake, my preparation for the Olympics was tough, my whole life revolving around getting myself in the best possible shape, mentally and physically, for 21 August 2004; but looking back it was pretty easy. Yes, I was training all day nearly every day, but the training programme was set, there were doctors, physios, dieticians, physiologists and sport psychologists working with us, the boats were bought and taken wherever in the world we needed them, and I was sponsored and supported by the National

Lottery. For this race, we had to do everything, from getting the boat built and paid for, to sorting out the sponsorship, planning our diet, setting a training programme and taking the safety and navigation courses, not to mention doing our normal day jobs as well.

To think Ben and I thought people were joking when they said they'd spent up to two years planning the project. When we really got stuck in to our preparations there were only four months to go until the start of the race.

By this point I'd inadvertently committed myself to the race without having secured any sponsors. As I remember it in my mind, I sat down and had a conversation with Bev about the pros and cons of doing the race and although she didn't agree about the pros or want me to do it, she said OK. Bev steadfastly believes that this talk all took place 'in my mind' and there was no discussion; one of us is wrong.

I had, though, avoided telling my rowing coach, Jürgen. I knew he wouldn't want me to take part in a race where competitors lose on average a stone and a half; having forced me to lift weights to build muscle for ten years, he did not want to see me lose it all in six weeks. I should have told him and let Ben get on with announcing to the press that we were doing the race. If we had done, getting a sponsor would not have been such a struggle against time.

I think, if I'm honest, I had concerns over people's reaction to me doing a race with a TV presenter. I was worried that it would look like I just wanted to race to be on TV, otherwise I'd have chosen a better partner to help win the race. Those concerns disappeared quickly over the course of our preparations, when I began to get to know Ben. The Atlantic Rowing Race is about far more than just being able to row. Two British international rowers started a previous race and lasted just one day before being rescued by helicopter, whereas Debra Veal had continued on her own when her husband, an experienced rower, had had to leave the boat because of his fear of the open ocean. This race is more about the mind and less about the body, and I was confident that Ben had the qualities needed to tough it out in a battle with the mind. He had completed the gruelling Marathon des Sables, spent a lot of time at sea and a year on a deserted island. As I said earlier, do not be fooled by the accent; competitiveness is not class-based.

What he can't do, however, is row. And by the time I definitely made up my mind to race he didn't have the time left in which to get the movement naturally engrained, which is vital when you're going to be rowing for twelve solid hours a day. Given more preparation time I would have had no worries, but as our boat was not due to touch the water until we were out in the Canaries, it was clear that Ben would have to complete all of his rowing education on the Ergo machine in the gym.

BEN

We were nowhere near ready. Not only did we have to build our boat, but we had to pass a Yachtmaster Ocean Theory course, and pass a sea survival test, not to mention organizing the shipping of our boat and equipment and addressing the small business of my learning to row. It was a mountain to climb, but James was still keen to keep shtum.

Without any sponsors, I was forced to buy the boat against my mortgage. James still hadn't confirmed his involvement – I trusted James, but I was again facing a nagging doubt in terms of his commitment. Why was he so eager to keep it a secret? We were running out of time, and by now I had invested nearly £30,000 of my own money in the project. It was nearly the end of the financial year and most companies and businesses had long allocated all their sponsorship budgets. If we didn't find sponsors now, we never would and the race would be off.

As for the boat itself, that was still just a wooden shell. I had a list of 200 components that would have to be fitted and added before she was ocean-worthy, and while James may have been a rower, neither of us had a clue about ocean-rowing boats. We had to find solar panels and batteries, a VHF radio and navigation lights, Sea-me and GPS units, antennae and a stove. Most people had been training on their boats all year. Ours wasn't even waterproofed.

As time marched on, I became even more concerned about our lack of preparation. James needed to make a firm commitment to the project, and we arranged to meet once again at the Hogarth.

We needed £70,000 and so far didn't have a penny. James assured me it would be fine, but I wasn't so confident. The problem was that few people had heard about the race; there had been little pre-publicity about the event and neither companies nor broadcasters were willing to invest in something 'invisible'.

The answer seemed obvious; we needed to make a big announcement, make a splash about our participation and then proactively target sponsors whose profiles would fit with the ideals of the race. I needed James's total commitment or we wouldn't make it to the start line. We had just four months until the off: it was now or never.

We had some positive leads, however. The *Daily Telegraph* were keen to be involved with the project. If we gave them the exclusive announcement then, depending on the news of the day, they would try to give us the front page. It was too good an opportunity to miss. I found an old Atlantic pairs boat that was moored up in London and towed it down to Putney, from where we had it tugged down the Thames to the Houses of Parliament. James and I took our positions in the unfamiliar boat and rowed up and down, while a photographer snapped away from an inflatable. The announcement not only made the front page, but also the double-page centrepiece. We were thrilled, the *Daily Telegraph* went on to ask for a regular diary, and BBC daytime commissioned a one-hour documentary. But we still lacked a sponsor and, more significantly, a rowable boat.

It was mid-August, and there was a great deal yet to be done. I discovered the name of a Devon-based boat builders called Rowsell & Adkin, which I was assured was the best in the business. Not only had Justin Adkin made and fitted ocean rowboats before, but he was also taking part in this year's event.

'Blimey, you're a bit late,' Justin marvelled.

'Yes, but can you do it?' I implored.

'Do what?'

'Get the boat ready.'

'From what?' he continued.

'I don't know.'

'What do you mean you don't know?'

'I've haven't seen it yet,' I admitted.

I explained that we had nothing and that we needed everything. I could practically hear him scratching his head down the phone.

'Yeah, I don't see why not,' he said finally.

At last we were going to have a boat, though we still didn't have any money to pay for it. I was now nearly £35,000 in the red and things weren't looking hopeful.

JAMES

In September 2005 we went down to the boat builders in Devon to see our boat. Woodvale ocean-rowing boats come in what looks like an Ikea flat pack. In order to decide how we wanted the boat set up, we took a finished one for a spin. It must be daunting for someone who can't row to go out in a boat with someone whose job it has been for over a decade. I should have exhibited patience and understanding – but then Ben should have got himself in good shape and made the effort to get down to a rowing club…

BEN

It was intimidating pulling into the Leander Club car park in Henley on a brisk autumn day. I felt rather inferior as I strode into this rowing Mecca, yet there was an almost businesslike air about the club as elite Olympic rowers chatted in pairs and downed vast jugs of fluid between gruelling sessions in the gym. I was about to have my first rowing lesson. As if that wasn't bad enough, I was going to undertake my first proper training session with James while the entire current Olympic squad, including their trainer, Jürgen Grobler, looked on. I had butterflies as I changed into my rowing gear and walked to the water's edge.

It was a beautiful day, and dozens of people – one of whom was Sir Steven Redgrave – watched from Henley Bridge as I stepped into the skinny boat. I was fairly scared. This was only the second time in my life that I had ever stepped into a scull, and I was being scrutinized by the rowing glitterati. My biggest concern was capsizing the boat with James in it. How would I ever live it down?

The boat was unfeasibly unstable, I thought as we pulled away from the safety of the shore. My poor strokes were punctuated by regular crabs, and swear words, and I would just get into the groove when I'd lose my balance. Sweat streamed down my face as we laboured upriver. Jürgen Grobler, James's mentor and trainer and perhaps the single most successful rowing coach of his generation, had observed me as I entered the boat and commented on my physique to one of his colleagues: 'Have you seen his hands? He has the hands of an office worker.'

Not exactly a ringing endorsement.

James was remarkably calm given that this was the first time he had been in a boat with me and that I quite obviously could not row, but he kept his cool as he coached me. All was fine until we decided to return to the club. A lone rower had turned back at the same time as us. We had 500 metres to go and before I knew what was happening, it became a race. I pulled as hard as I could on the oars as James bellowed instructions, and yet even with the two of us, he started to close in on us. The closer he came the more I panicked. Soon he was alongside, and with a quick flick of his oars he edged ahead. 'No!' I screamed pulling harder still. We had just been beaten by a single oarsman.

'Jürgen was watching you,' James said casually as we changed.

'What did he say?' I asked nervously.

'He said you're going to have a very sore back.'

JAMES

I was shocked by how little natural feel he had for a boat, and he was stunned by my lack of sympathy with him being, well, crap. I could have shown more patience but there was no point in hiding from Ben the massive improvements he needed to make in his technique and his fitness. If he didn't sort out the fundamentals we could find ourselves in real trouble at sea. Luckily our Atlantic boat required far less technique than the type of boats used at the Olympics, but he was going to have to put more effort into getting the movement as flowing as possible, though

15

most of that work would have to be done on land now. I, on the other hand, had to temper my frustrations at his rowing ability. I should have realized that would be his level when I signed up to race with him, but the problem was that as the race approached, my competitive spirit well and truly kicked in. I just couldn't imagine starting a race knowing that we didn't have a chance of winning. To have any chance at all, Ben would have to make some huge steps in fitness. The trouble was, he was going to Africa for three weeks.

We had an honest chat after the session; I promised that I could not and would not expect Olympic performances from him, saying that there would only be anger on my part if he had not got himself to the start line in the best shape possible. That was vital not only for him but for me as well. If he arrived at the start line not having prepared it was going to hurt him physically and he wouldn't enjoy the experience but, more importantly to me, it would affect our boat speed. After all, I'd promised my wife it wasn't going to take us that long.

BEN

James's agent had decided to pull in a big gun, Justin 'Muzza' Murray, a sponsorship agent whose last project had been London's 2012 Olympic bid. If anyone was going to help us with a sponsor, it was Muzza.

Meanwhile, as we moved into September, I found a sailing instructor willing to guide us through the gruelling ocean Yachtmaster Ocean Theory course, a week of intensive astro-navigational training followed by an exam. The certificate was an obligatory requirement for the race.

We had just a week to take the course and pass the exam or we wouldn't be going anywhere. To make matters worse, this was the last free week either of us had before the race. We had discovered that another rower, Andrew Morris, a shipping magnate from Nottingham, also had to take the course and so he joined our little group as we learnt all about astro-navigation in my Notting Hill flat. It must have been a strange sight, the four of us standing in the middle of Notting Hill Gate, sextant in hand, calculating our position from the sun, pretending houses were ships and roofs, masts. I was overwhelmed by the theory and number-crunching involved in the course.

Classes began at 8 a.m. and finished mid-evening. I laboured into the middle of the night to work on the homework, bamboozled by the complex mathematics.

'Most people spend months learning the theory,' explained Mike, our instructor, as he talked us through another complicated equation. My head hurt. I hadn't used maths so much since school; not even university taxed me as this course did. I couldn't sleep for the numbers spinning in my head.

'How can everyone have passed this course?' I wondered as I struggled through. James on the other hand seemed to take it in his stride; he appeared to have inherited his father's numerical mind. It was the first time we had both spent any time together though, and I enjoyed his company. It was the start of us working as a team.

Exam day was a daunting prospect. If either of us failed, the project would collapse. The two-hour exam seemed to take an eternity, while Mike immersed himself in various sailing books.

It was unbearable waiting for the results. Failure wasn't an option.

'Hello, Ben, I've got your results,' said Mike tantalizingly down the phone. 'You've both passed.'

'YEEEESSSS!' I punched the air. 'Thank you, thank you, thank you.'

We had done it. We had worked as a team. I immediately called James with the news.

'Who got the higher score?' was his immediate question. I hadn't even thought to ask for individual marks, let alone find out who got the higher one. We had passed, wasn't that enough?

It was a simple question, but one that was to define each of our characters very neatly indeed.

At last we were making real progress. The boat was under construction, we'd passed the exam, and the TV production company Twofour had begun work on the documentary, but what we really needed was money.

To make matters worse I had to spend October in Namibia filming another series of BBC's *Wild in Africa*. We held an emergency meeting during which we divided up tasks. James, we concluded, would be responsible for getting the boat ready and securing sponsorship, while I would acquire all the equipment we needed and organize shipping, logistics and communications.

I bought life-rafts, EPIRBs (emergency position-indicating radio beacons, which send a distress pulse to a satellite that is picked up by Falmouth coastguard in the UK – we had four, one fixed to the boat's bulkhead, a hand-held one in our grab bag and we each had one built into our watches), flares (red and white), expedition food, a computer and satellite phones capable of reaching the outside world from the middle of the ocean. My house was brimming with strange and unfamiliar equipment, while my bank manager called on a daily basis.

Training was still proving a problem. James had organized for a Concept 2 rowing machine to be dropped off at my house and I had been using it in my garden, but with so much planning and organizing to do, exercising had fallen by the wayside. I was dangerously unfit for the race ahead and would have to take the rowing machine with me to Africa.

'What's that?' asked a customs official at the airport in Windhoek.

'A rowing machine,' I explained, gesturing a rowing movement with my arms.

He looked perplexed.

'A boat?' he puzzled, looking at the bubble-wrapped contraption.

We were, of course, in Namibia, one of the driest countries in the world, a vast, rolling expanse of desert and scrubland.

'For the land,' I explained

'A land boat?' he asked.

'Sort of.' I smiled.

'Why?' he continued.

Here we go, I thought. This will really stump him.

'To row across the Atlantic Ocean.'

He stared at me unblinkingly.

'OK,' he nodded, 'pass,' and he ushered me through.

For a month I rose at 4 a.m. every morning to row for two hours before we began filming, and then again in the evening. I rowed in the desert, out in the bush, on the beach, in front of elephants, and more often than not in front of dozens of Namibian children, who would flock around the bizarre machine to watch the crazy Englishman making wind with the flywheel of the machine that propelled him nowhere at all.

While I made progress with my training, the same couldn't be said of our finances. We had simply left it too late. A number of companies had registered interest but that was about it. According to Muzza, some of them were worried about the implications of something going wrong; after all it was a dangerous race and they didn't want to be accountable. There had been a suggestion that a less sensitive sponsor might be keen to secure the keel of the boat – a relatively large expanse on a 23-foot rowing boat – so that should the worst happen and the boat be capsized any photographs would be dominated by the logo on the bottom of the boat, but it was an incentive none of our potential sponsors was seduced by.

And then came the breakthrough we needed.

'EDF want to sponsor us,' said James. He explained that they wouldn't sponsor us for the whole cost of the expedition but that they wanted to be the major sponsor. Now all we had to do was to find a number of companies prepared to invest small amounts and we would be out of the red. Costs had spiralled and we had now invested nearly £70,000 of our own money. EDF's involvement as major sponsor had the desired effect and by the time I flew back to the UK, Vodafone, MITIE, The Glenlivet and FRL had all joined. We were in the black and in business.

I hit the ground running; with just a few weeks until we were due in the Canaries, we still had the sea survival course to pass.

The boat, christened *The Spirit of EDF Energy*, had to be collected from Justin's workshop in Devon, packed in London and then delivered to PA freight in Newark. James and I drove down to Devon in my Land-Rover to collect our precious boat.

It was strange seeing her. We had done the one thing everyone had advised against us doing: we had got someone else to fit her. We knew nothing of her wiring, or fixings. She was as much of a stranger as James and I were to one another, and we didn't have a great deal of time to get to know one another.

We hauled the trailer out of the workshop and connected her to the back of the Landy and started the long journey home. Neither of us was used to pulling loads, and it was only after we got to London that we discovered that she hadn't been tied down properly and that during the journey she had shifted and fallen from her frame, damaging the keel. She hadn't even been in the water and already she had taken a knock. It was not a good omen, I thought, as we parked her at Chiswick Rowing Club by the river Thames.

She was due to be shipped in just a few days and we still had to pack her with our equipment. We unloaded the kit to James's home, emptying the food in piles. It seemed impossible that we would ever get it all on board. Time was running out and we eventually resigned ourselves to pack everything, and to edit out things that we wouldn't need when we were in the Canaries. The next day I drove the half-ton boat up to Newark and bade her farewell. The next time I'd see her was in La Gomera in three weeks' time.

In the meantime the RNLI had invited James and me to a sea survival day, not normally open to the public; they had heard about our exploits after my girlfriend Marina and I took part in the RNLI raft day at Marlow on the Thames. Marina, her sister Chiara, Chiara's boyfriend and I had built a raft for the race that subsequently sank before we even made it to the start line, warranting a health check by the St John ambulance crew, a cup for 'First to sink' and now an invitation to the RNLI HQ in Poole.

'We thought it might be useful after your Marlow experience,' explained Jo, the press officer, looking genuinely concerned.

The course included learning about flares, life jackets and EPIRBs and culminated with us aboard a life-raft in a full-blown storm. It wasn't a real one of course, but it surely felt like it as they started the wave machine in the cold pool and turned off the lights. Rain poured from the ceiling and lightning flashed, while wind machines tossed our little raft around the huge waves. Water hoses were directed at the raft's exit flap to ensure we stayed inside.

James and I wallowed around in the water, dressed in our heavy foulies and wellies. We bailed and took sea sickness tablets that turned out to be Smarties. James went green but before he could be sick I snapped one of the light sticks I had been given in case of 'emergency'. I had heard the bass thud of a helicopter above and concluded that it would be clever to snap the stick and wave it so that they knew where we were. Of course this was only a simulation, but I was sure they would be impressed with my ingenuity.

Suddenly the wind and waves stopped and the lights came on, as half a dozen RNLI staff dived into the water, and a whistle blew. 'Are you OK?' screamed the instructor.

'You dick,' laughed James. I'd just ruined the whole exercise.

Chapter One

La Gomera

BEN

'Ladies and gentlemen, please welcome on to the stage Antony Worrall Thompson, John Humphrys and James Cracknell!'

It was the eve of our departure for La Gomera in the Canaries and we were at the BBC's *Children in Need* telethon, where James had been roped into a spot of tap dancing, complete with hat and cane.

We had decided to nominate Children In Need as our charity in the hope of raising thousands of pounds through our rowing efforts, and we were using the event as a chance to announce our adventure. Rather disappointingly, however, we were relegated to the studio audience, where we were interviewed alongside a girl who was doing a charity skip and brushed aside by a troop of singing newsreaders.

As I sat listening to the story of the skipping fundraiser I was struck by how well our place in the audience summed up the difficulties we were having drumming up support for our Atlantic row. Despite our very best efforts – articles in the *Daily Telegraph*, press conferences and topless photo shoots – interest in the race was minimal. It had become apparent at the outset that in order for us to succeed in our enterprise it wasn't only our bodies that needed to be in good shape, it was also our wallets. The cost of the boat alone ran into the tens of thousands of pounds and I had managed to persuade my bank manager that remortgaging my flat was a sensible way to fund our endeavour. If we couldn't secure enough support to persuade sponsors to commit themselves, rowing the Atlantic wouldn't be my toughest challenge, it would be persuading Marina to set up home in a 23-foot flat-pack boat on our return. I thought about being forced to sell the flat to cover our debts. A skipping-rope couldn't cost more than a few pounds; what could James and I achieve with a simple piece of string? I wondered. As I reflected upon our adventure and the enormity of the risks we were taking I began to question quite what we had got ourselves into.

The next morning Marina, James and I all set off from Luton for the first leg of our journey. We were heavily laden with boxes of equipment and supplies, which included four pairs of 12-foot-long oars. We must have made a strange sight as we checked in for Monarch flight M605 for Tenerife. I handed over my very well-used credit card, and confirmed our flight details. It seemed ominous, buying a one-way ticket.

JAMES

I felt out of place in a plane filled with couples heading out to the Canaries for some partying and winter sun. Not only was I travelling alone but upon arrival I was planning to row the Atlantic. The lovebirds, Ben and Marina, weren't helping, chatting away in the seat next to me. I was the definition of a gooseberry. I stared out of the window at the sea below as I have countless times before on plane journeys but never have I felt my stomach as I did there. Like a slug in salt, it seemed to shrivel inside me. My throat went dry and my bacon and egg sandwich lost its appeal. The reality of what I was about to let myself in for was being unveiled below me: the Atlantic Ocean from 35,000 feet looked very different from the map on the wall above my desk at home.

In the past when I'd questioned myself about the task ahead a glance at my teammates would make a huge difference. The shared experiences and level of trust are enormous. I looked at Ben whispering sweet nothings to Marina. I realized two things: I hardly knew him and he was no Steve Redgrave. What had I done?

BEN

La Gomera, the national park and starting point for the Atlantic Rowing Race, heralded a new chapter in our adventure. I was apprehensive about the monumental task that lay ahead of us, but excited by our ten days of preparations. England had been enveloped in a low-pressure cold spell and the prospect of some sunshine and warmth was particularly alluring. Marina had taken time off work, and had been designated official team helper. In fact Marina, James and I *were* 'the team'; we were distinctly understaffed, a fact that would become glaringly obvious in the week ahead.

Event rules had stipulated that teams must arrive in La Gomera no less than fourteen days ahead of race day, but James and I had been given special dispensation by Woodvale in light of the *Children in Need* telethon. We arrived three days later than the rest of the crews and unbeknownst to us, Lin, the Woodvale safety officer, was apoplectic with rage at our arrogance.

It was dark by the time we touched down in Tenerife. We had to find a taxi capable of carrying our 12-foot oars, as well as a dozen bags and boxes that we had brought with us. As we negotiated the logistical difficulties of getting our equipment from the airport to the ferry I was struck by quite how many new ways we could be surprised by the demands of this race. I didn't know the half of it. We made our clumsy way to the ferry terminal for the final leg of our journey to the tiny island of La Gomera.

One of our first duties on our arrival was to comply with a newspaper interview we had set up with the *Daily Telegraph*. We headed straight for the boat to prepare it for the photographs that would accompany the interview, which we hoped would appease our sponsors. That initial sight of our boat was shocking. Stranded totally unprepared in a group of lovingly equipped vessels, it stuck out like a sore thumb. We were nowhere near ready.

La Gomera is one of the smallest of the Canary Islands, a rugged mass of volcanic rock about the size of the Isle of Wight that rises sharply out of the clear blue Atlantic Ocean. It was from La Gomera that Christopher Columbus set off on his voyage into the unknown in 1492, and the tiny, picturesque harbour of San Sebastián formed an historic, if somewhat sleepy setting for the start of the 2005 Atlantic Rowing Race. Against a striking backdrop of rippling green volcanic hills, dozens of rowing boats sat on their wooden cradles in the pretty marina like an assortment of brightly coloured sweets, while, all around, rowers and their support teams buzzed about painting, sanding, screwing, sawing, packing, tweaking – and sneaking peeks at rival boats.

Nobody was in a hurry to spy on our boat. Set amongst the other craft *The Spirit of EDF Energy* looked barren, unfinished and distinctly unseaworthy. It had looked positively majestic when we had collected it from Justin's boat yard in Devon, but now it became clear quite how much we had to do to get the boat in the water for its first practice session at sea – and we had just a day to do it. To cap it all, somehow we had already managed to lose half of our sponsors' stickers somewhere between boarding the ferry and arriving at our apartment. I had to admit – if only to myself – the initial signs did not bode well.

Marina set about painting the boat (and herself) in our chief sponsor's colours, a sort of turquoise blue. The problem was that we didn't have their colour, and it was only after a number of experimental mixes that we settled on a near-enough hue. Meanwhile Lin, the race's chief safety officer, summoned James and me into her office: 'I want to carry out the safety vetting this afternoon,' she explained. 'You'll have to get everything out of the boat and into the hall.'

With that single sentence we were forced to face up to the realities of committing to this race and adhering to its strict rules, and in that moment I was aware of the pressure on us. How could we undergo the scrutineering process *and* get the boat seaworthy, in just one day? While Marina painted, James and I ferried the gear into the hall, creating a mountainous pile of equipment, alongside a veritable Everest of food. It looked strange seeing all our kit in one place. It was difficult to imagine how it was going to fit into our 23-foot boat.

We started out with nearly 409 main meals, 170 puddings, 242 packets of breakfast muesli and 60 of porridge as well as 100 bars of chocolate and 100 'Go' bars, although not all of these rations would make the final cut. We had a further 700 sachets of Lucozade, two EPIRBs, two GPS units, two satellite phones, a laptop computer, cameras, a sea anchor, a drogue (a sort of mini-parachute needed to stabilize the boat in rough conditions), a VHF short-range radio, a water maker, flares, first aid kits, torches, a cooker, thirty gas bottles, life jackets, a life-raft, survival suits, harnesses, Thermos flasks and loo rolls, not to mention all our clothes, film kit and eight oars.

The scrutineering process was not simply an inventory of the boat. It was also a thorough assessment of how ready for the ocean the vessel itself was. Woodvale had stipulated everything from the maximum height of the Sea-me radar device, to the size of loop in the grab line and even the position of the fire blanket and extinguisher in the cabin. Time was running out and to make matters worse James and I both had to be present for the safety kit check. For two long hours Lin picked through the gargantuan pile of equipment, quizzing us along the way to make sure that we knew how to use it.

JAMES

Arriving at a race venue, the first thing I'd normally do would be to sit and watch the other boats training. With national colours painted on the spoons (the end of the oar that goes in the water) and their rowing style it was easy to see which country they were from and to work out whether they'd pose a threat. Similarly, in the boat-park any blokes hanging around a boat built for four people were presumed to be opposition and by seeing familiar faces or identifying new ones that looked like good athletes it wasn't difficult to spot where the challenges were going to come from.

The boat-park in La Gomera was different. To start with there wasn't the same need to identify the opposition. At a World Championships, of the 1,000 people competing only about a hundred would be in our event, but in this race, apart from two crews of four people, a few mixed crews and two crazy people doing it on their own, everybody else was in a two-man boat racing against us.

Here so much more attention was paid to the boats. At the Olympics, while watching their rowing and seeing who was in the crew I'd have a cursory glance at the make of boat they were in but no more than that. As Lance Armstrong's book said, 'It's not about the bike'. The same applies in Olympic rowing: there are strict rules governing weight, materials used and substances rubbed into the hull to make it travel through the water faster. Any design innovations that aren't available to every competitor are banned. The boats are carefully examined before racing and at any time during the regatta, violation of the rules means disqualification. The rules are in place to ensure the boat itself has nothing to do with the result, and by limiting innovations and setting a minimum weight limit both boat design and the use of expensive ultra-lightweight material are reduced, keeping the price down so that every country can afford to participate.

In the 'pit-lane' of the Atlantic Rowing Race that clearly wasn't the case, despite the rules stating everybody must row in identical boats. The theory is sound but in order for that to work the rules have to be rigorously enforced. This hasn't happened in previous races, where boats with significant alterations have been allowed to compete – keels have been shaved down, stabilizing fins added and smaller rudders made – so the temptation is for people to bend the rules, confident that they will get away with it.

This meant boat watching was the sport of choice for the first week on the island and was made easier by the whole fleet being placed on trestles in close proximity while final preparations were undertaken. In international rowing it is the quality of the crew and the way they are rowing that are the talking points; here it was the boats.

The first victims of this were Boat No. 1, *Digicel Atlantic Challenge*, crewed by two Irish boys, Ciaran Lewis and Gearoid Towey, both of whom had international rowing experience. Gearoid had competed at the Sydney and Athens Olympics so naturally anything different about their boat caused a stink. Shit had already hit the fan before we got to La Gomera concerning the size of their rudder (and a couple of others in the race), which was not only smaller but made of different material; in the end, the organizers allowed the smaller rudders. Not everybody was happy but with people spending over £70,000 just to get to the start line, it wasn't feasible to tell them they might not be allowed to race because of the size of their rudder when they'd bought the boat off a previous competitor in good faith. We weren't exempt from suspicion: our boat had been sitting there for a few days before we arrived and questions had been raised about the depth of our keel – and we'd bought our boat straight from the organizers.

Certain boats became the focus of my frustration (Ben might call it paranoia) with the way the rules were applied. But however cathartic I found focusing on other teams' boats, it was a mistake. There was much more to the race than the boat and the athletes on board. Sea experience and organization were also vital components to any race plan. We had underestimated the importance of these criteria until we were out there. The Danish crew of (Boat No. 27) *Team Scandlines*, Christian Petersen and Søren Sprogoe, had both of these in bucket-loads. They were big strong coastal rowers who were very well prepared and confident. I asked them how many days they were hoping to get across in and they said 'Thirty-nine.' The record is forty. In the race around the harbour held when the start was delayed they were the quickest. Ben and I didn't compete but nobody needed a conspiracy theory to see why – we weren't ready. The *Spirit of Cornwall* (Boat No. 9) was similar to the Danes in both organization and sea experience. The crew of Bob Warren and Chris Barrett were relaxed and friendly but clearly looking forward to the racing.

There were other oarsmen in the race with international rowing experience. *Team C2* (Boat No. 8) had ex-rowers Chris Andrews and Clint Evans on board. Ben called them the 'Shire Horses' because of their size and strength, and because he envisaged seeing them plodding all the way across whatever the conditions. Their boat didn't look the most organized and certainly wasn't the lightest, but they knew exactly how to work everything on board as they had to repair most of it to pass the scrutineering. Not to mention the fact they were competitive buggers.

There was no doubt which category was going to get across the quickest – the fours. With two people rowing at any one time they would be much faster, but the downside for them would be the lack of space. Our boat felt full with two people on board and the ones the fours were using weren't much bigger. This event was a straight shootout between Boat No. 24, *All Relative*, which included Justin Adkin, who had helped build our boat, and Boat No. 6, *Atlantic 4*. Justin also had the unique advantage of having built both his and the opposition's boat. I can't say I'd have enjoyed racing in a boat built by another competitor.

The most courageous crew in the race was Boat No. 20, *Bout de Vie*, not because Dominique Benassi was brave enough to row with a guy called Franck Bruno (honestly), but because they had both had a leg amputated. They were inspirational characters and veterans of many different endurance races, and had a wicked sense of humour. Yachts sometimes have a sticker indicating 'No shoes on board'. They had one banning people with two legs.

A light boat was vital, as were the oarsmen and the organization, but what was becoming clear watching the other crews prepare was the importance of having a strategy that both crew members agreed with. How hard were you prepared to race and what were you willing to do in order to get the finish position you wanted? Ben and I had skirted round these issues and our energy would have been used more productively sorting that out than worrying about the opposition. Without a strategy we both signed up to, there could be some serious conflicts on board.

BEN

Race day was Sunday, 27 November – we were just a week away from the start – and so we decided to start work on readying the boat itself. James and I were both anxious about this part of the proceedings as the boat was still a stranger to us; we weren't even sure where equipment was, or how it should be stored on board let alone how it worked. For over an hour, Lin and her colleagues forensically analysed our equipment.

The scrutineering process had highlighted the fact that we were missing a large amount of kit, including rope, floats, a hand-powered water pump, tools, water containers and some essential medical kit, all of which were in acutely short supply on the tiny island of La Gomera, whose shops had already undergone fours days of ransacking by dozens of other rowers.

'You boys are going to be quite busy,' was Lin's parting remark as she left us to consider our predicament. Aside from the substantial amount of missing equipment we also had the small matter of getting the boat ready for the water, both inside and out. Time was running out, and the *Daily Telegraph* pictures had been a stipulation in our sponsorship contracts. If we didn't get the boat in the water by the morning we would miss the paper's deadline and break our contract, thereby potentially jeopardizing our financial support. It was a deadline we couldn't afford to miss.

I had been so immersed in getting *The Spirit of EDF Energy* ready that I had been virtually oblivious to the army of rowers that had been beavering around us all day. I wended my way past boat after boat, each one brimming with equipment and the fruits of scrupulous preparation. I peered into hatches and under gunnels where neat pockets bulged with supplies. Compared to ours these boats looked so much more complete, and indeed the majority of them were veterans in this race; one or two of them had several crossings under their belt. As I stared at these battle-worn boats I felt rather vulnerable. *Spirit* was brand spanking new, untested – rather like me and James. Seeing the well-stocked, meticulously organized competition drove home that we were ill prepared for what lay ahead. There followed a sleepless night.

The next morning we launched *Spirit* into the marina. She wasn't even close to being ready but the organizers, contrary to Lin's protests, had given us a dispensation to get her waterborne. It was the first time James and I had been aboard, and indeed the first time we had rowed together in an ocean-going boat. Without all her equipment she was high in the water and without her rudder, which still hadn't been rigged, she was almost impossible to steer. But James and I set off with Martin the photographer aboard nonetheless. Marina followed in a small fishing boat we had chartered for company in case of disaster.

We had barely pulled five strokes on the oars when I fell off the seat. My heart sank. 'What must James think of me?' I wondered, let alone all the other rowers who had gathered along the pier to check out the competition. My fall pretty much dashed any hopes of demonstrating our prowess. We can't have looked half as threatening as James would have hoped. I imagined this sort of thing didn't happen at the Olympics.

We rowed on in silence, while Martin did his best to stem his nausea as he took his eyes from the horizon to snap us. Without the rudder the steering was difficult, but more worryingly my rowing position at the front of the boat felt particularly heavy and cumbersome. The seat kept slipping from under me and the oars dug heavily into my ribs with each small wave. For an hour or two we beat into a heavy sea, before relenting and agreeing to the offer of a tow from Marina's fishing boat. Those hours were a reality check. We had a mountain to climb before we would be ready for the off.

JAMES

With none of our supplies, no ballast, no rudder and a photographer clambering all over the boat while we were rowing, we weren't going to get a truly accurate reflection of what it would feel like when we set off. I was, however, expecting a more positive experience. We pushed off from the dock, Ben put both oars in the water and then fell off his seat. If he'd been in a normal racing boat he'd have been swimming – that would at least have told him he needed to get his ass down to a rowing club to acquire the rudimentary components of a rowing technique. Fortunately for Ben the Atlantic racing boats are much wider and take a lot more than falling off the seat to capsize them. I put my head in my hands, Ben went red in the face and kept apologizing and Martin (the photographer) shook his head as if to say, 'Oh dear, boys, what are you doing?'

When we'd reassembled Ben's seat and started rowing my concern over him suffering another self-imposed ejection dissipated as the boat felt very heavy despite the fact that both of us were (vaguely) rowing together (which makes it faster and lighter). We still had 400kg of supplies and ballast to go on board. The problem was, there was very little we could do about it as the oars were at their lightest setting. I tried telling myself it wasn't that hard, it was simply a case of getting used to it. I reminded myself that the boat we used at the Olympics was only 50kg and there were four of us to pull that along and here we were about to spend most of the time rowing on our own in a boat that when fully loaded would weigh about 700kg. It was bound to feel bloody heavy, yeah, that must be it and we'd get used to it.

BEN

Spirit was hoisted back out of the water and on to a cradle, on a patch of concrete pier next to the ferry terminal. By now the majority of the boats were waterborne, moored along the jetty like an assortment of polished gems glinting in the sunshine. I envied their crews and fretted about the state of our own boat. It was Tuesday, 22 November. We had less than a week till the start.

Our preparations continued apace but James had become increasingly preoccupied by what I considered to be the niceties of our boat, and by the hulls of our competition and the size of our blades. Unfortunately, he discovered a hole while sanding the hull. It was only a hairline fracture but it needed significant work to repair it and ensure the boat's watertight integrity. James set about repairing the hole, an essential task, and yet I felt that his meticulous repairs were not solely about getting the boat 'race fit'. Something about his endless tweaking seemed misguided to me. Of course, I couldn't hold a candle to James's rowing expertise – I wouldn't dream of trying – yet I was unable to shake the feeling that this was about so much more than just rowing. For the next three days James sanded and filed and tweaked and sanded some more, until our hull was as smooth as a baby's bottom.

Meanwhile, I assigned myself the task of packing the boat. The food had to be counted, assigned a place, logged and stored, and safety equipment had to be mounted and the boat rigged appropriately. To make matters worse, we had been told in no uncertain terms that we had purchased the wrong electric water maker.

The water maker we had bought initially, we had been warned, could be temperamental and complicated, and what's more neither James nor I understood a thing about it. But the cavalry were arriving. James's family joined us on the Wednesday, followed by my family on the Thursday. My mother had been apprehensive about coming out, but my father and my sister, Tamara, had quashed her concerns by persuading her to meet other rowers and their families. My other sister, Emily, had even flown over from Dubai, and Marina's sister Chiara had come out as 'team doctor'.

With eight extra pairs of hands we began to make some real progress. We had taken the difficult but important decision to replace the water maker with a more efficient one. This new and improved water maker didn't come cheap at £3,100 but we had no option. Scott, a mechanic and a competitor, had offered to fit it professionally and more importantly instruct us in its use, maintenance and repair.

Thursday, 24 November, with just three days to go until race day, and word had reached Lin that we still weren't prepared. Virtually every other boat was on the water, fully packed and signed off. We, on the other hand, were a long way from being ready, and Lin was concerned about our progress. It was 6 p.m. when she arrived with three other members of her team, all ready to assess our safety. Her expression said it all, and the sprawl of equipment did nothing to allay her fears. Scott was busy installing the water maker, with components strewn around the boat; in the meantime James worked on the hull with the only electric sander we had to patch up the hole. It looked like a workshop and Lin wasn't happy.

'We have a BIG problem,' she announced. 'Firstly, this boat is illegal – I've been through your paperwork and you don't have a ship's radio licence,' she continued. 'And where is your VHF radio licence, James?'

'I don't have it,' he whispered.

'Doctor's certificate?'

He shook his head again.

'Where's the fire blanket?' she demanded.

'It's just there.' I waved ambiguously in the general direction of the cabin.

'Where?' she pressed, at which point I slowly edged my way into the cabin, scanning for the elusive blanket.

'Here!' I announced proudly.

'Where's the life-raft?' she asked, not letting up for a moment.

It was in the hall with lots of other bits of equipment, but Lin wanted to see it in its position on the boat.

James and I hauled the 65kg raft up on to the deck and into the footwell.

'Ah,' I exclaimed. Try as we might to wedge it in, it was simply too wide to fit into the narrow gap.

'It's too big to go there,' stated Lin, 'so where are you going to put it?' She knew very well that this was the only space nearly big enough on the boat. Anywhere else and the massive raft would be in the way of the rowing positions, and it was far too big for the forward cabin.

We were well and truly snookered.

'Are the axes mounted'?

I shook my head.

'Grab bag packed?'

Another shake of the head.

'Is the rudder connected?'

This time James shook his head.

Lin's face became red and her eyes opened wider. I could have sworn I saw steam coming from her ears.

'Where's the medical book?'

Shake.

'Hand bilge pump?'

At last, a piece of equipment we had! The problem was that it was still packaged and neither of us had had a chance to open it. More to the point, we hadn't tested it, something that became blatantly obvious to Lin after she asked James to prove we knew how to use it and he stuck the wrong end into a bucket, furiously pumping air into the water.

Lin had had enough, and she wanted us to know about it. I felt like a schoolboy as she berated us for our lack of planning, commitment, and organization. Pooh-poohing our excuse that the hole repair and water maker change had set us back, she suggested that the hole itself was a manifestation of our lack of care and judgement, insinuating that the damage was our fault.

'But what really bothers me is that neither of you looks nervous,' she continued. 'Every other team seems to understand what they're undertaking, but I haven't seen any of that in you two and that really, really worries me.'

She paused, ominously.

'If you can't convince me of the contrary and get yourself ready, then you won't be going,' she said simply.

I was incredulous. Had she just threatened to withdraw us predominantly because of a lack of fear?

'And,' she continued, 'there's the small matter of sea trials. The rules clearly stipulate that crews must row together for a minimum of twenty-four hours before the start of the race, twelve hours of which must be rowed at night.'

'Shit,' I muttered under my breath.

'We need to hold an emergency meeting to discuss this further,' Lin concluded. 'I'll see you in half an hour in the ferry terminal bar,' and with that she left.

Half an hour later, James and I found ourselves surrounded by three stern-faced Woodvale staff, including Simon Chalk, the owner of the race.

If James and I hadn't cocked up yet, we unquestionably did our best to now, as James, brilliantly misreading the mood of the meeting, launched into a diatribe about how rubbish the race's reputation was, and how unfair it was that we had to carry the same amount of ballast as everyone else when we were already carrying a further 40kg of extra film equipment.

JAMES

Wandering over to the meeting I knew we were in trouble; we were underprepared but I felt that we were equally underestimated. I understood and agreed with the safety guidelines but was frustrated by their insistence that all the boats were the same when they clearly weren't. I figured rather than look at our feet and be chastised for our preparation like two schoolboys in the headmaster's office, attack was the best form of defence. I chose 'Your race is bollocks!' as my opening line. I could see Ben shaking his head in disbelief out of the corner of my eye.

BEN

Lin explained her concerns to the group about our lack of planning, training and knowledge, highlighting my query in one of the briefing meetings about whether we should go north around the island before heading out into the open Atlantic.

'Have you looked at a chart?' she demanded. 'Have you ever *seen* a chart?'

'Actually I navigated in the Royal Naval Reserve for four years,' I explained. 'I already had my "day skipper" sailing licence before getting my Yachtmaster Theory qualification and I'm a very competent sailor –'

'DON'T SAY ANOTHER THING,' she seethed.

'I –'

'I mean it, one more word like that and I WON'T let you go.'

Between us we had succeeded in alienating the entire group. We had until 4 p.m. the following afternoon to tick every box in our new extended 'to do' list, and then – and only then – could we begin our sea trials. We would have to spend Friday night at sea and miss the pre-race party.

Our predicament was further complicated because James's wife Beverley was due to arrive the following evening. The non-negotiable sea trial that night would mean we'd pass Beverley's ferry on our way out to sea. James wouldn't get to see her until the day we set off. I couldn't really imagine how things could be going any worse. As I pondered the sheer awfulness of our situation I realized that there was nothing for it, there was only one thing left for me to do. So I did what every depressed, humiliated person does: I went and got completely pissed.

Friday, 25 November 2005

My alarm didn't go off.

I turned on my phone. Beepbeep, beepbeep, beepbeep, beepbeep! it went as a dozen messages and missed calls screamed on to the little screen.

'Ben, it's James, where are you?'

'Ben, where are you?'

'Where are you?'

'Ben?'

Shit, I thought. And then to make matters worse, I had a message from Justin. I had managed to track down a suitable replacement life-raft in Essex, and though most airlines had refused to take it as it was a safety hazard with its gas canisters and emergency flares, it had finally arrived. Justin and his cousins who made up the *All Relative* team of four had all gone to Tenerife for a last, big night out and I had bribed him with ferry tickets and beer money to pick up our new life-raft from the airport cargo.

'Beeeennn, it's Justin. I'm reeeeelllly pished, I can't find the air – airport.'

Just when I didn't think things could get any worse, Justin was drunk and lost in Tenerife. And he had my passport with him.

While I had been sleeping off the night before, James had found a local sailing school that agreed to give him a speedy VHF radio course, and had spoken to his Olympic team doctor, who had been able to sign his medical certificate. Now up and running I got on to the phone to the radio licence office and begged like I've never begged before. Incredibly, my sweet-talking did the trick and they agreed to dispatch one within the hour; my only problem now was getting it on to the island by the day's end.

It was all hands on deck as the Fogle and Cracknell families and all the friends who were now helping out were thrown into action, packing, cutting, and rallying. We even drafted in other rowers, who descended on our boat in swarms. Ex-ocean rowers gathered around, awaiting instructions. As we once again scrambled to meet Lin's deadline I had a surge of optimism. I loved the fact that everyone helped out. The Guernsey girls had a team of thirty people to help them back in England yet they also lent us a hand. There was something amazing about this collective effort.

At that moment my phone rang again. 'Help me, Ben, I'm lost and I'm reeeellly drunk,' slurred a familiar voice.

'Justin, listen to me, you HAVE to get to the airport and pick up that raft. Go and get a strong coffee to sober up!' I pleaded.

It was nearly noon, and we had only a few hours to get everything done.

JAMES

Sitting through the VHF radio course as I learnt my Alphas, Bravos and Charlies I was aware that Ben would be rushing around while I was doing something I had had months to organize at home. However, my guilt lasted only so long as I enjoyed the air-conditioning, a glass of Coke and not being stuck under the bottom of the boat. But I had to get through the course by lunchtime to have any chance of getting the boat ready in time. Fortunately I passed, getting the second highest score on the island – unfortunately I was second to someone whose first language wasn't English, and given that the exam was in English it wasn't much of a victory – obviously I didn't tell Ben that part.

BEN

James soon returned clutching a certificate. 'I passed,' he sighed, 'highest score on the island… ever,' he added with a smirk.

The radio licence had been an extraordinary collective effort (and involved an enormous telephone bill) but had been delivered to the UK airport by my *Animal Park* co-presenter, Kate Humble, who had begged an air stewardess to take it to Tenerife. James's mother-in-law Joyce headed off to meet the flight.

Like a frenzied, erratic production line, *Spirit* was taking shape before our eyes. The rudder was assembled and the boat's various ropes rigged. Tamara and Marina fixed pockets to the deck and the cabin, while Chiara labelled all the drugs in our medical kit and mum packed snack bags.

It was nearly 4 p.m., and Lin would soon be back to find out whether or not we had managed the apparently impossible. The boat was almost ready, but there were two critical exceptions: the life-raft and radio licence. With just one ferry due in to San Sebastián from Tenerife before the final scrutineering, if either Justin or Joyce failed to make the ferry we would be disqualified.

I felt sick as I watched the ferry appear on the horizon. It pulled into the little port, overflowing with tourists and the families and friends of various rowers, but there was no sign of Justin. He had been ominously quiet since his drunken calls in the morning.

'One ship's radio licence,' announced James's mother-in-law, proudly handing over the valuable document. One down, one to go.

I felt a tap on my shoulder; it was Justin, looking distinctly the worse for wear. 'Here you go,' he said sleepily, dumping a heavy box at my feet: the life-raft.

Right on cue, Lin and her team appeared.

My heart was in my mouth as we went through the checklist. No part of the boat was left unchecked as she went through our paperwork with a fine-tooth comb.

'Medical certificate?'

Check.

'VHF licence?'

Check.

'Life-raft and certificate?'

Check.

'And now for the biggy,' she announced after a theatrical pause, 'the ship's radio licence.'

'Check,' I confirmed.

Her eyes widened and a furrow appeared on her brow. She looked at me suspiciously as I handed her the certificate.

She examined it, and then re-examined it, 'How did you get it?' she stuttered with genuine astonishment.

She went through the remaining list, and was amazed to find that we had managed to do everything that had been required of us. 'I'm speechless,' she said, genuinely flabbergasted. 'I never thought you'd be able to do it,' she admitted, 'but I have to say you have both REALLY impressed me.'

I beamed.

'That means you just have your twenty-four hours of sea trials left to do,' she added rather deflatingly. I knew it was in our best interests, but part of me hoped that we would be excused. We had only a day until race day and I wanted to spend my last precious hours with Marina and my family, not aboard *Spirit*. But Lin wasn't about to let us off that easily.

The organizers had decided that we should be accompanied by the race safety craft, a rigid inflatable boat (or RIB) that would be crewed by Mick, one of the Woodvale staff and himself a veteran ocean rower, and Simon Chalk. They would test us on a number of tasks, including deploying the sea anchor, using the water maker and the cooker, as well as plotting our position and navigating.

It was 6 p.m. on Friday, 25 November, by the time we set off into the stormy ocean. A strong northerly wind had been building and the sea was whisked into an angry mess. Waves crashed against our newly painted hull, washing away the autumn leaves that still littered the deck of *Spirit* from her short stay in London.

The boat was much heavier now that she was laden with kit and supplies.

'Dig harder,' implored James. 'I can't hear you pushing yourself.' We rowed on hard, as the sun began to dip into the rough Atlantic swell.

I stared dead ahead, eyes fixed on James's movements in order to keep up with his rhythm. All the time, Mick and Simon followed alongside in their boat, watching and analysing our progress.

The oars were digging painfully into my chest, occasionally wedging against my thighs as I fought to keep up with James. Every so often I would miss a stroke, and knock into James's back as we slid out of tandem.

'Fucking hell!' he screamed.

'Sorry,' I'd reply as the pressure mounted.

On we rowed as darkness slowly enveloped *Spirit*. I turned our little navigation light on, which blinded me to the tumultuous sea. We pitched and reared as the invisible waves tossed us around like a toy boat.

'DEPLOY THE SEA ANCHOR,' hollered Mick above the cacophony of the howling wind. I had been dreading this moment. A sea anchor is basically a kind of parachute that, when deployed, secures the boat in the water. The parachute fills then holds the boat in one place when there's a headwind or when it is too rough to row. I understood the theory, but was still bamboozled by the assortment of ropes needed, one 80 metres long, one of 60 metres and a third of 20 metres.

I had drawn a diagram on a scrap of paper, but couldn't remember which line to deploy first. Was the longer rope attached to the top of the chute, or the bottom? Which line should be cast first? Should I unfurl the parachute before casting the ropes? What was the float for? What should have been a straightforward procedure had assumed baffling proportions. I clambered around in the darkness, as much struggling to untangle my thoughts as the lines themselves.

At long last I cast the chute over the side, followed by the first rope, then the second and very quickly by the last. I sat on my seat, crossed my fingers and prayed. Mick and Simon were there to reassure themselves that we would be safe and competent at sea. I had taken nearly fifteen minutes to deploy the sea anchor already and if it failed now they were sure to lose confidence in us. As we waited *Spirit* began to pull around, her nose into the wind. Incredibly, I had got it right.

'GOOD,' shouted Mick, 'the anchor's deployed, now make us a cup of tea.'

'Blimey, that was lucky,' I thought as James struck a match and lit the gas stove. For several hours we rowed on with intermittent tasks set by Mick and Simon. All the while James rowed and vomited, rowed and vomited.

JAMES

I was convinced that a long night's rowing was just what we needed to familiarize ourselves with the boat before the race started the next day. Rowing under the watchful eye of the organizers created a pressurized environment and the fact that the session was in the dark just made things more difficult, although not as difficult as my phone call to Bev telling her of our plans. She was travelling from the UK that day and was due to arrive on the ferry from Tenerife that would dock before we headed out to sea.

The first problem became clear pretty immediately: the steering wasn't working well. It wasn't surprising, I'd watched boats train all week and almost every time they came back to the marina work on the steering would begin. Although the boats came with a rudder, the system to make it work was left to the crew, so it was a case of coming up with an idea and then using the advanced technique of trial and error to get it to work. We only had one trial and that had identified an error straight away: there were too many pulleys, making the wires too tight. This wasn't a big issue to address and I felt confident of sorting it out before we set off the next day. What I wasn't as confident about was our not discovering another problem once we'd rectified this one.

More worrying again, however, was the GPS (or Global Positioning System – now a prerequisite in your average car). The main control unit was inside the cabin and a small repeater screen on the outside showed the important information such as bearing and speed. No matter what buttons we pressed we couldn't get it to work so we were effectively rowing blind as the compass we'd bought was hard to read at night. I had no idea how to fix this and did not want to begin the race without a fully functioning navigation system. We had roughly four hours on land to fix it before the race started.

We headed straight out to sea and as we emerged from the shelter of the harbour wall the swell picked up and the boat started getting thrown about. The rowing had started off better than the other day – at least Ben had stayed on the seat this time. I wanted him to realize how tough the race was going to be for us, but that was impossible to achieve in the few hours we'd had at sea. I thought he'd underestimated the physical toll the crossing was going to put on our bodies and I felt the best way to show him how hard it was going to be was to set a relentless rhythm, and make him pull harder and harder. He would be forced to feel the resistance we would be rowing against for the next couple of months.

The black skies and strong winds made for a tough night-time initiation, especially as any communication meant shouting over the wind – a 'request' for extra effort sounded more like an order. It sounds cruel but I thought it was better to demand more from Ben than he was expecting so that the start of the race wouldn't come as too much of a shock. It was going to be difficult enough being isolated at sea. If he thought the race was going to be gentle stroll, tomorrow lunchtime would be a huge eye-opener.

The rough water was causing us problems: our blades were banging into the waves on the way forward for the next stroke. We couldn't push them any higher because our hands were already rubbing along our thighs. Fuck! I'd had the seats built up too high. The angle of the oars to the water was exactly what I'd wanted when I designed the set-up. But with the boat pitching and rolling in the waves it was impossible to row – I hadn't allowed enough clearance between our hands and legs. If we were struggling a mile out to sea how were we going to cope with the huge waves in the middle of the Atlantic? We didn't have time to lower the seats (a huge job that would have meant demolishing most of the decking and rebuilding it). I had to find a short cut because we were going to end up banging our legs for 3,000 miles, probably breaking an oar or a gate (the plastic oarlock that holds the oar in place) when the oars inevitably stuck in the water.

Simon Chalk stopped us and made us put down our sea anchor, and this is where it became clear how much we needed each other on the trip. We were so behind in our preparation we'd had to divide and conquer to get everything done. I'd spent the last few days under the hull mending the hole whereas Ben had packed up the boat and sorted out all the safety equipment. The long and short of it was that I wasn't sure how to put the anchor down without tangling up the three ropes that came with it. Ben sprang into action and, with the help of a crib sheet, managed to put the anchor out. I would have applauded him if I hadn't been throwing up over the side of the boat. Just over half an hour from pushing off to being seasick had to be some kind of record. The first four days weren't going to be a barrel of laughs for me, while Ben looked as though he'd have been happy to tuck into some *foie gras*.

Simon and Mick eventually took pity on us and decided that spending your last night before rowing the Atlantic stuck on a boat wasn't good for the soul, or in my case my marriage. They pointed back to shore and we headed home via a big headwind.

The boat was moving along fairly well and despite the problems with the blades she was coping well with the conditions. If the worst came to the worst we could race like this but it wasn't ideal and it wouldn't be comfortable. That wasn't good enough. It had been my job to get the boat design right and I'd failed.

Mick and Simon seemed pretty pleased with our outing and were surprised by our speed coming back into the wind. The speed didn't surprise me, we had a heavy gearing – meaning the blades were hard to pull through the water, but with every stroke the boat went a lot further – so it was always going to be fast when we were both rowing. It was when we would be rowing one at a time that it might be hard work but right now that was the least of my worries. As Simon was speaking to us one of our gates caught my eye. The pin that closed it had bent after only a few hours' rowing: they had to last for over a thousand. I had to think of a short cut to lowering the seats – I didn't want breakages to be the reason we didn't get across, but we didn't have enough time…

BEN

'Right, you can head back in!' shouted Mick.

We had been on the water for only six hours, but already my back was sore and my hands were rubbed red raw. For an hour we beat into the northerly wind. Sweat streamed down my brow as I struggled to keep up with James.

'Harder, Ben, for fuck's sake!' cried James.

It was after midnight when we pulled alongside the jetty and I prised my weary body from the seat. I was aching, tired and above all worried. I had seen a side to James that I hadn't witnessed before, and it concerned me. As I nursed my new blisters I reflected upon the pressure I'd felt out on the water. We had both been under immense pressure to perform for Mick and Simon, who we knew would both report back immediately to Lin, but I had also been under the fierce spotlight of James's attention, and the difference between training and the real thing had become impossible to miss. When I invited James to row with me I'd had some idea of how hard he pushed himself: he has a reputation and I couldn't blame anyone but myself if I was finding his standards exacting. I knew that there would be tensions for sure. Yet those months of Ergo training simply hadn't prepared me for the realities of life at sea.

James and I sat on the pontoon, reflecting on our short practice session. It had been a reality check, but more than that it had highlighted a drastic flaw in the boat's design. The seats were too high – far too high – and my oarlock (the loop that holds the oar in position at the side of the boat) had been bent and twisted into an arc by the power of the waves. If we left things the way they were, we wouldn't last a day, James warned. The boat needed to be stripped down and rebuilt, a huge task. There were just thirty hours to go until the start, and once again I could feel the race begin to slip from our grasp even before we set off.

'If I didn't know any better, I'd think someone didn't want us to take part,' I smiled to James.

I understood that the seats were too high, but I couldn't grasp the importance of changing the height at the eleventh hour. It seemed crazy to consider such significant structural alterations just when we'd got *Spirit* ready, and what's more we simply didn't have time for such fundamental changes.

James and I unenthusiastically made our way to the remnants of the party we had been forced to miss by our last-minute sea trial. We walked along the deserted streets in silence, lost in our own thoughts.

Several dozen rowers and their families mingled around the detritus of a barbecue, while my family and friends huddled in a corner. They seemed downcast.

'Have you heard?' asked Marina.

'Heard what?' I asked.

'A tropical storm is on its way, we think they're going to postpone the race until Wednesday.'

James and I looked at one another and grinned; maybe someone did want us to take part after all. The delay would give us just enough time to make the seat adjustments, as well as some other last-minute tweaks. Every silver lining comes with its cloud, of course. Marina and my family still had to leave on Sunday. They would miss the start of the race.

JAMES
Saturday, 26 November 2005

The rumours were confirmed and at the 1 p.m. race briefing it was announced that we would begin the race on Wednesday, 30 November. The tropical storm had given us a reprieve. Since hearing about the delay I'd wrestled with whether or not to lower the seats. I'd designed them to put us in the best biomechanical position for rowing and in flat conditions they would be fine, but the odds on having blue skies and calm seas for the next two months were pretty slim, especially as the race had just been delayed by a storm.

We had to make the change. Apart from its making rowing much more comfortable, which after a few days at sea would be more important than we could possibly imagine here on land, we couldn't afford any equipment breakages caused by the oars continually hitting the water, as we hardly had any spares. I knew Ben wasn't going to be happy with the decision but he'd have to trust me.

It would have been easier to leave it – Ben wouldn't know a comfortable boat from an uncomfortable one – especially as on a scale of one to ten both set-ups were down at the low-scoring end. It was a big job but we had been gifted extra time and I could envisage us being out at sea after a couple of days wishing we'd done it.

The downside to making the change was not being able to row again until the morning of the race. Ben wanted to get more practice in but was this the best use of our time? He'd have plenty of opportunity to make up for lost practice. I had to back myself and get him to trust me, although why should he? I'd screwed up once already. But it was my mistake and I'd rectify it.

BEN

On what should have been race day James began work on the height of the seats. The boat became a workshop once again, a task made more difficult by the approaching tropical storm, which deluged the island. Marina and my family were set to leave on the afternoon ferry to connect with their flight back to the UK. It was devastating walking them down to the terminal. They had been an immense support through the week. From my journey out with just Marina to help me and James to my dad's purchase of the new water maker, my family had rallied round and I knew that without them I would have cracked under the pressure. They had offered not only practical help but unswerving emotional support.

My mother, who had aired her concerns and reservations about the race, had still come along and not only supported me but actively helped us with our mad venture. She had had to suffer Woodvale's reaction to our slapdash preparations, as if confirming her fears. I was so anxious that she would leave even more terrified for me than when she had arrived. I would have done anything I could to assuage her nerves but with just over a day to go I just couldn't find the words.

Marina had been my stabilizer, my rock. She had not only supported us with the hard graft, but she had calmed me and provided me with a rational perspective when I couldn't see how we could complete all the tasks in hand before the race. In my lowest moments, when our life-raft was abroad and our plans were in tatters, she had appeared like a soothing angel, her very presence providing an element of calming rationality and reassuring familiarity.

La Gomera was the first time I really got to know Marina. We had been dating for nearly eighteen months and had been on countless holidays and breaks, but this was different. Until now I had never truly relied on her. Where my week had been plagued by chaos, confusion and turmoil, she had been judicious and sanguine, the perfect antidote to my pessimism and despondency. When all the world appeared to be against me, Marina had been there, and now she had to leave me.

I held her tight to my chest, breathing in her scent one last time, our salty tears merging on our cheeks. Neither of us had ever seen the other one cry and I was as astonished by her tears as I was by mine. I loved her more than I had realized and I was overcome with the need to show it. A little voice in my head was saying 'Propose' but I knew it was the wrong moment – I still had to row the Atlantic – and the departure I had envisaged had been reversed; it was no longer me disappearing over the horizon in a boat, but Marina and my family.

I stood there, and the glowering cloud mirrored my sense of impending doom, as the ferry pulled away. Tears distorted my view, but I could just make out my family and friends: Mum, Dad, Tamara, Emily, Jake, Chiara and of course my darling Marina, their arms waving farewell. I trudged back along the pontoon, forlorn and lost. What was I doing here? It wouldn't be the last I'd hear of that question.

Sunday, 27 November 2005

As James and I rushed to make the urgently needed (or so I had come to be persuaded) alterations, the race organizers decided to stage a race of their own to alleviate the pressure building on all the rowers as we waited for the storm to pass. With the first ever 'La Gomera Cup' the majority of the other teams had something to concentrate on. As I walked around the harbour, wishing we'd had the chance to get in a bit more ocean-rowing practice, I thought about one of the most striking individuals I had met on La Gomera.

As we had busily prepared the boat in its cradle a friendly older guy named Graham Walters had quietly worked alongside us, refitting a cheerful old tub of a rowing boat called *Puffin*. A veteran of three transatlantic rows, Graham was readying the old boat for a single-handed crossing to raise money for the Red Cross the following year, and all of the Woodvale crews had chipped in with bits of spare kit and equipment to help Graham prepare for his voyage. With its fresh new coat of blue, red and yellow paint, it was hard to imagine the 20-foot

Puffin, looking for all the world like a bath toy, venturing into the harsh seas of the north Atlantic. And yet upon examining Graham's boat, I saw that its hull carried a sobering message painted on its side, a reminder to James and me of both the sense of history behind the Atlantic race and its all too real dangers.

Atlantic crossing 2006 in remembrance of David Johnstone and John Hoare 1966. Only the boat survived.

On Sunday, 22 May 1966, *Puffin* and her crew of two had set off from Norfolk, Virginia, intending to be the first boat in modern times to cross the Atlantic Ocean by manpower alone. Almost simultaneously, hundreds of miles further up the coast in Cape Cod, a young paratrooper called Chay Blyth and his rowing partner John Ridgeway set off in their own 20-foot boat, *English Rose III*, with exactly the same goal in mind. When news of the rival attempt reached David Johnstone, he remarked: 'We never wanted a race, but of course it is.'

Compared to the heavy, clumsy boats used by these two pioneering crews, our boat – which to us had come to seem so woefully under-prepared – was a luxury yacht. Neither Hoare and Johnstone's *Puffin* nor Blyth and Ridgeway's *English Rose III* were fitted with GPS, Argos tracking systems, satellite telephones or even a water maker. The boats were powered by heavy wooden oars instead of the carbon ones that James and I were using, all the food supplies and drinking water needed for the entire trip had to be carried on board, and the crews were forced to navigate with only the stars for guidance. More ominously, the rudimentary cabins offered very little protection from the harsh conditions of the north Atlantic ocean and, crucially, the boats were not designed to self-right in the event of a capsize.

The race may have been on, whether Johnstone wanted one or not, but things began to go wrong for the *Puffin*'s brave crew very early in their voyage. After narrowly avoiding being blown up on a US Navy gunnery range, the pair covered only twenty miles in their first week at sea. While the *English Rose* powered on along its more northerly route, ultimately

49

arriving in Ireland after a punishing ninety-two days at sea, nothing was heard of the *Puffin* for weeks until, 990 miles east of Boston, she was spotted by a US steamship called the *Ashley Lykes*. Carrying enough food for the sixty-five days the pair had reckoned it would take to cross the Atlantic, after fifty-one days had passed Johnstone and Hoare still had almost 2,000 miles to go. According to the men's diaries, the *Ashley Lykes* had slowed down and asked them if they needed anything; they said yes, food, but inexplicably the ship turned around and headed off without helping them.

With Hurricane Faith gathering menacingly off the coast of the United States, Day 106 of their diary, the last recorded entry, stated simply: '3 September. No rowing due to Force 2 NNW winds.' On 14 October, some six weeks after these words were written, a Canadian ship, *Chaudière*, spotted *Puffin* drifting aimlessly in the middle of the Atlantic Ocean. There was no sign of life on board.

As James and I worried and grumbled our way to the start line, frustrated by the seemingly unnecessary bureaucracy of the organizers, the fate of *Puffin*'s crew, starved, alone and apparently swept away by the force of Hurricane Faith, offered a stark reminder of what we were letting ourselves in for:

> If we don't have a go, we shall live the rest of our lives wondering if we might have made it – and knowing that only fear persuaded us from the attempt.
>
> David Johnstone and John Hoare

Chapter Two

Race Day

JAMES

Wednesday, 30 November 2005

I always simultaneously loved and hated the nerves and energy that pulsed through my body as I woke up on the morning of a big race. Invariably I would have spent most of the night tossing and turning, the upcoming race running continuously through my mind, forbidding my body to switch to standby. Under any other circumstances, after such a terrible night's sleep I would wake up absolutely exhausted, but race days were different. I would be awake before the alarm sounded, whatever the time – 4 a.m. in the case of the Athens Olympics – just lying there, eyes wide open, the race going through my head for the thousandth time; my body ready to produce the performance that all the training guaranteed was within me; confident in the belief that I had done absolutely everything possible to give myself the best chance of winning. Prepared for the chance to prove that all the sacrifices had been worthwhile.

It would still be dark as I flicked on the light. My roommate and crewmate Matthew Pinsent would groan as the room exploded in light, but even he would be focused and alert within a matter of seconds. No words would be said but a habitual nod would be exchanged, letting each other know that today was the day and we were there for each other, however tough it got.

Breakfast was an impossibility, my throat tight with the knowledge that any food that made its way to my stomach was only going to be coming back up shortly after. And yet over the years, I got used to the almost paralysing nerves and stomach cramps on the morning of a World Championship or Olympic Final. They became my bedrock, my comfort blanket – a reassurance that my body was ready for what it was about to go through. If I'd woken up without them, I would have been worried.

Our crew liked to be first down to the regatta site on the big day, normally around dawn. The venue would be deserted and as we approached our boat it would seem to shine more than the others around it, cleaned and polished to within an inch of its life over the previous week; every nut had been tightened, checked and rechecked.

We would make a point of being the first on to the water when the course opened for training before racing started. Slicing through the virgin waters made it feel like it was my lake, my home. By the time we took our boat off the water, I would always be convinced that no other outcome was possible. We were better prepared both physically and mentally, we knew the course better than anybody else and our will to win was stronger.

As with any other big race I woke up before the alarm, and again I was in a twin room. This time my roommate would not be sharing the experience with me. In fact my roommate did not even want me to go through the experience at all – despite being my wife. The two single beds had not been pushed together; our last night before the start of the Atlantic race had been a tense and tetchy affair.

Over supper the night before I had started to withdraw into myself. My answers to Bev's questions were at first monosyllabic and then little more than unintelligible grunts as my mind drifted out to sea. I was starting to realize the scale of the task that lay ahead. Having spent the last ten days frantically trying to fulfil the race criteria in order to be allowed to start, I had had no time to think about what was going to happen at sea.

The tropical storm that had delayed the race was still raging, pummelling the boats in the marina. Bev and I wandered down after dinner to check on the boat. Standing on the dock looking at the tiny boat, the piercing noise of wires banging against the masts of sailing boats exaggerating the strength of the wind, there was no doubting what Bev and I were thinking. What happens if a storm hits us out there? The tension between us grew again, although it stemmed from more than just the risks of the crossing.

Bev did not want me to take part in the Atlantic race, she felt that I was selfish for going. Not only was I leaving her to look after Croyde single-handedly, I was placing my life in jeopardy when I had clear responsibilities as a husband and father; and if that wasn't enough, she seemed to think I was happy not to see her or Croyde for two months.

Bev has a huge sense of justice and speaks her mind, two qualities I adore about her. She said she couldn't have been away from Croyde for that long and even if she'd wanted to be 'it wasn't an option'. In her opinion, mothers don't have the same choices as fathers.

Admittedly I should probably do more than I do to help ensure parity between the sexes, but part of me felt some of the anger directed at me was frustration because she believed she wouldn't have been able to go away for that length of time. I tried explaining that I'd support anything she wanted to do, but the thought of me and the little man looking after each other for a few months obviously didn't fill her with much confidence.

Our relationship had been a struggle over the previous few months. Living in a small flat with a young boy and both working from home a lot of the time, we'd become like two rats in a cage. As the race approached, Bev had expressed to me a number of times that she was worried I was rowing to get away from her. I tried to reassure her that that wasn't the case, but failed. Empathy, sensitivity and spontaneous shows of affection are not my strong points, so I was unable to set her mind at rest.

Perhaps the problem was that I shared her fears; not that I was going to leave her, but that there was a chance she would prefer life without *me* while I was away. The extra space and freedom would be liberating and empowering. Daily life in the flat for Bev would involve less tension, fewer arguments and fewer piles of clothes. I was convinced I'd miss home stuck on a seven-metre boat with one other guy more than she would miss me at home in the flat. But I'd be lying if I said there was no part of me that was looking forward to the space and time the trip would give me to think about our relationship. Our marriage used to be fantastic, but when I signed up for the Atlantic race, I think we'd both admit it wasn't in the best shape.

Even for those rowers who had complete support from their partner the violent wind and vast expanse of angry ocean would have tested it that night. In the case of Bev and me where that support for my adventure was very limited, the storm increased the tension between us. With the start of the race looming, it would only take something petty to act as a spark and light the fire: sure enough we found it.

Marina had written a couple of riddles on the outside of the cabin facing the rowing positions:

> What is greater than god, more evil than the devil, the rich want for it, the poor have it, and if you eat it you die?

> A man is looking at a picture of a boy. He says, 'Brothers and sisters have I none, but this man's father is my father's son.' Who is this?

I'd solved one earlier that afternoon while I was fiddling around on the boat. Ben never managed to work out either of them despite staring at them for twelve hours a day while on the oars. Joining me on the quayside, Bev read the riddle and asked me what the answer was; knowing how intelligent and competitive she is, and knowing that if I could solve it she definitely could, I didn't tell her the answer the first time she asked. Big mistake.

In hindsight I should have realized that her mind was a thousand miles out to sea imagining a little boat being pounded by the waves – not concentrating on solving a riddle. Bev instantly got wound up because I didn't tell her the answer. Her aggression over such a small issue collided with my stubborn streak, which resulted in a cold silence and the beds remaining on either side of the hotel room. Our last night together involved no touching or holding. The atmosphere was one of anger and resentment, something I bitterly regretted when I was out at sea.

As usual on race day, I ate no breakfast – this time not because my nerves wouldn't allow me to eat, but because the hotel kitchen hadn't opened at 6 a.m. when I headed down to the boat to work through the long list of things we still had to do before the 11 a.m. start. As predicted, the storm had blown over. We would set off today.

BEN

Beeep beeep beeep beeep beeep.

'This is the last time I'll wake up,' I proclaimed as I rolled out of bed and back into my grubby shorts. It wasn't a Captain Scott moment, nor portentous of an ill-fated voyage. It was a reference to my unease about the sleep deprivation that lay ahead. Sleep is right at the top of my list of basic human necessities. I'll sleep till I'm woken up, pretty much without exception. My mother used to remark that I was the only child she knew to actually come and say, 'Mummy, can I go to bed now?' This morning the possibility of a full night's sleep ahead ended.

It was 5 a.m., I was hung over and the sun was still to rise. It was race day. Charts were strewn across my hotel room floor, while the computer and satellite phone buzzed away in the socket, squeezing in every last amp of charge for the long, long journey ahead.

I knew that I should set about packing, but we had been so preoccupied with getting the boat ready that we had never discussed how much, or indeed what, to pack. James had supplied me with a vast pile of sportswear, but what about wet-weather gear, fleeces and pants? I knew it would be hot, but wouldn't it be chilly at night? Did I need shoes and if so, would socks be useful? I had a mountain of kit with me that I'd brought out from England – three enormous bags, to be specific – from which to choose. James had supplied me with a small waterproof plastic bag, closely resembling an oversize freezer bag, out of which we could extract air in order to minimize its size. I took it as his subtle suggestion to pack light.

I picked up two pairs of Lycra shorts (my least favourite item of sportswear, I usually avoided them at all costs but I couldn't dispute how easy they were to pack), two T-shirts, a pair of pants and a pair of tracksuit bottoms. The bag was already bulging to capacity. James had pooh-poohed the idea of foul- or cold-weather wear – 'After all, we won't be wearing anything most of the time,' he had reminded me – but I wasn't so sure. I scooped up my fleece and squeezed it into the bag. In five minutes I had packed what would be my wardrobe for the next few months. It wasn't much. I slipped on my well-worn and well-loved Converse trainers, rolled up the charts, packed the electronics into waterproof aquapacs and made my way out into the chilly morning with all I could squeeze on to the boat, leaving the rest of my now discarded kit to be transported home by Alexis Girardet, the director filming our adventure.

The harbour was a hive of activity as rowers buzzed back and forth, strutting proudly in their team colours, their muscles bulging under Lycra plastered with sponsors' logos. Small round paunches indicated that this was no ordinary race. Most teams had been 'eating up' for months, to create a layer of fat that could be used by the body during the race. I hadn't eaten, let alone 'eaten up', for a week. My tummy grumbled with hunger; or was it trepidation? For the first time since my arrival on La Gomera I recognized the unpleasant sensation of wings fluttering in my stomach.

It was calm and cloudless as the sun began to rise. A seagull watched as I struggled with the still unfamiliar hatch. I squeezed my meagre possessions into the tiny cubby-hole that I'd been allocated for the journey. The ocean is no place for comfort, nor for materialism.

We had been on La Gomera for nearly ten days, but this morning everything looked and felt unfamiliar, not just the surroundings but my feelings too.

JAMES

For the last week I'd watched as the other competitors fine-tuned their boats. Making sure the weight was distributed evenly, essential items were within easy reach; cabins were decorated with family pictures and messages of support from loved ones, an inspirational reminder of home and a refuge from the ocean.

It was time to put the suppliers' stickers on the boat; all those companies who had donated equipment, food, energy drinks and even plane tickets got some space on the boat. I'd left it until this moment as a symbolic act – a declaration to ourselves as much as anything that we were ready. Like in *Days of Thunder*, where Robert Duvall unveils the gleaming car covered in new sponsors' stickers and an amazing paint job for Tom Cruise to race in and against the odds (surprisingly) win the Indy 500 and get the girl. Our unveiling was not quite as spectacular; after its hasty reconstruction the boat was ugly and efficient rather than aesthetically jaw-dropping. Even after the stickers were on I had to remove an angle-grinder, a jigsaw, a belt-sander and countless other tools from the cabin before we could even begin to start packing our personal belongings in.

Ben arrived just before 8 a.m., his cheery 'Morning' not hiding his apprehension. Seeing the weather he must have been hit by the reality as well: the race was going to start today. I left Ben sticking nets to the inside of the cabin, pockets that would hold all our essentials: Vaseline, seasickness pills, iPod, sunglasses and toothbrush – although I'm disappointed to say this became a non-essential and worryingly underused item.

I walked back to the hotel for one last meal that I wouldn't have to add water to. But before that could happen there was some conflict resolution required between my wife and me. Going to sleep on an argument is one thing; going to sea for two months is another. Wandering through reception I heard a voice shrieking 'Daddy! Daddy!' from the restaurant; Croyde was there having/wearing his breakfast with my mother-in-law Joyce, who'd looked after the little man the night before to give Bev and I some quiet time to ourselves. Our room had certainly been quiet.

I'd explained to Croyde that I was going across the sea in a boat with Ben to Antigua. I would be gone for a while but he'd get to come on an aeroplane (his favourite mode of transport) to see me. He seemed to understand that I was 'going rowing in a boat with Ben to America'. I thought that was close enough and Ben came with a ringing endorse-ment from Croyde because he'd seen him with a tiger on TV (Croyde's preferred animal, with the possible exception of dinosaurs).

Sitting there eating cereal topped with orange juice – a taste sensation courtesy of Croyde – I knew I'd underestimated how hard I was going to find it being away from him. When I'd originally agreed to race he was so much younger and the ratio of effort in to pleasure out was weighted mightily in his favour (my dad would say the ratio never changes). Since then he'd turned into a chattering ball of energy that lit up both our lives, and leaving him was going to be incredibly hard.

Although I've lived by the rule that if somebody can say something to my face then they are free to write about it, I hadn't expected Bev to voice our disagreement about the race in a national newspaper. That's the way I approached this book: anything I've written about Ben I'll either have said to him during the row or told him prior to publication; being honest and consistent is the best policy. It does seem to get me into heated discussions (arguments) but, despite that, I like to think of it as one of my endearing qualities. Climbing the stairs back to our hotel room I hoped Bev was of the same opinion. As with many of our arguments there was no real resolution; neither of us wanted to apologize, despite both of us knowing we were wrong. Instead we got on with the few hours we had left, both harbouring regrets but still seething about what had happened.

I packed a bag to go back with my family to the UK and a smaller one for the boat. Weight was still the biggest influence over what did and didn't make it onboard. The result was that the bag to go on the boat contained two pairs of shorts, a T-shirt, a singlet, a long-sleeved top, photographs of Bev and Croyde, a letter each from my parents (including one for Ben), two letters from Bev – one for Christmas Day and one to be opened when I was at my lowest point on the trip – two Christmas presents and my passport. The bag home contained everything else I had and hadn't needed over the previous ten days. Almost immediately another argument erupted, as a pram, a two-year-old and four bags were going to make the journey back to the UK almost impossible.

Armageddon was avoided by me leaving half my belongings on La Gomera, and a timely interruption by Ben phoning to say the race had been delayed until 12 p.m. to let the 11.30 a.m. ferry leave without a fleet of rowing boats littering the harbour. This created another problem: Bev and Croyde had tickets for the 11.30 a.m. ferry. I tried to explain this might be for the best: watching your husband or your daddy row out to sea, getting smaller and smaller until disappearing over the horizon, is not the last image I'd want to be left with if I was the one standing on the beach.

Down at the boat, I climbed aboard and squeezed into the cabin, banging my head and elbows simultaneously (an initiation ceremony for the daily abuse they were to receive) as I forced myself in and out of the two-foot-square hatch. Inside the cabin I could just about sit up by the entrance but at the stern there was only room to lie down. I slid back on the mattress and realized this was my first time lying in the cabin. The roof was less than eight inches from my face, with bare wood staring down at me: our own private coffin. I had known it would be small, but tried to convince myself it would be cosy rather than claustrophobic and that once the race started I'd be too tired for the size of the cabin to bother me. Even so, I put my personal effects into the pockets on 'my side of the cabin' and got the hell out of there as fast as possible.

Less than an hour to go. I wanted to say goodbye and good luck to the other competitors, some of whom I knew from international racing and others who had become friends during the build-up to the race. I hiked round to the other side of the marina – the most organized crews had grabbed the berths which required the least walking, vitally important when you're loading up. The rush for the best spot had resembled a supermarket car-park on a Saturday morning, where the best spaces are taken five minutes after the shop opens. Ben and I had been left with a berth the equivalent of parking next to the recycling bins.

Wishing a competitor good luck is not something I would have done before an Olympic Final. There might have been a nod to the opposition if we walked past each other or happened to be taking a piss at the same time close to the race, but no more than that. At the Olympics people are there for one reason: to win, or at least to try to get a medal. Because it happens once every four years the stakes are huge, and your opponents stand in the way of what you have sacrificed so much for. Baron de

Coubertin's maxim, 'It's not about the winning but the taking part,' is not the ethos of the modern Olympics. The ancient Latin motto *'Citius, Altius, Fortius'* ('Faster, Higher, Stronger') is more applicable and what the athletes are really striving for.

An Olympic rowing final lasts about six minutes. In a race that short there can be no mistakes, everybody has to contend with the same conditions and it's not dangerous. Crossing the Atlantic couldn't be more different. There is plenty of time to both make and recover from mistakes; but unlike in the Olympics, those mistakes could cost you your life.

This final point was emphasized as I wished the others good luck; the last thing everyone said was either 'Be safe' or 'Look after yourself'. I didn't think I'd been flippant about the dangers at sea but having looked at previous races where nobody had to be rescued I was absolutely confident we would get there. It was just a case of being mentally and physically strong.

Had we been blasé and underestimated the ocean, as the organizers had said? Were we really ready for this? These questions were bouncing round my head as I wandered back to our boat. I bumped into Peter Haining on the way, a former British international rower and three times world champion, who was on La Gomera to support his girlfriend. He had taken part in the inaugural 1997 race and before setting off had tipped himself to win; he lasted just hours before being towed back to the start line suffering from chronic seasickness, which was followed by chronic piss-taking when he got back to the UK. I didn't think we'd be the quickest but I was in no doubt we'd make it to Antigua. And yet standing in front of me was a lesson in what happens when you underestimate the ocean. Being able to row was no guarantee I was going to get across.

BEN

We hadn't even begun the race and already I needed a break from the boat. I made my way to one of the cafés on the square. 'This is really it,' I thought as I sipped on my milky coffee. I felt sick and very alone.

'Mummy, we're off,' I spoke softly into the phone. I knew they were not the words my mother wanted to hear, but it had been a stressful ten days and I think part of her was actually relieved. 'Be careful, darling,' she ended tearfully.

Tears brimmed in my eyes as I dialled Marina's mobile.

'This is it, darling,' I sighed.

We chatted and laughed and cried. 'I'll call you from the ocean,' I ended.

'I LOVE YOU.' Her departing words echoed in my head as I walked back down to the harbour. Why was I doing this to her?, I wondered. Why was I doing this at all?

'Why on earth would you want to do that?' had been the common reaction to the revelation of my forthcoming adventure. 'Because it's there,' had been my customary answer, although this hadn't been sufficient for my mother or granny, who were both uncustomarily opposed to the row. Despite the regularity with which I'm asked the question, even now I struggle for a rational, reasonable answer.

I have been attracted to adventure ever since I was tiny. After school I set out on a 1,000-mile bicycle ride with two friends from London to Monte Carlo (interestingly, one of those friends, Cass Gilbert, never stopped and is now on his third circuit of the world). I went on to sate my itchy feet with a gap year in South America, which began with a 3,000-mile boat journey from the mouth of the Amazon to the source in the Andes. The year was a catalyst for my travels and I spent a second year working on a turtle conservation project on the Mosquito Coast of Honduras before studying for a degree in Latin American Studies at the University of Costa Rica.

But the defining moment in my life came after I applied to spend a year on the BBC's millennium social experiment, *Castaway 2000*, in which thirty-six men, women and children spent a year on the Scottish island of Taransay in the Outer Hebrides. The year not only gave me the opportunity to break away from city life, but proved to be a life-changing adventure. Indeed my friends and family all thought I was crazy when I first announced my plans to resign my job at society glossy *Tatler* and 'live like a hippy for a year'. They simply couldn't comprehend why I would want to do such a thing. I received a similarly incredulous reaction when I announced my plans to row the Atlantic.

My general outlook on life changed after *Castaway*, there was a real sense of 'If I can do this, I can do anything'. I had spent a year battling the elements, and fighting to preserve my sanity on a treeless island, and having overcome what had felt like insuperable obstacles to make my situation on Taransay viable no challenge seemed too great.

For the next few years, I sated my wanderlust with dozens of adventures around the world. I was arrested and deported from Pitcairn, the remote Pacific island home of the mutineers from the *Bounty*, on suspicion of spying; I relocated rhinos in Nepal, went husky dog racing in the Arctic and chased cheeses down hills in Cheddar, to name just a few. But all these paled into insignificance after a drunken bet in 2005.

Over a pint, a friend suggested I run the London Marathon. I announced that if I was to run any marathon, it would be the Marathon des Sables, a 160-mile self-sufficient race across the Sahara desert. Pride won and just three months later I found myself hobbling across vast sand dunes in 100-degree heat with 700 international runners. I returned to London a new person. I walked taller, with a strut to my step. It was one of my proudest achievements. I can remember striding around Notting Hill Gate in my surgical socks hoping people would ask what had happened to my feet.

A psychologist would probably call it a reaction to my distinctly unsporty childhood, but I think it was deeper than that, perhaps a primal attempt to test myself. Indeed, human physical endurance is in many ways the twentieth-century form of exploration. Amundsen, Livingstone, Bingham et al have all but mapped our world, and even today's great explorers like Sir Ranulph Fiennes, who recently attempted to run seven marathons on seven continents, have resorted to physical endurance in order to find new ways to test the limits of our existence. We are no longer able to 'discover' our world and so the same tests of mental and physical strength are internalized. The test is the same – man versus environment – but the subject of the experiment is me rather than the ocean. For me the Marathon des Sables, or Sand Marathon as it translates, was a catalyst for my self-confidence. I love challenging people's perceptions. I work in a business where one is so often pigeon-holed and stereotyped, and I am always trying to test that typecasting.

But it wasn't just challenging people's stereotypes that attracted me to such adventures and challenges, it was also the chance to take myself out of my comfort zone. We live in a society of excesses, where just about anything and everything is available at our beck and call. It's not that I don't enjoy my comfy, contented life with my beautiful girlfriend, Notting Hill flat and loyal friends, but I have always enjoyed leaving those environs to test myself outside the circle. There is something so sweet about returning to life's luxuries after a period of abstinence. Everything, from tastes and textures to feelings and conversations, is much more vivid, and somehow also more precious.

I live my life by the adage 'Add life to your days, not days to your life', and for me, every experience is another ingot in life's treasure chest. It is no coincidence that Woodvale's literature states, 'One life, live it,' and for me the best answer I can give as to why I should want to row across the Atlantic Ocean is my other favourite maxim, 'If not you, then who? If not now, then when?' The day of the race had finally arrived and I knew the answers to those questions:

It was ME, and it was NOW.

James was busy making some last-minute tweaks to the oars. 'What's this?' he asked, holding up my fleece. 'We're not going to the Arctic,' he continued. I rolled my eyes and ignored him.

Beverley appeared looking remarkably calm and glamorous, clutching two enormous bags bulging with bread rolls and sandwiches. Marina had discovered that rowers in past Atlantic races had lived off fresh rolls for the first week and in her absence Beverley had promised to stock the boat. Twenty Marmite-and-cheese rolls were carefully placed into one of the deck stores, alongside the Vaseline and sun cream.

Croyde explored the boat for one last time as we finalized the packing and discarded anything deemed unnecessary, which despite our stringent rules about extraneous kit seemed to be almost everything. James's obsession with weight continued. I was surprised not to be weighed myself before being allowed to come aboard.

JAMES

Watching Ben disappear into the cabin clutching a huge pile of letters, one for every day of the race, I bit my lip; despite all our discussions on keeping the weight to a minimum, not much seemed to have sunk in. Admittedly letters don't weigh very much but if we'd had that mindset about everything on board then we would have been lugging a hell of a lot more weight across the Atlantic. I was convinced that having a light boat was psychologically invaluable: if we believed it was lighter, we'd go faster. But in order for us to truly believe it was lighter it was important for us to go without some comforts. I thought a letter a day was excessive but with less than two hours to go until the race this was no time to raise the issue, and given the stress of the last ten days, it seemed petty.

BEN

A stream of rowers came along to wish us luck. One boat handed us a small Christmas present. James responded by giving them his 'gift': 'Why don't you take Christmas Day off on us.'

Oh James, I thought as I packed away their present. It was 11 a.m. In just an hour we'd be off. I sat on my sheepskin-padded seat and smothered myself in sunscreen as James kissed Beverley and Croyde goodbye on the jetty. I really felt for James, waving goodbye to his little boy. I recalled Croyde singing 'Row row row your boat' as we had struggled to finish our preparations. I couldn't fault his logic, but I wondered what he made of it all. I wished my family and Marina had his naivety. I watched transfixed as Beverley and Croyde disappeared down the jetty, his little hand waving over her shoulder, and then it dawned on me: this had been my idea. I had asked James along. If anything happened to him it was essentially my fault. I had a commitment to Croyde.

JAMES

I don't know how soldiers, astronauts or anyone in a profession where death is a real possibility say goodbye. Is it something that gets easier?

Or is it because it is their job that makes it easier for both parties to handle?

Either way, our farewell wasn't a memory to cherish, despite Bev saying for the first time that she was proud of me. I knew she didn't want me to go; and combined with my guilt for leaving her to cope with Croyde, the stress of the building work that had just started on our house and the prospect of spending Christmas alone, there were too many emotions and issues for it to be a simple loving goodbye. Saying farewell to Croyde was harder for me than for him. I told him I loved him and was going on the boat now. I got a cheery 'OK Daddy, see you later'. I'd have liked to have seen him slightly disappointed, but the prospect of a trip on a ferry was the only thing on his mind and compared to his dad going to sea for a few months was a far more pressing issue.

We were being given a final run-through of the camera equipment from Alexis, the director of the BBC documentary about the race, when we were told by the organizers to make our way to the start area, just outside the marina. We said our last goodbyes; having decided to catch the next ferry and risk missing their plane, my sister and her fiancé were still by the boat. My sister and I had a combustible childhood together (a worryingly common denominator seems to be developing here) but have grown closer as we've got older. When we hugged goodbye it was the first time I've ever seen concern or worry for me in her eyes. It made me glad Mum had gone home the day before. I'm not sure how she would have coped watching her baby boy head out to sea.

BEN

This was it. Our families and partners were gone and we were on our own, just the two of us. Months of planning culminated in this moment. We hadn't even set off and already I felt like I'd rowed an ocean. The stresses of the week had overshadowed the reality of the coming months. I had been focusing on the practicalities rather than the realities of what lay ahead and now, for the first time, I was scared. Really, really scared.

Chapter Three

The Start

Wednesday, 30 November 2005
Woodvale press release:

At 1130 hours GMT, the first of the rowing boats left the marina, Boat No. 14 – *Atlantic Prince*, leading, closely followed by the rest of the fleet. At 1200 Hours GMT, a five-minute Woodvale preparatory flag was hoisted onboard official start boat and primary support vessel *Aurora*, allowing the fleet to strategically position themselves on the start line.

At 1205 hours GMT, the Woodvale flag was dropped to indicate the start of the race by three times Atlantic Ocean rower, Graham Walters, coinciding with a sound signal operated by the president of La Gomera, Casimiro Curbelo.

First across the start line was Boat No. 14 – *Atlantic Prince* rowed by Dan Darley and Richard DeWire closely followed by Devonshire based Boat No. 24 – *All Relative* and then single-handed boat, Boat No. 5 – *Pacific Pete*. The celebrity team of BBC 1 presenter Ben Fogle and double Olympic Gold Medal rower James Cracknell were not far behind the first three, crossing the start line in fifth position.

With a following wind of 18 to 20 knots from the NNE, the conditions on race start day were perfect for an exciting sprint start and the fleet overall left the shores of La Gomera at an average speed of 2.5 to 3.5 knots on a heading of 190 true. Once past the second support vessel, *Sula*, positioned some three miles off shore, the teams were clear to take their preferred course across the Atlantic Ocean, bound for Antigua.

BEN

We cast off the lines and manoeuvred our cumbersome craft from her mooring. 'Ditch the fenders,' ordered James. I donated them to a passing yacht as we carefully rowed out of the marina and into the harbour where all the boats had congregated.

I was filled with apprehension. I was dreading the start of the race more than anything. I knew that James wanted to hit it hard and that a weak start would be a disastrous beginning to our voyage. We had not taken the oars together more than five times and this was the first time we had rowed competitively.

Adrenaline was running high. James's eyes flicked from side to side as he weighed up the competition. We had sized up one another's boats on dry land and in the marina, but out on the ocean they looked different; despite their similarities to our vessel they all appeared to be sturdier and faster than ours. Most families and friends had been forced to leave early owing to the original postponement, so the beginning of our adventure was marked by a small crowd of locals and tourists who had lined the breakwater to watch our momentous start. I felt hopelessly ill-prepared as James rowed us past the dozens of increasingly vast yachts.

JAMES

We waited at the marina entrance as the 11.30 ferry left; I looked for Bev and Croyde hoping for a last glimpse of them waving frantically at the balcony but couldn't see them. Ben was busy putting his oars in the gates – the wrong way round: not a good start.

I'd hoped to improve his rowing in the week before the race, naively thinking our boat would take only a couple of days to get ready and that we would be able to spend the rest of the time enjoying the sun, beach and local restaurants as we fattened ourselves up for the journey. However, during the previous ten days the things that had seemed important before we arrived had been shoved way down our list of priorities. One of these was Ben's ability to row; it had been a major concern in the UK but amongst all our other problems in the Canaries it had barely crossed my mind. As we were paddling towards the muster area I remembered why I had been worried. I didn't want to be teaching Ben how to row when we were out at sea; it wouldn't help either of us. You don't want someone telling you what to do when you're exhausted, but on the other hand you don't want to be rowing for 3,000 miles with someone who can't row.

I remember thinking, 'Why didn't you take yourself down to a rowing club a few times a month? You've known you're doing the race for a year!' Realizing that wouldn't be a particularly inspiring comment ten minutes before the start I broke the habit of a lifetime and bit my tongue. I decided I'd give Ben some gentle tips during the first week (although I'm not sure how gentle he thought they were) and then when fatigue had settled in not say anything else, as the chances were it would create more problems than it would solve.

The start procedure had been fully explained using twice as many words and taking twice as long as necessary. Basically we had to be in the start area five minutes before the off and anybody who drifted through the start early would receive a 24-hour time penalty. A harsh punishment for jumping the start in a 3,000-mile race, but it had the desired effect of controlling people's enthusiasm to lead the field out of the harbour.

I was looking forward to seeing how fast we were. Having not had the opportunity to practise, we had no idea how quickly we could perform. Ben, on the other hand, didn't really care. As the minutes counted down, all my thoughts were focused on the start.

One minute to go. I wished Ben good luck and waited for the flag to drop.

BEN

We pulled alongside the cow stripes of *C2* as the boats jostled for position.

'Where's the start line again?' I asked nervously.

'Between *Aurora* and the red buoy,' James muttered.

Brrrrrrrrrrrrrrrrrrrrrrrrrrrrrrrrrrrr!, sounded the claxon before I could hear the answer, as a long banner unfurled on the support yacht..

We were off. Three thousand miles of ocean lay between us and the finish line.

JAMES

Nobody was sure whether that was the start or not, then I heard 'Good luck everybody' come drifting across the water and I yelled 'Go!' to Ben. I was pretty sure the boats that were serious about racing all the way to Antigua would go off hard and make their intentions clear from the very beginning.

Despite knowing the race was 3,000 miles and going to take around seven weeks, it wasn't enough to change my default mechanism. When the guy says go: race. As we left La Gomera harbour behind and headed out into the Atlantic it still hadn't really clicked what we had undertaken. I was too busy comparing our speed to that of the other boats, and the reassuring sight of land meant my brain hadn't truly grasped what was happening.

With the sun piercing a hole in the bright blue sky and a following wind blowing us along, the tropical storm and our problems on land were already becoming a distant memory. We were on our way and nobody could stop us now. We were also holding our own in the race. Having started just behind the first line of boats it now looked like we were catching them up. I glanced over my shoulder and saw the Irish boys on board *Digicel* – Boat No. 1 – and we were definitely catching them. Admittedly neither boat was doing a pace we could keep going for 3,000 miles.

I no longer had to turn round; I could see them in my peripheral vision. A few minutes later that became redundant; they were behind us: we'd overtaken the pre-race favourites and only had 2,998 miles to go!

It felt amazing. The pressure we'd been under since arriving in the Canary Islands was disappearing with every stroke. There was only one boat ahead of us: *Atlantic Prince*. It didn't have the best rowers in the race on board but they were well prepared, which I'd learnt over the last week was probably more important. Squinting into the harsh midday sun, I was sure we were catching them.

All crews were required to stay on a bearing of 190 degrees for the first three miles, and then we were free to choose our own course. I set myself a target of leading at that checkpoint, the last and indeed only one until the finish line 2,997 miles later. Ben agreed to up the effort and reel *Atlantic Prince* in before the checkpoint (at least that's what I think he said); either way it worked, and we moved steadily past them and took the lead. I was amazed. I thought we'd improve as the race progressed – we had so much to learn about our boat that the other crews already knew about theirs and Ben's rowing could only get better. To be going this well straight away, and with the boat coping with the sea so well, it was going to be plain sailing to Antigua.

With *Atlantic Prince* slipping further behind I felt a familiar buzz starting to flow through my body, a surge of endorphins that I only get when I'm racing, or to be more precise that I only get when things are going my way in a race. If I was leading a major final they would start to pump through my body, making all the training I'd done and sacrifices I'd made during the year worthwhile; I'd feel stronger and stronger as the race went on and at that point, I always knew I was going to win. It is a feeling that is impossible to re-create any other way. Was I going to get to feel like this for two months? I hoped so.

BEN

In and out, in and out, I dragged my oars through the azure water as beads of sweat streamed down my face.

'Pull a little harder,' implored James calmly. 'Long, slow strokes,' he added. 'Good, Ben, good.'

I smiled as we began to break away from the fleet. The RIBs, sturdy little vessels that populate any coastal resort, buzzed around as we rowed on into the increasing swell. The sun beat down on us as we thrashed onwards and upwards. We were soon alongside *Atlantic Prince*.

James looked at them, they looked at James, James looked at me, I looked at them. We picked up the pace and edged ahead.

'Good, Ben,' whispered James, as we dug in. 'We're going to be in first place at this rate,' he announced triumphantly, before disaster struck.

JAMES

The endorphins were still pumping, but something didn't feel right; the oar in my left hand was not locking in the water, it felt loose. I glanced quickly at it; everything seemed all right but then I saw that the gate (which holds the oar to the boat) was rocking violently, when it should be locked in place. There wasn't much time before the nut locking it to the side of the boat would come off and we had no spares. I threw my oars down – if the nut fell off and went overboard we would be down to one rowing position after less than an hour of the race – but I was too late: the nut came off, clanking on to the deck and rolling towards the scupper (the hole in the side of the boat that lets any water, or stray nuts, drain off the deck). I made an uncoordinated lunge to my left and missed the nut; fortunately it stopped before disappearing out and down into the Atlantic.

I couldn't believe I hadn't double-checked the nuts. In any previous races I've done, this kind of mistake would have guaranteed defeat. Luckily because of the distance we had left to cover it was irrelevant but I was embarrassed, frustrated and starting to think that the organizers might have been right when they said Ben and I weren't properly prepared for the race.

The boats we'd spent an hour overtaking were gaining on us hand over fist. Ben dug the tool bag out of the bow cabin; I was impressed by how relaxed he was about equipment failure so early in the race, especially since, for all he knew, it could have been race-threatening.

Earlier in the morning I'd been complaining that the tool bag wasn't made of see-through material because it would mean emptying everything out unless you got lucky and the required tool was on top. Obviously now that I needed a tool in a hurry I wasn't lucky: the 17mm spanner was at the bottom of the bag.

I fished it out just as *Atlantic Prince* was overtaking us, shouting across, 'Bit early for a re-rig!', a term used in 'normal' rowing where a lot of time is spent setting up the gearing of the boat perfectly for the people rowing it and the conditions. They'd used it either as an attempt at humour or as a dig at us, unless I was being oversensitive. *Atlantic Prince*'s crew, Dan and Rich, were club rowers who had spent a long time preparing and considered themselves favourites. In fairness they had come second in the four-mile race around the harbour held just a few days previously when the tropical storm had delayed the original start. It was a race Ben and I hadn't been able to take part in because we hadn't been ready.

The atmosphere during the build-up to the race had been incredibly friendly, with everybody pitching in to help each other out, and despite their scepticism about us – Ben and I expected favours from the organizers, were underprepared and were not taking the event seriously – many other competitors had lent us a helping hand during that week. *Atlantic Prince* had been the exception, despite being one of the first finished boats.

There is of course no reason why they should help a competitor but with the general feeling among the racers that the real opposition was the Atlantic, everybody mucked in. Dan and Rich's most helpful contribution was a comment they made in the chandlery that 'We have every faith you'll beat Roz' (referring to Roz Savage, a lady racing on her own who completed her crossing in 102 days).

It wasn't just the comment that wound me up, since it was probably meant as a joke (although if that was the case then some work is required on the boys' comic timing), but it revived a question that I'd been asking myself ever since I agreed to row with Ben, a question that I'd failed to come to terms with: would other people think I was doing the race with Ben just to have a documentary on TV, instead of giving myself the best chance of winning? As the start had drawn nearer this had become more of an issue. I'd never entered a race where I'd knowingly lessened my chances of success. In the past even if I'd been in crews that weren't favourites to win, they had still been made up of the best people available. I couldn't say that on this occasion. In fact, I didn't need to say it; plenty of the other competitors were quick to point out weaknesses in my partner. And yet while I agreed with them on Ben's rowing pedigree, they had overlooked qualities that I was sure would serve him well at sea and I was surprised by the arrogance of others taking part in the race. It is always dangerous to underestimate people, and I stored the comments up as a source of motivation.

In retrospect my concerns were not so much due to what others thought, but what I thought. I'd tried to convince myself that as long as Ben and I were amongst the leading boats and gave everything we had during the race, I'd be satisfied. Looking back, I was kidding myself. There was no way I'd be truly satisfied with anything other than arriving into Antigua first, which was not the kind of news Ben was hoping for.

As I was hunting for the 17mm spanner, the smiles and comments of *Atlantic Prince* as they glided past gave me, and I also hoped Ben, some extra fuel for the fire. Anything at that point would have wound me up; I was so angry with myself for letting an elementary mistake like this lose us the honour of leading the boats away, and for giving the organizers any reason to think they had been right about us.

A minute later the nut was tight and we were both rowing again and *Atlantic Prince* was still in sight. The extra adrenaline from our early and unplanned pit-stop giving us, or at least me, extra energy to retake the lead, we reeled them in once again. Our fast boat speed wasn't a fluke after all. It transpired that we were naturally pretty quick.

When we moved into the lead for the second time, however, there wasn't the same euphoric excitement. We had found out how quickly a lead could be overturned. Our boat felt like it was going quickly but as we passed *Atlantic Prince* I could see how slowly both boats were actually going. The speed on the GPS of 3.5 knots confirmed it: we were managing little more than a quick walking pace. We were effectively playing a game of 'Pooh Sticks' across the ocean. It finally began to dawn on me: it was going to be a long race.

We passed the three-mile mark; we were free to choose our own bearing. Ben had decided to steer a course of 200 miles on a bearing of 220 degrees, so we changed course from our 190 bearing and headed off. This was our first big decision; nobody had told us where to steer. Unlike in a polar race, where you are given a course and only allowed to walk for a certain number of hours a day, our course and the number of hours we rowed a day was entirely down to us. Having said that, there hadn't been much more science in planning our route than Columbus used five hundred years ago when he'd said, 'Go south until the butter melts, then turn right.'

In previous races the faster boats had tended to row a 'rhumb line' (straight course) from the Canary Islands to the Caribbean. People sailing across travel south to take advantage of the stronger trade winds and currents, their higher boat speed and the benefits they get from the wind making this an easy decision. We had to try to work out if the benefit of helpful winds was worth the extra miles we'd have to row; in the end we decided to split the difference.

As we turned we could still see most of the fleet stretched out behind us. I waited to see how many would steer our course, but only one boat came our way; the rest seemed to be heading for the more direct route. It wasn't the ringing endorsement of our decision I was hoping for, and I was tempted to alter our course and mirror that of the majority of the fleet. But Ben had spent more time looking at the charts than me and in our division of roles on board he was 'Captain of Navigation' and had the final say (and at that point was the only one who'd read the GPS instructions). I was reassured that the only other crew who had come our way were the pre-race favourites *Digicel* and their support team included some experienced sailors, so I figured if it was good enough for them, it was good enough for us.

BEN

Of the two of us, I had the most experience on the ocean. Indeed I had spent four years as a midshipman in the Royal Naval Reserve. Midshipman is a pretty lowly officer-class but it was a stripe that I had worn with real pride, although I have to say not necessarily with immense skill. As we'd toiled to equip *Spirit*, for example, I had been pleased – and not a little relieved – by James's failure to notice that whilst my bowlines were pretty much perfect they were also the only knot I was able to tie. However, my limited knowledge of knots notwithstanding, my experience at sea would, I hoped, prove invaluable to myself and James in other ways.

As a midshipman one of my regular duties when we set out into the Solent week after week was to 'nav'. In fact, my last tour of duty had been onboard a P2000 (best described as a small floating caravan) which had escorted HMS *Britannia* on its final journey into Portsmouth. I was sure that my hours huddled over gyroscopic compasses taking more-than-averagely-rhumb fixed bearings couldn't fail to stand James and me in good stead. I would never claim that navigation was my forte – my fixed bearings had always resembled a rather unfortunate triangle as opposed to the more useful single intersection – but I had taken on the mantle of 'Captain of Navigation', based mainly on the premise that James would be 'Captain of Rowing', and I would do my best to fulfil that role. My confidence had been dented by Lin's assertion that I couldn't navigate, but I had endeavoured to establish a tactical route. It resulted in my being bombarded with conflicting advice on the best bearings for our journey.

Historically, the fastest rowers had taken the shortest route from A to B, but tacticians, including sailor Emma Richards, whom we had met before we left London, had suggested a southerly route in order to pick up the trade winds and the prevailing currents. By rowing an extra hundred or so miles south, we stood to gain not only stronger winds but an extra knot of current. But it was a gamble: if we went too far we could get caught in the westerlies and be blown into Western Africa.

As the necessity to plot our course loomed into view I pored over the unfamiliar charts, and deliberated over the best route. Neither of us had fully appreciated just how important our decisions would be. It seems strange now, but we had spent so long worrying about everything else, that the small matter of course had been somewhat overlooked. Admittedly, it was my department, but I had been so preoccupied with getting race-ready, that the mechanics of direction had seemed academic. Now in the hard Atlantic, the bearing became increasingly relevant, and I, as the Captain of Nav, felt increasingly that I had a great responsibility.

On the advice of a number of individuals, including a meteorologist, who supported Emma's recommendations, I established a course of 220 degrees for 200 miles. It was a risk in terms of the extra mileage it added to our trip, but if it worked it would set us directly on course for Antigua. If I got it wrong, we could end up in the Cape Verde Islands.

JAMES

As the field spread out it was becoming difficult to see other boats, and even harder to tell who was in the lead. Crews kept disappearing into the trough of a wave and we'd struggle to spot them again.

We were holding the course well despite having problems steering. Olympic rowing boats are steered by a rudder about three times as big as a postage stamp. These ocean boats came complete with a rudder measuring one metre by 30cm but no steering system, so it was up to individual crews to invent a mechanism. There seemed to be plenty of ways to skin a cat looking at the other boats before the start; no two appeared to have the same steering system, and whereas some boats had automatic rudders, others were toe-steered, heel-steered, or even controlled by hand.

The rigging of the rudder had been left to me. I decided that, rather than make it toe-steered (where the steering wire is connected to the top of the shoe) as in conventional rowing boats, we would instead have a heel-steered system, because of the greater force required to turn the rudder in ocean conditions. The foot is in a stronger position pivoting from the heel than the toe, and I also thought it would be better to have a steering foot in each rowing position because then Ben and I could have our own rowing set-up for the entire race. The only problem was, that meant a lot of steering line was required, a complicated tangle of knots and pulleys.

In the week leading up to the race, crews were adjusting their steering after most training sessions. Ours had to be right first time. If we'd managed that, it would be a landmark event in our preparation.

We were close but it wasn't perfect; the steering moved freely and worked well in Ben's position up in the bows, but in the stern, where the rope passed through a number of pulleys, it was too stiff to move. Until it loosened up, it was up to Ben to steer. The only problem was he couldn't see the screen to know if we were on the right course or not.

BEN

For James, rowing is second nature. By his own admission, he could row in his sleep, but for a novice like myself I found it difficult to sync the action of rowing with the movement of the boat, and to make matters worse, I was struggling with the steering.

'My steering doesn't work!' screamed James above the din of the wind. 'You'll have to steer.'

When I tried to control the boat's direction I was doing my best to synchronize my oar strokes while also struggling with the unfamiliar footplate steering. I was confused and disorientated by the backwards steering.

'Left!' James would cry, at which point I would inevitably steer right.

'Left, I said left!' he would bellow. Did he mean my left or the boat's left, and if he meant the boat's left, then was that from the front or the back, in which case did that mean twisting my foot to the left or the right? If I twisted my toe left, then that would send the boat right, but because I faced backwards, it was in fact left…

My mind felt clogged with the concentration of steering as I strained to keep up with the punishing rhythm of James's oar strokes. 'Harder,' he demanded as we beat into the waves. 'I want to hear you breathing,' he urged as I rowed with all my might. The oars were digging painfully into my chest, occasionally wedging against my thighs as I fought to keep up with James. Every so often I would miss a stroke, and knock into James's back as we slid out of tandem.

'Fucking hell!' he screamed.

'Sorry,' I'd reply as the pressure mounted.

'Left!' he instructed. The boat turned to the right.

'No, LEFT, Ben.'

I have never been good with my lefts and rights, let alone ports and starboards in reverse. Indeed, I was once voted off the BBC's *The Weakest Link* first with the question: 'When laying the table, on which side does the fork go?' I of course answered, 'The right', despite three years as a silver-service waiter. As I say, I have never been strong in the directions department and now, hungry, sore and dehydrated, I was more confused than ever.

It drove James crazy. He simply couldn't understand how I could mix up my lefts and rights. If we were heading, as we often were, on a course of 265 degrees, and the GPS screen was showing 290 degrees, then I knew I had to decrease my angle, but did that mean toe to the left or the right? I racked my brain each time. Even now as I sit at my computer and recount my confusion, I can't for the life of me remember which way was which. The result, of course, was trial and error and therefore a vastly inefficient course of weaves.

JAMES

The race officials would have felt fully justified in not letting us race if they'd seen us trying to steer; it was an object lesson in miscommunication. I'd see we'd drifted off course and would shout, 'Left!' Ben would say, 'What?' I'd shout, 'LEFT!' a bit louder, I'd hear, 'OK', which was normally followed by me saying, 'Other way!' or Ben saying, 'Which way do I point my foot?' I explained before we left, and almost every time he had to steer, that all you had to do was point your foot the way you wanted to go. It wasn't rocket science but according to Ben it was too difficult a concept to grasp if you were trying to learn how to row at the same time. 'You shouldn't have waited until now to learn how to fucking row,' I said. Luckily this line got swallowed by the wind and Ben didn't hear it.

Once we'd got the boat steering in the right direction I then had to say, 'Foot straight!' because Ben couldn't see the screen to know when we were back on course. I kept forgetting he couldn't see the screen and that he therefore couldn't know when to take the rudder off, so we kept over-steering and then re-correcting, which meant yet more miscommunication. End result: zigzagging our way out into the Atlantic.

In spite of the minor tacking and teething problems though, we headed out pretty much on the course we wanted and as far as we could see, were still leading the fleet, when I heard Ben say, 'James, something appears to have gone wrong with the steering.'

My heart rate increased and I instantly felt sick. My head snapped round. 'What's happened?' I shouted. Inside my head I was yelling 'no, no, no', a mixture of frustration, anger and self-pity testing my self-control.

'Er, it's snapped,' came Ben's response.

'No, no, no, no!' I squealed. I saw the metal tensioners we'd attached in order to keep the steering line taught had separated and were lying on the deck. Thankfully it was a case of just screwing them back together, and at least this time there were no boats in sight to cruise past us as we carried out our second running repair in as many hours. Getting the boat set up was my responsibility and already two things had gone wrong; Ben had every right to be furious.

BEN

One hour, two hours, three hours passed. My mouth was parched; my hands were already scarred with ugly welts, my fingers sore with rapidly forming blisters, fourteen of them to be exact. They were everywhere: on the palms, on the joints, even on my fingertips.

By now we had lost sight of all other competitors. We had pulled ahead of *Atlantic Prince* and for several miles we had rowed with *Digicel*, James's main perceived rival; our boats weaved in and out of each other's course, passing dangerously close. At one point our oars had clashed. It seemed incredible that in this huge ocean we were fighting for space with another tiny boat. James relished every moment as we pulled ahead of the Irish internationals, his face beaming with satisfaction. It had been a strong start. Thank goodness.

My back ached; my hands and feet were blistered raw. I was hungry, thirsty, tired, bored, depressed, homesick, lonely, sad and scared and we were only a few hours into the race. What had I done? What were we doing here? Why hadn't Lin prevented us from taking part? She was right, I thought, as the long afternoon turned to evening. We weren't ready for this. As we rowed on I began to understand why other teams had spent a year or more planning for the race. Not only was the boat strange to James and me, but we were still strangers to one another.

As the sun began to set, we prepared to break into our watch system. We would each row for two hours, followed by a two-hour break. We would repeat this system, twenty-four hours a day, seven days a week, until we reached land on the other side, or that at least was the plan.

The boat pitched and fell with each wave. All around was darkness, the faint lights of La Gomera and the distant glow of Tenerife twinkling as we rowed away from the sanctity of land and into the unfamiliar ocean.

JAMES

I took the first shift, pausing as Ben clambered past and disappeared into the cabin. As the sun set the wind had dropped and the sea flattened out. The only boat in sight was the yacht chartered by the BBC to get some outside shots for the documentary we were making (the rest of the filming was to be done by us). I'd like to say the two hours flew by but they didn't. The boat felt really heavy. Too heavy? Two hours was the longest rowing session I regularly did in Olympic preparation; admittedly it was more intensive, but then I didn't have to get up two hours later and do it again and again and again. Ben came out of the cabin and by the look on his face the previous two hours hadn't been spent in a relaxed sleep. He said nothing, filled up his water bottle and started rowing.

Seasickness was my biggest fear in the first few days but as yet it hadn't materialized. When the race officials made us go out to sea to prove we knew one end of the boat from the other it took just thirty-five minutes until I was throwing up over the side. It was horrible. Our sea survival teacher had said, 'For the first two days you'll feel like you're dying and for the next two, you'll want to die.' It wasn't nice hearing it the first time in a classroom but when it echoed round my head as I threw up over the side, it sounded even worse. But with the combination of a following breeze, relatively flat seas and so much else going on I hadn't had time to even think about being seasick. I also realized that I hadn't been in the cabin or tried to eat anything.

I was about to attempt to do both. I dug out one of Bev's sandwiches, but missed the fruit she also packed (indeed we didn't even know it was there until we smelt it a few weeks later). Peeling off the clingfilm I realized how hungry I was and was delighted to be about to bite into a cheese and ham baguette rather than a dehydrated meal. I'd been rowing for nearly eight hours without eating anything, but one bite told me I wasn't yet that hungry. I wasn't feeling seasick, but I wasn't ready to eat anything either. I dived into the cabin to rest up before my next shift.

When I say dived into the cabin, it wasn't exactly graceful. Ben had already mastered a fairly elegant entry, sitting down in the hatch bum-first, bending forwards and going in backwards. The size of the doorway (for want of a better word) or my lack of flexibility meant I couldn't get in that way; instead I entered head-first, planting my head on the mattress, moving my arms through and using them to pull myself inside the cabin, scraping my knees as my legs came in. Stylish it wasn't, but throughout the journey I struggled to find a better way of getting in. At least it amused Ben.

BEN

As James squeezed himself into the cabin I prepared for my solo row. The initial six hours had been gruelling but nothing would hit me as hard as those first two hours alone at the oars. The weight of the boat seemed to be carried entirely in my back as I struggled to maintain my balance in the face of the waves. As I strained to sustain some kind of rhythm I became conscious of every gram of the half-ton boat under my (very weak) control. With every stroke the oars scraped my knees, seeming to confirm my lack of prowess as a rower. The not yet sea-worn skin on my fingers and palms yielded to the repeated action on the oars and the only possible positive was that I was now no longer concentrating on the pain in my back. I had new aches to consider, broken hands and scraped knees.

As my rowing position deteriorated over the course of the second hour I realized that everything about me and this boat was mismatched. I have never felt so totally uncomfortable. But with the two hours up I was at last free from the oars. I lay in the tiny cabin, rigid with fatigue, my eyes staring at the roof just a few inches above. My mind was contorted with confusion. I was shell-shocked. The rowing had kept me distracted, but now in the cabin the cold hard reality of life on board had begun to sink in. I had struggled to row, and now I struggled to sleep. I couldn't do anything. I felt insecure and inadequate.

Tears streamed down my cheeks as the reality of what lay ahead sunk in. The first few hours had been disguised by endorphins, but now in the solitude of the cabin, my real emotions were exposed. I felt such a tremendous responsibility towards James. It was agony. I was the one who had suggested the race. I had dragged him away from his family, causing a rift with Bev. And now here we were just a few hours into the race, and already I was deflated and defeated. I was embarrassed and felt like a fraud. What was I doing rowing across an ocean with a double-Olympic gold medallist with a reputation for determination and perfection?

JAMES

I'd felt alone rowing that first shift but it was nothing compared to that first two hours in the cabin. That was when the reality of what was ahead of us hit me. I now understood why Ben had looked so haunted when he came out for his first rowing shift. The immensity of what we had started and the lack of thought we had given to life at sea were rapidly becoming apparent. When Lin had said that she was really worried because we weren't afraid enough it had seemed offensive at the time, but now her words made total sense. We'd got the boat ready in time but mentally we weren't anywhere near the start line.

I'd thought we'd row two hours on and two hours off and then approximately fifty days later we'd get to Antigua. It sounded so easy on land, but I'd not given any real consideration to what those fifty days would be like.

It didn't help seeing Ben silhouetted against the night sky, clearly struggling to row. Anger started pulsing through my body; why hadn't he gone down to a rowing club and learnt the basics before he got out here? I'd promised myself I wouldn't look at his speed and compare it to mine. According to previous competitors that would drive me insane; as long as we were both doing our best it didn't matter, but knowing that Ben had handicapped himself not getting suitably prepared made it difficult.

Ben could have said the same about me. I hadn't done my job properly; the last-minute adjustments to the boat and today's problems were my fault. The squeaking I could hear coming through the hatch was a reminder of the drastic alterations to the seating position I'd insisted on to correct my design fault; we had had to chop the seats out and they had not been put back together exactly in line, hence the squeaking. I was still convinced that the boat felt too heavy. Were the oars too long? In heavy seas we were going to struggle.

I lay there staring at the cabin roof six inches above my face, unable to sleep, unable to eat and with the same question going round my head: 'What have you done?' Tears started rolling down my cheeks.

Chapter Four

'Ten Minutes To Go': Settling into the Routine

Thursday, 1 December 2005, 9 a.m.

1 *Spirit of Cornwall*, 54 miles

2 *Atlantic Prince*, 53 miles

3 *All Relative* (four-man boat), 51 miles

4 *Team C2*, 49 miles

5 *Digicel Atlantic Challenge*, 47 miles

6 **Spirit of EDF, 47 miles**

Woodvale press release:

Boat No. 88 – *Charmed Life*, with Andrew Morris and Mick Dawson on board, were towed into San Sebastián on Gomera on the evening of the race start. Both crew members are well. More information as it unfolds.

Posted 01/12/05 02:17:56 PM

BEN

Two hours on, two hours off. Two hours on, two hours off.

'TEN MINUTES TILL YOU'RE ON.' Those simple five words were always received with a sunken heart. Not once did I relish them, and what's more they seemed to linger like a bad smell, invading every pore of my body. The instruction was issued and I could often gauge James's mood by his wording:

'Ten minutes, buddy,' was a good sign.

'Ten minutes till you're on,' suggested indifference.

'Ten minutes' meant he was in a bad temper.

'BEN' was a sure sign of a filthy mood.

Somehow the more words used to wake the other person up, the more inoffensive it was. I hated being woken with a single word.

JAMES

'Dude, ten minutes to go.' A phrase that still haunts me now. I must have fallen asleep, the demons raging in my head finally surrendering to the tiredness in my body. But as soon as my eyes opened, they were back. I put on my gloves and trainers over hands and feet that were already badly blistered, and opened the hatch to reveal a clear black night, full of stars. Under normal circumstances their brightness would have me staring up at the sky in wonder; instead all I was thinking was, 'How am I going to get through this?'

'You OK?' I asked Ben, although his face told me the answer. He looked like I felt, haunted by what we were facing. 'Not really,' was his response.

'Let's get through tonight and talk about it in the morning,' I said.

'OK,' he muttered as he went straight into the cabin.

The sandwich I'd left on deck was now sodden with salt water, even more unappetizing than I'd found it earlier. I managed to force a couple of army biscuits down and started rowing.

I wasn't totally alone on this shift; I thought I could see a light in the distance just ahead of us, possibly the running light of one of the other boats. To get me through the shift I set myself the task of catching it up.

Ben came out at 2 a.m. for his next shift and we changed over in silence. The pattern that would define our existence was starting to take shape. It was the only thing we had to keep us going.

Our plan had been to row together for about six hours on the first day, using the extra energy and enthusiasm of the first day before switching to rowing two hours on, two hours off, all day, all night, all the way across.

Again there was no real science in choosing this shift system, but I thought that two hours was the maximum time we could row in one go without the boat speed dropping significantly and without having to dig deep into energy reserves that would be hard to replenish in time for the next shift. Whatever system we employed, it had to be sustainable for nearly two months. The other side of the equation was the need to sleep – obviously the more the better, but with a two-hour break, grabbing something to eat and snatching an hour and a half of sleep was possible. My theory was backed up by Rob Hamill (a Kiwi former international rower), who had won the inaugural race. Rob had used the same system, and a submariner we'd met on our sea survival course had said that the body sleeps in ninety-minute cycles. If you wake up after ninety minutes you feel pretty good, but after two hours you feel terrible from waking up mid-cycle. The next complete cycle would be three hours in duration, and that would mean making the rowing shift too long.

Not everybody agreed. Simon Chalk, the owner of Woodvale Events and a veteran of attempts to cross the Atlantic, Indian and Pacific oceans, said that every team rowing two on, two off had ended up in pieces by the finish. I had avoided eye contact with Ben at that point. Despite never having practised the shift system, this was the only thing on board we had given any thought to. Everything else to do with the reality of rowing across an ocean was a case of finding out how it worked when we were out there.

For me rowing was a release, preferable to the confines of the cabin because at least I was doing something to get us closer to Antigua. Lying in the cabin on that first night, watching Ben struggle and seeing how slowly we were progressing, was torture. Bev had given me two letters for the journey, one to be opened on Christmas Day and one when I was at my lowest point. It took all my strength not to open the latter that night.

It was during my shift that the sun came up the next morning. As it rose above the horizon I could feel both my energy levels and mood rising with it, not by much, but nevertheless, we'd got through the first night. I called Ben for his shift; the new day had improved his mood but, like me, he wasn't himself. We both seemed to be shell-shocked by what was happening.

Me, Marina, Inca and Maggi relaxing at the seaside. *[Antoinette Eugster]*

Me and Bev enjoying a night out. *[Peter Andrews, Corbis]*

Our first proper training session out on the Thames at Henley, Autumn 2005.
[Alexis Girardet]

I give Ben tips on improving his technique as we practise topless on Ergos
to drum up publicity, August 2005. *[EDF Energy]*

All the family members join in with helping to make the boat seaworthy: John Cracknell and Roger Turner work together to mend *The Spirit of EDF*'s fixtures and fittings. *[Bruce Fogle]*

Preparations continue in La Gomera as I oversee *The Spirit of EDF*'s lowering into the water. *[James Christian]*

James fixes the hole and puts the family hairdryer through its paces. [Alexis Girardet]

James continues tweaking Spirit's design. [Alexis Girardet]

Ben goes shopping for 150 litres of ballast water. [Alexis Girardet]

BEN

Morning broke as the sun painted the sky pink, and daylight returned. As I came to I tried to get some sense of our progression. It seemed as if we hadn't gone anywhere overnight; the vast mountainous peak of La Gomera appeared to be exactly where it had been the night before. According to the GPS we had covered fifteen miles overnight. We still had 2,970 to go, an inconceivably depressing distance.

Alexis, the director of our documentary and a key member of our team, had tracked us through the night. I had seen his mast light in the distance, rising and falling in the increasing north-east swell, and now he quietly buzzed around us aboard the yacht chartered by the BBC. He was up and down the mast, in and out of the dinghy and the water, as he filmed our funereal progress.

Contemplating our position and our progress – or lack of it – I wanted to be anywhere but on that boat. I'd made a huge mistake, but there was no way of getting out of it. We would be letting too many people down; we could never survive the humiliation of returning to London now. What would everyone think of us? We'd be a laughing stock, a shame that would haunt us for the rest of our lives. I'd really done it this time, I thought, as I tortured myself for my stupidity.

How could I get us out of this mess? We couldn't just give up, but what if we were forced to withdraw? What would happen if some vital piece of equipment broke, like the water maker? We couldn't continue without such a key piece of kit, I thought as I rowed on, lost in my increasingly desperate fantasies. Perhaps I could break it? But I didn't even know how to do that, I lamented.

Dark thoughts punctuated my every stroke. I considered 'falling' overboard, or 'injuring' myself, anything to avoid the indignity of giving up. We can't just withdraw, there *has* to be a reason, I decided. Why was everything working so well? Why couldn't something else break?

The conversation between James and me had been limited to 'You're on in ten minutes', and in no time at all we had both disappeared into a solitary world, a melancholic space which we weren't prepared to share with one another just yet, though our silence spoke volumes for our sentiments.

JAMES

We'd left the comfort of a hotel room for a seven-metre boat which we'd never spent a night on before. Our bodies were being bombarded mentally and physically by new experiences. I'd never rowed so much in twenty-four hours before, never slept on such a small boat and never been this far out to sea. Ben had no experience as a rower and had never been on such a small boat at sea. Our world had literally changed overnight: food, sleeping patterns, amount of exercise. We hadn't adjusted with it.

We both knew there was no option but to fight through it. Having made such a song and dance about this adventure, asking for media attention in order to secure and then satisfy sponsors (and our egos), not to mention making a television documentary, there was no way we could quit.

I rehydrated a packet of muesli and forced myself to enjoy the experience of eating breakfast with an ocean view. I tried to imagine my favourite breakfast venue, a restaurant high in the Austrian Alps where the British Rowing Team has its altitude training camp. We would train early and be eating scrambled eggs on the balcony as the sun rose above the mountains and the lake we trained on, knowing the hardest session of the day was over.

It didn't work – I was starting to realize that there were going to be no days for us, only shifts of two hours at a time; days were going to become irrelevant, reduced to a simple question of rowing in darkness or rowing in daylight. We would never complete the hardest session, because another identical one was just around the corner.

BEN

'TEN MINUTES TILL YOU'RE ON.'

Two hours on, two hours off. The same phrase signalled the start of another seemingly interminable four-hour cycle.

I'd lie like a soldier, arms stretched down my sides, and stare up through the hatch window to the sky above. With a fleeting glance my spirits would either be lifted or plummet. There were two quick telltale signs to look out for: the first was the amount of cloud cover and the second was our little Spanish flag, which fluttered from the VHF (short-range radio) mast.

If it was cloudy, then despite the promise of a welcome respite from the sun, an overcast sky was actually something of a bad omen, reducing the effectiveness of the solar panels and therefore the amount of fresh water we could produce. More crucial still, however, was the movement of the little Spanish pennant itself. If it was pointing towards the front of the boat then all was well and it meant we had a strong stern wind from the north-east, helping us on our way to Antigua. If, however, the flag pointed to the stern, as it often did, then it meant we had a brisk head wind, which would push us back towards Africa.

It's strange how symbolic that little Spanish flag became. Throughout the race it stood as an emblem of my hopes and fears, directing my mood and forewarning me of difficulty even before James called me for my shift. It was the first indication of our progress each session and my eye sought it out before I was even conscious of what I was looking for. I never imagined that a piece of yellow and orange material could have such a profound effect on my mind and therefore my well-being, and little did I realize how much that image would plague my waking and sleeping thoughts even long after the race.

Two hours on, two hours off. Getting ready in a small dark cabin was anything but easy, but as with everything in life we each soon worked out a routine. I began to leave key items in exactly the same places so that one lunge in the dark would invariably fish out my Lycra shorts, or a T-shirt.

As part of my attempt to make the most of those precious moments away from the oars I developed over the course of those first few days an efficient way of dressing while still lying down. I would leave my shorts, shoes and gloves by the hatch. Through trial and error, I then worked out an intriguing system that I can only base on our close relation to apes. The ceiling of the cabin was too low to allow me to sit upright, which meant that reaching with my arms was often simply not an option, so in a Darwinian tumble of evolution, I learnt to grab things with my toes. At first I was clumsy and often caught the wrong things, but before long I could feel textures with my feet and differentiate between shorts and T-shirts. With one deft movement I could grab an individual glove and pass it straight into my right hand. I became so proficient and agile with my feet that I even managed to pick up the satellite phone, my diary and once even my evening meal and a spoon, though I never resorted to eating with my toes.

Once I had my clothes – Lycra shorts, gloves and shoes if it were day, and an added T-shirt if it were night – I would feel for the label to ensure they weren't inside out, and then dress while still lying down. All of this would either be done in pitch black or boiling heat, depending on the time of day.

Once dressed I would lie on the sticky mattress for thirty seconds to regain my composure, and then with a quick twist of the body, wriggle my way to the hatch, often wedging myself beneath an awkward panel or instrument. The foam lagging that had been fitted to protect us from sharp edges only enhanced the cabin's 'wedgability', and I often spent thirty seconds prising my head from an awkward angle.

Once I'd made the transition from the bottom of the cabin to the top, a monumental challenge in itself, I would peer at the GPS screen to see what sort of speed James was making:

4 knots – amazing

3 knots – healthy

2 knots – manageable

1 knot – oh dear

I'd slip my shoes on, sigh deeply and then unhook the hatch door, opening it just a fraction. 'I'm coming out!' I'd holler. Invariably my words would be snatched by the wind and I'd often surprise James by my appearance, which would surprise me in turn. You might think he'd have expected my arrival, especially as he had just called me, yet despite the regularity with which I would appear from the cabin I often startled him, lost in concentration at the oars.

We soon found that it was impossible to row while the other clambered through the hatch, a task which would have troubled an

Olympic gymnast, especially if you wanted to avoid soaking your feet in the footwell, or 'cesspit' as it soon came to be known. This was several inches of water that the bilge pump comprehensively failed to drain, which seemed to attract all things nasty and dirty on the boat; everything from pubic hair to small fish, which would begin to rot in the water, creating a soupy concoction to be avoided at all costs.

To avoid the bilge water meant opening the hatch and sliding out head-first rather than feet-first. I would grab on to the top of the cabin, and haul my body through facing backwards; then, as my hips emerged, I would twist around, planting each foot on the storage bins, while slamming the hatch closed between my legs. It sounds simple on paper, but it required maximum mental awareness and dexterity and took me weeks to perfect. My aim was to minimize my impact on James's rowing. Occasionally I'd get it wrong, or mistime the routine and catch James's fingers on the door, or slip into the noxious soup, neither one of which can be recommended for the start of a session. With the exit from the cabin complete, the next stage was to negotiate a course past James, down the side of the boat to the spare seat at the bow.

Walking on the boat was simply not an option, we soon discovered. The movement of the boat was too erratic and invariably resulted in bruises and scrapes as one found oneself tumbling across the deck. We quickly established that the safest and most efficient way of moving around the boat was like a monkey, on all fours. My feet had already become my hands, though, so I suppose it was only a matter of time before I used my hands as feet. Once again James would be forced to miss a stroke as I crawled over his oars, with my sheepskin seat under my arm.

Now that I had got to my position in the bow seat, which had also become the preparation area, I could begin the next stage of my routine. I usually managed this first period of my ten-minute call in around three and a half minutes, giving me a further six and a half for the next, rather more complicated stage.

Peeing on the boat was not a simple procedure, even for a man. For the first few days of the race we had peed over the side, but, as with walking, we had both lost our nerve after several near-tumbles, and in my case, a rather messy accident. Haunted by images of Robert Maxwell, weeing was soon confined to the onboard bucket. The race rules stipulated that every boat must carry two buckets: one for washing and one to be used as a loo. When we had been stocking up for our trip I had spotted wonderfully practical, lightweight buckets in Purves & Purves, which I arranged for my mother to collect. She chose one pink, one yellow so that we could clearly separate the bucket for washing from the poo-bucket – and the real bonus on such a small boat: they were collapsible.

In La Gomera we replaced our yellow bucket with a sturdy window-cleaner's bucket – space was at a premium but trying to poo on a collapsible toilet was sure to end in disaster – so when you had to go you'd sit on the 'seat', pull down your shorts, hold the bucket between your legs and answer nature's call.

Number twos, despite our careful planning and our specially selected bucket, were still surprisingly complex and required considerably more foresight and planning. The bucket needed to be filled with around three inches of seawater and then placed in the centre of the deck. The wet wipes – we had rationed ourselves to three sheets per day – then needed to be placed nearby, as both hands were required for balance. The bucket was then dumped overboard and given a quick rinse. Although neither of us talked about it, for the sake of modesty and to avoid blushes we tried to answer this particular call alone, while the other was sleeping. But when you gotta go, you gotta go, and our prudishness soon waned.

Ablutions complete, it was time for a quick meal. Cooking on board developed into a finely executed task which involved boiling the kettle twice a day, and filling our two Thermos flasks each time, thereby ensuring we had a ready supply of hot water for our rehydrated foods. A quick dip into the food bins beneath the deck would result in a 'surprise' choice of meal, which in my case seemed to be chilli con carne or chicken curry, my two least favourite flavours; it was never the surprise I was hoping for. I'd fill the bag with the appropriate amount of water, which would be amended according to the type of meal, and leave it to sit for thirty seconds, during which time I'd refill my water bottles, one with plain water and the other with a Lucozade energy drink.

By now I regularly had a minute and a half left until I was due on the oars. I could eat the entire bag of food in thirty seconds, allowing me a minute to put Vaseline and sun cream on all the relevant places. I'd stare at my watch and wait until the second hand hit the twelve, not a second earlier. With every passing session I became obsessive. I'd never been a clock-watcher before, in fact, I'd never worn a watch, but I'd been warned by previous ocean rowers that a regular second of lateness would result in huge animosity.

'Time, dude,' I'd announce.

As with most movements around the boat, James and I had choreographed a clever little clockwise strategy, whereby James would rip his sheepskin padding from the seat at the same time as I would slap mine into place on the Velcro. I would sit down and place my arms behind me, at which point James would place two bottles of water in my hands and I would pass him his empties.

And so begins a two-hour rowing session.

I can't say I enjoyed rowing. Unlike to James, the whole process was alien to me. I had spent several months preparing on a rowing machine prior to the race, which had bored me to tears. I had found it difficult to last an hour on my Ergo during training, and here I was faced with an interminable set of two-hour, cyclical sessions.

Everything ached for the first few minutes of each set. I used to dread clenching on my hands the oars, as my tendons had invariably started to seize up in the gap between each row. I'd grimace and grit my teeth for the first few strokes and then slowly ease back into it. The only words that can accurately describe these two-hour shifts are: 'boredom', 'monotony' and 'tedium'. In these initial days of the race each session felt like a life sentence, the oars my ball and chain. The only way to cope, I began to learn, was to make my imprisonment more manageable by compartmentalizing each two hours spent at the oars into sections.

The first fifteen minutes were invariably taken up with James faffing around, and though sometimes irritating, it was also a welcome distraction from the ennui of rowing.

With the first quarter of an hour under one's belt it's amazing how easily the rest of that first hour passes. It was the second that dragged horribly. This was probably in part because I became acutely aware of that second hour and often began time-keeping, but it was also due to the sheer repetitive mundanity and loneliness. I had never expected loneliness – after all, that was something one suffered on one's own, not in a pair – but I was amazed at how lonely I often felt. It wasn't James's fault; it was rather a symptom of our routine. We were rarely up and around together, and when we were, conversations were generally limited to monosyllables and grunts.

Despite the enormous pressure I felt at the oars I never found the rowing physically exhausting. It wasn't like an hour in the gym because I was trying to conserve my energy for the long row ahead, but I was tired at the end of every rowing session. I think the emotional and psychological work of coping with such endless repetition was almost as tiring as the physical exertion. Whatever wore me out, when those 120 minutes had passed it was an immense relief to hand over the oars and, above all, to give my bottom a rest.

The final fifteen minutes of each shift were the worst; they seemed to drag and drag, and my chocolate would regularly have run out, after a two-chunk binge at the half-hour mark.

'Dude, it's ten minutes till you're on,' I'd holler above the din of the wind. (Naturally this was fifteen minutes before James's session began.)

I'd watch as James's head-mounted torch cast little shadows around the cabin as he struggled to get dressed. Without fail he would take an eternity. How I sighed with relief when he appeared from the cabin and made his way to the bow seat.

I would row with extra vigour when James was about, not because I was trying to pretend that I had been rowing like that for two hours, but because I wanted his approval, which in fairness to James he often did give me. I would clock-watch from the minute James sat in the bow seat. The seconds would tick away agonizingly slowly as he peed, made food and water and prepared to take the oars. Invariably the second hand would strike the hour and James would still be unfinished. I could usually manage fifteen seconds more, before putting down the oars whether he was ready or not. I wasn't angry, more frustrated that he wasn't planning to the second, but I was surprised at my lack of patience. As I became increasingly frustrated at James's tardiness I began to understand the warning about delay on board. It was early days and already I was annoyed by James's behaviour. He seemed to have the longest wees I'd ever heard, prolonging my agony on the oars, as I waited for him to finish his preparations.

We'd then repeat our little clockwise ballet around the seat and I'd return to the bow seat for a packet of muesli. The mueslis were a significant part of the voyage. Not only were they the most prolific food aboard, but they were also one of the easiest and tastiest, requiring just a dash of cold water to create a thick, gloopy mulch.

Before we had set off from La Gomera, on the advice of Rob Hamill, the race's previous winner, Marina had spent a whole afternoon chopping off each and every corner of the square muesli bags in an effort to save weight. The problem, bless her cotton socks, was that often she cut into the airtight bag itself. The result was a couple of hundred 'holey' cereals. It was a bit like Russian roulette: you'd grab a muesli from the food bin and rip off the top, and pour in a dash of water. I'd scrunch my eyes together in anticipation of a rush of rehydrated milk powder as it escaped through one of Marina's holes. More often than not, it made me smile as I watched half my cereal escape on to the deck; it reminded me of her. James was never quite so amused.

I'd eat my muesli as fast as I humanly could and then make my way back down the boat towards the cabin. I hated wasting my valuable downtime, especially if it were night-time. Once again, I'd contort myself into the cabin, using the exact reverse of my exit strategy. It was ungainly, but worked. I was back in the cabin, free from responsibility for another two hours.

I'd spread my damp towel on to the sticky mattress and remove my Lycra shorts, which were usually soaking with sweat. One of the most pressing problems before I could get some sleep was 'bottom maintenance'. Bottoms are often underrated, the fat between you and a chair, but when you are rowing the Atlantic they become invaluable parts of the anatomy that need to be cared for and nurtured. I had never really been aware of my bottom before, but it was now both the most important and the most uncomfortable part of my body. We had an enormous pot of Sudocrem for nappy rash, but the problem was that it needed to be left on the skin in order to sink in naturally. This was all very well when you could get a full night's sleep, but nigh-on impossible given just an hour and a half. However, a few 'Sudocrem-free' days made me recognize its importance so I employed a strategy that involved lying on my front, naked on my towel, then rubbing in a dollop of the thick white cream and then putting on a pair of baggy shorts. Of course half the cream vanished into the fabric, but for a while my system appeared to work.

I have never suffered insomnia before, but stuck on a tiny rowing boat in the middle of the Atlantic, I found myself so over-tired that sleep was often impossible. It was never the light or noise that kept me awake (we played music at full volume twenty-four hours a day for those first few weeks so I would lie in the cabin with James's iPod selection blasting out to sea). It was my mind running out of control. I would toss and turn for an hour. Desperate for sleep but unable to drift off, eventually my brain would succumb to my body's needs and I'd sink into slumber.

'Sorry, sorry, James, I'm really sorry,' I'd utter as I prised open the hatch.

'Mate, you're not on for an hour,' James would answer breathlessly.

'What do you mean?' I'd ask, disorientated.

'Go back to bed, you're dreaming,' he'd continue.

At which point I would quietly close the hatch and return to my pit, close my eyes and drift off for another ten minutes.

'Am I on yet?' I'd holler, pulling my shoes and gloves on again.

'GO TO SLEEP.'

Once again I'd drift off.

Ten minutes later:

'Sorry I'm late,' I'd apologize, once again opening the hatch.

'BED,' he'd shout.

And so on for a further fifty minutes, never settling, never quite comfortable, waiting for the next shift to begin.

Two hours on, two hours off, twelve times a day, and at least fifty days to go.

Chapter Five

The Real Race Begins

JAMES

We had to talk about what was going on in our heads. For every other boat in the race that would have been easy, as the other teams were made up of people who had known each other for years. Ben and I didn't know each other at all. We'd spent a lot of time together in the last month but we had had other people to go home to and share problems with. It was just the two of us now and I realized how little we knew about one another. I couldn't tell what Ben was thinking from his body language or how he would respond to things I said. We had to communicate honestly, emotionally and freely about whatever was troubling us without fear of being judged, knowing we would be supported. This is hard enough with best mates on land but with a relative stranger in the middle of the ocean it was going to be almost impossible.

'Is this what you were expecting?' I asked.

'Not really.' That reply again.

I tried to lighten the mood. 'You know I hold you personally responsible, you asked me to do this stupid race.' That made Ben smile; the first time I'd seen that since the start of the race.

Figuring the best way to get some dialogue going was to tell him what I was thinking, I tried to open up a little. 'I had some dark thoughts in the night; I just wanted to be off the boat. I thought about jumping overboard. I couldn't even look at my picture of Bev and Croyde without crying. I can't believe how naive I've been, thinking it would be easy once we got going.'

Ben stopped rowing, took a drink and although his eyes were hidden behind sunglasses I could tell he was welling up. 'Me too. I just want to be back at home with Marina. I never imagined it was going to be this hard.' His voice cracked as he said this and tears rolled down his face.

I was relieved he was feeling the same way, it made it easier to share my thoughts with him. 'I knew it was going to be hard but I wasn't prepared to feel this lonely, isolated and emotional. We've got to help each other through it and not be afraid to say exactly what we are thinking. We need each other to get through this.'

We made a pact not to use the satellite phone until we had come to terms with what we had let ourselves in for. Phoning home in the state we were in now would have only upset and worried our families even more than they were already. Having said that, phoning home might have been easier for Ben than me. Marina had been nothing but enthusiastic and supportive of Ben, even taking ten days off work to help get the boat ready in La Gomera. Without her we wouldn't have made the start line. Ben could be assured of a sympathetic and supportive ear.

Bev had not wanted me to go, of course, only coming out to the Canaries the day before we started. Phoning her up and saying how hard it was and that I wished I hadn't done it would get me no support and more likely a retort of 'you wanted to do it, you deal with it'. But she was the only person I wanted to talk to.

At least by going through the same problems and emotions we were building up the reservoir of shared experiences that forms the basis of any lasting friendship. I was convinced that would help us; there were going to be times when he was down and I felt OK, and times when I was down and he felt good, but being able to sympathize with how he was feeling meant I could help. I hoped that we would both be more able to open up as a result.

BEN

In those first few days at sea the sense of loneliness, combined with facing up to the realities of the race, was overwhelming. We each knew the other was suffering and we retreated into our shells to try to cope with feelings that were almost impossible to describe, let alone discuss. Unlike James, I had real reservoirs to draw upon when it came to being alone. *Castaway* had tested my ability to feel secure in a completely alien environment and to rely upon no-one but myself. But one day out, with thousands of miles stretching before me, I came to realize that drawing on the strength of those experiences wasn't going to get me through this. I didn't know what was.

JAMES

In the meantime there were other things on board to do apart from row, eat and sleep. The squeaking from the seat as we slid backwards and forwards grated like fingernails down a blackboard and there was no way of escaping it. The sound was bad enough but the friction that caused it was going to damage the equipment and we had very few spares, so it was vital to look after it.

The squeaking wasn't going to be solved by oiling the slides, firstly because we forgot to pack the oil and secondly because it was caused by a bigger problem: the slides weren't set parallel. It was like a train trying to run on a track which is slightly too narrow for the axles – it won't run smoothly and sooner or later something will break. That's what we were faced with on the morning of day two. We had no option but to stop and re-drill the slide beds.

It's not the most challenging DIY job even for my limited skills but trying to be accurate when you're being tossed around by the sea was like trying to fix it blindfolded. I was rapidly learning that everything takes at least three times as long to do at sea as it does on land.

I tried not to think too far ahead, concentrating instead on each two-hour block at a time. I was listening to the Prodigy album *Music for the Jilted Generation.* It has seen me through hundreds of training sessions and I hoped it would help me settle into the routine, but I couldn't stop thinking how much I missed home and how much longer I was going to be stuck here for. It didn't make sense then and it doesn't make sense now. I'd only been away from Bev and Croyde for twenty-four hours and I was more homesick than I'd been when I was away for two months training for the Olympics. Ben felt the same: he'd been away from home for a year while he mucked around with sheep in *Castaway* but was struggling after only a day at sea.

In the afternoon of the second day the BBC yacht which had dropped back during the night to let us get used to being at sea alone came alongside. Ben and I struggled to look at it; this was our route back to dry land. Ben later admitted that he'd contemplated smashing a hole in our boat forcing us to abandon ship and ride back to the Canaries with the BBC. I wanted off as well but was not cunning enough to think of that. Both of us though were too stubborn, too proud and too egotistical to fail so publicly.

Alexis, the director of the documentary, who had been instrumental in us getting to the start line in time, was loving it. He was up the mast getting some aerial shots and started shouting at us with a grin on his face. 'You're in second, you're in second a few miles behind the Irish!' It meant I hadn't been imagining the light during the night but I didn't care what position we were in – right now I would have accepted last place just to be in Antigua and off this boat. Something I would never have contemplated before the start twenty-four hours earlier.

BEN

Time passed agonizingly slowly. It was 4 p.m., and all day long Alexis had shadowed us in the yacht. Now it was time for him to leave us to face the ocean alone. His presence up until now had been comforting, a 'Get out of jail' card, but he was about to vanish along with his yacht.

'We're going back,' he hollered from the deck. 'Are you OK?' he asked. I didn't answer. James was in the cabin. I knew he was awake but he didn't emerge. Alexis must have realized our torment as I held my hand aloft in an ambiguous gesture of goodbye and STOP.

'Five days, boys, give it five days and it will become easier,' he bellowed as he and the yacht began turning and disappearing slowly over the horizon. This was really it, there was no way out now and we both knew it. 'You bloody idiot, Ben,' I thought as I slipped even further into depression. 'You've really done it now.'

JAMES

As the sun was setting on day two it was time for the yacht to head back to the Canaries. I couldn't watch as our only way out of this enforced nightmare turned around. I wasn't on shift and went into the cabin. I heard Ben shout 'Goodbye.' He must have looked terrible because I could hear Alexis shouting 'Just give it five days, five days.' We'd managed one.

I knew I'd be rowing twelve hours a day and before we'd left it was one of the few things I'd prepared for. When I thought about the journey I automatically saw myself rowing during the day, after all, night-time is for sleeping or if it's not for sleeping it's definitely not for rowing. At our latitude the days and nights were almost identical. The days went by pretty fast but the nights dragged on and even though Ben was just a few feet away and I saw him every two hours when we changed shift I felt incredibly lonely. I knew it was going to be another long night as both of us battled our demons. Despite not feeling like eating I was trying to force down as much as possible knowing that if I felt bad now it would be a hell of a lot worse with no energy. Ben wasn't doing the same; he'd finish his shift and disappear straight into the cabin. I tried not to take it personally. I know my conversational skills aren't brilliant and any dialogue would have consisted solely of us telling each other how miserable we were, so perhaps the silence wasn't such a bad thing. But I was starting to get concerned that Ben wasn't eating or drinking enough. When I suggested he should eat something before lying down he muttered, 'I'm not hungry.' I thought better of telling him that wasn't the point; you can't row for twelve hours a day on water alone.

I got stuck into my shift; we'd decided to play the library of songs on the iPod from the start to the finish. At home time is a luxury I don't have and having the opportunity to do something as indulgent as that

I can't understand, looking back, why I hated those first days so much. The shock to the system of such a change in environment and routine must have knocked me off my axis. My emotions were so sensitive that when we got to 'C' and The Carpenters' 'Top of the World' began playing I started crying. Memories of walking back down the aisle having just married Bev, with all our friends and family packing the room out, came rushing back, throwing me off kilter. Luckily I had fifteen minutes to compose myself before Ben came out for his shift. If he wasn't worried about my mental state before he would have been if he'd witnessed that.

When he came out for the next shift some of his enthusiasm that I thought would serve him, and indirectly me, well on this journey was back. He was looking forward to rowing under the stars; a pattern was starting to develop. Ben would enjoy the night shifts but struggle in the day whereas I was the opposite. For the first time we were able to start helping each other out.

Friday, 2 December 2005, 9 a.m.

1 *All Relative* (four-man boat), 108 miles
2 *Team C2*, 107 miles
3 *Spirit of Cornwall*, 106 miles
4 *Atlantic 4* (four-man boat), 104 miles
5 *Atlantic Prince*, 103 miles
6 *Mayabrit*, 103 miles
7 **EDF, 99 miles**

We'd rowed 100 miles, a pivotal landmark not because of the distance we'd clocked up (3,000 minus 100 still leaves far too many to start celebrating) but because up until now the boat (with us in it) could have been towed back to land. From now on we would have to sink our boat (you can't leave deserted vessels floating in the ocean) if we bailed out. Not only that, if we did run into trouble we'd end up on a tanker which could be going anywhere in the world, or on board the support yacht, which would stay with the slowest crew in the race. With some people rowing solo (why?) this guaranteed our quickest way off the ocean now was to row as fast as possible to Antigua.

As Bev's treasure trail of baguettes on board ran out and the fresh water we'd brought with us had been drunk we switched to the supplies and equipment that would see us across. The most vital piece of equipment being the desalinator/water maker: seawater is pumped through a membrane that draws the out the salt resulting in just about drinkable lukewarm water. We did not carry enough water on board to get across; the desalinator above everything else was our lifeline.

Fortunately the desalinator was working like a dream and we had plenty of water, so our major worry seemed to be under control. The water was used for drinking, cooking and washing. Half the 10–12 litres of water we drank a day was mixed with either isotonic or protein powder, the other half we drank as plain water. Two litres were boiled for using in hot dehydrated meals and half a litre was used for washing. When I say washing, invariably it was used for splashing areas where the sun don't shine. The problem was that as soon as you'd washed you were back getting sweaty an hour or so later and there wasn't enough water to wash after every shift. It was already clear we weren't going to win any awards for hygiene.

No Michelin stars were going to be awarded for culinary excellence either and definitely none for variety. But the meals provided us with the energy we needed. Having cooked the same meal of pasta, tuna and ketchup almost every night for a year because it was easy and provided me with enough energy and protein for training, I didn't find the lack of variety too bad. We would boil two litres of water at lunchtime and load it into Thermos flasks for use throughout the day. This meant the water wasn't piping hot by the evening but that was preferable to having to boil up another load of water. The simple task of boiling water meant filling up the kettle, connecting the stove to its mounting on the cabin bulkhead so allowing it to swing and keep the stove level, letting the water boil then filling a Thermos and repeating the process twice more. This took about forty minutes. Without the Thermos flasks we would have had to fire up the stove at least three times a day. I'd like to claim their presence on the boat was down to good planning but I thought they might be useful when I was doing a last-minute shop in Blacks the day before flying out.

Apart from energy the meals gave us a huge amount of entertainment and there hadn't been many laughs in the first few days. So far neither of us had needed to frequent the alfresco toilet, which was located alongside the kitchen, shower room, restaurant and laundry in the bows of the boat. Only under very unusual circumstances would there be another diner in the restaurant when the 'bucket and chuck-it' toilet was in operation.

We'd been warned that rehydrated food and army rations (our staple diet) are designed to 'bung you up', reducing the need for 'comfort breaks' when on the march and for those regiments in the army where it's important not to leave a trail behind. So when I was the first to test the rest room it was a moment of history. I filled the bucket with the regulation six inches of water so as to avoid any Michael Schumacher 'tyre marks' collecting in the bucket and then proceeded to dispose of the biggest turd in my life. With the sombre mood on board the decent thing would have been to throw it overboard, but then I risked losing the chance of a witness to a potential Guinness World Record for size. In true British style it had amused me enough to crack a smile, so I decided to introduce my turd to Ben, who was busy only two feet in front of me.

'Buddy, you got a sec?' I asked.

'Why, what's up?' Ben replied. The delivery of the line and slump of the shoulders told me he was preparing himself for some more bad news.

'Nothing important, I just err … I just wanted you to, er, see the size of the shit I've done.'

A disbelieving 'What?' came back.

'No honestly, mate, you'll want to see it.'

He put the oars down, turned round and looked in the bucket. For the first time since we set off I heard him laugh; it was infectious. Soon we were giggling like schoolboys, concluding that the British Army wouldn't be hard to track if they were leaving these monsters strewn around a combat zone.

BEN

'Oh my god,' stuttered James behind me. 'Mate, you've got to see this, you won't believe it,' he announced. I turned around to be confronted by the most enormous poo I had ever seen in my entire life. James proudly held it aloft in the bucket, three feet of curled-up turd. James beamed with a cheeky schoolboy grin. We broke into uncontrollable, eye-wateringly unstoppable laughter. It was like a pressure valve being released. The poo had precipitated a truce to our glumness and, more to the point, to our self-imposed silence.

'How's it going, dude,' I asked for the first time since we'd left La Gomera. I had wanted to ask the question dozens of times, but it had somehow seemed futile, like asking if a stab wound hurts.

'Not great,' he answered, his mouth full of shepherd's pie.

'Me too,' I replied with a smile. It was our first open acknowledgement of weakness and it felt good, even liberating.

And with that exchange we slowly began to adapt to life on board.

Saturday, 3 December 2005, 9 a.m.

1 *Atlantic 4* (four-man boat), 183 miles

2 *Spirit of Cornwall*, 175 miles

3 *Team C2*, 174 miles

4 *All Relative* (four-man boat), 169 miles

5 *Atlantic Prince*, 166 miles

6 *Mayabrit*, 163 miles

7 **EDF, 160 miles**

JAMES

My emotions were at least starting to fluctuate. Although I was still feeling very low at certain points, especially during the night when the isolation and task ahead seemed larger, overall I was getting more positive. Ben had started eating properly, as was evident from his offerings in the bucket, where he continued the precedent of displaying your wares. To my mind, he had some work to do before mounting a challenge for the boat record.

According to the race rules we had to have our satellite phone switched on between 12 and 1 p.m. GMT every day so we could be contacted and receive a daily weather report. It was during this window that I spoke to the outside world for the first time. Although feeling better I still wasn't confident of being able to speak to Bev without breaking down. Luckily it was my dad calling to say 'Hi'. I tried to sound upbeat, I told him how hard we'd found the first few days but we were settled into a routine and had started looking forwards not backwards. He'd been tracking our progress and our course on the internet; we were in seventh place and heading further south than other crews, the majority of which were now on a rhumb (straight) line to Antigua. I asked him to call Bev and say that I was OK.

I came off the phone concerned for the first time where we were in the race. Up until then all I'd been worried about was surviving, but finding that I was frustrated with our position meant I really was coming to terms with life on board. I wasn't surprised we were in seventh – after the first few hours of racing our speed had dropped while we tried to overcome the mental barriers that blocked our path to the Caribbean.

Ben had said on numerous occasions before the start that his aim was solely to get across. This simple ambition had been tested since we'd set off, and although that desire was back, the will to win was non-existent. I got off the phone and came out of the cabin. 'We're in seventh place, buddy.' I told him.

'That's fantastic!' he replied.

I shook my head. It was going to be a long journey if our aims differed so much. 'We're a lot further south than the crews ahead of us. I think we should start heading west now,' I suggested.

Ben's lack of concern at our position contrasted enormously with me questioning our course. He was our 'Captain of Navigation and Safety' – we'd divided up certain roles so that somebody had the final say (I was 'Captain of Rowing and Equipment'). I'd agreed with the course we'd set and now I was questioning whether we should turn because the others had.

'Are we going to steer whenever they do?' he demanded.

'There is only one turn in the bloody race! Head south and then turn west on a bearing for Antigua. Why not turn if everybody else has?'

'Because we have to have confidence in what we're doing or we'll never get there.'

A fair point. We had to back ourselves. Maybe everybody else was behaving like sheep and following the flock; we should stick to our guns. Ben had chosen the course; his was the final say so I agreed to stick to our original course regardless of what anybody else did.

That left the issue of speed. I couldn't make Ben competitive. The only way I could get more speed out of him was by using his desire to get to Antigua as quickly as possible – his source of motivation. Every 0.1 knot increase in average speed over the 3,000 miles meant arriving a day earlier, an average speed of 2.5 knots would get us there in fifty days. Ben's major worry was that his body would fall apart before we got there if he pushed or was pushed too hard, too early. I told him to trust me and that I'd make sure he got there in one piece. That was easy for me to say and probably harder for him to do. He'd trusted my rowing experience to set the boat up properly and mistakes I'd made meant we'd wasted three days' practice on La Gomera. My experience was of racing over six minutes, not fifty days, and Ben wasn't 100 per cent confident that I wouldn't burn him out.

Something that I'd tried to keep from him had been bothering me since the first night. The gearing on the boat was much too heavy. The gearing is the load in the water, which is determined by the length of the oars and the position of the pin that the oar levers on. It wasn't possible to move the pin. So if there was a problem with the gearing the only option was to shorten the oars. There was one way to do this and it was irreversible. I'd have to saw the handles down and use gaffer tape and strips of T-shirt to try to make as soft a grip as possible on the carbon loom.

Ben wasn't convinced; yes, it felt heavy to him but as he'd never rowed before he knew no better. He quite rightly reasoned that, yes, I'd rowed before but not in an Atlantic boat. It was a difficult decision to make. We had one spare pair of oars and if shortening the oars didn't work we'd have no spares for the rest of the journey. I said I'd give it more thought and we agreed to make a decision the next day.

Sunday, 4 December 2005

I was just finishing the dawn shift; Ben was out early grabbing a muesli before getting stuck into his shift. 'I'm gonna chop the oars down, buddy. It feels too heavy and we haven't even had any real wind yet, even a crosswind will make it really heavy and I'm not sure my back will last with this load all the way.' No response. 'Did you hear me?'

'Do what you think is best, you know more about it than me.'

Not the ringing endorsement I was after but not surprising given the problems we'd had with the boat so far. As the boat was my responsibility I decided to go for it. Pleased that I'd chosen the £2.99 deluxe hacksaw from B&Q rather than the budget £1.99 one, I set about chopping the oars down. Considering the conditions and equipment I was working with I was pleased with the results. The improvised handles seemed OK and the oars were shorter. Would they make the boat feel lighter? I used them on my next shift: it was definitely easier to move the oars through the water and the boat speed was faster. Happy days.

We'd passed through the five-day barrier and I decided to call home, I was feeling more positive than at any point so far but when I heard Bev's voice I broke down. Despite her anger towards me for going she was amazing, supportive and encouraging. Croyde was missing me, doing OK, but he kept asking why Ben wasn't with daddy as he kept seeing him on TV playing with the lions at Longleat.

Ben had spoken to Marina and in spite of it making him miss home we were convinced we'd been through the worst. As if to confirm this, that night a tailwind picked up, blowing us exactly on our bearing. This was what I'd signed up for; at last we had some easy speed. The wind was strengthening all the time and by the time Ben came out for the 2–4 a.m. shift we were being blown along at 3 knots without even paddling. It was a dark night. The moon had just ended its cycle and wasn't going to come up, and clouds had arrived with the wind, covering the stars. Ben wasn't confident about the waves that over the last couple of hours had grown to over fifteen feet.

I'd experienced surfboat rowing in Australia and compared to that this was a relaxing pleasure. At no time did I have to pull a pair of Speedos up my crack or have waves crashing over my head. Ben had made great strides with his rowing but the waves were a step too far.

'I'm just going to sit here, not row, and steer. We're going 3 knots now and you said that was a good average speed.'

'That's an average speed twenty-four hours a day all the way. Some days we won't be able to move at all, we have to use the wind when we've got it.'

He wasn't having any of it and I was too tired to argue with him, if he was scared of the waves there was nothing I could say that was going to make any difference.

BEN

When I clambered out to begin my shift I was immediately struck by the size of the waves, which looked to me to be between fifteen and twenty feet high. I knew that if one had hit us side on we would have capsized – the physics was obvious. As I prepared for my shift I couldn't help feeling what little confidence I'd gained over the last few days begin to seep away. I'd already struggled with the steering – making myself row double the distance with over-correction – and it was clear that in this weather good steering would be fundamental. If the wave was surfed correctly it could triple our speed. I knew it would take most of my energy to get the steering right so I was anxious about trying to steer the correct course and row simultaneously.

I also saw the following wind as an opportunity to recoup our strength and energy, a chance to take a break after the days spent rowing so hard. I bit the bullet and told James that I wasn't going to row; I was going to ride the waves instead. James went for his shift and I could tell it was driving him crazy that I wasn't rowing with the waves, I was surfing, not rowing and surfing. What James seemed to forget was that this kind of surf-rowing was not something I knew how to do. In fact I was a complete novice, never having done anything even approaching this, and the combination of my lack of rowing experience with these new and challenging conditions was too much for me. While James was inside I dug out a life jacket and a harness and put them both on.

JAMES

I lay on the mattress, looking at the speed on the GPS. It was a constant 3 knots. We'd have been delighted with that speed on any other day of the race so far, but as I'd been averaging between 4 and 6 knots I couldn't let that free speed go to waste, however tired I was.

BEN

When James reappeared he failed to disguise a wry smile at the fact that I was wearing not one but two safety devices. I ignored his smirk. I was really unnerved by the whole thing and with my Royal Naval background the need for safety at sea had been thoroughly instilled into me. As I dismissed James's humour at my belt and braces approach I remembered that when we'd been at the RNLI for our safety training James had announced that he would never wear a life jacket at sea. At that point I had presumed this was bravado and that when he saw the oceans we would encounter he would 'belt up'. A presumption that would be proved flat wrong when were at sea. In the end we both became far too complacent about the ocean. This would be the last time I would wear a life jacket, but it wouldn't be the last time I would need one.

Having let James take over from me on the oars and vent some of his frustration at my tactics I decided to get outside and try to understand what it was that he was doing. By observing James I learnt how to row the waves, and having studied him carefully I thought it was my turn to try it.

JAMES

I went back outside. 'Mate, I'm going to get on the oars, we have to take advantage of the wind. Go and get some extra rest.'

'If you're sure, I'm happy to stay out here and steer.'

'No, it's OK.' I spat the last line out through gritted teeth.

Any anger was forgotten as the boat got thrust along by the wind and waves and I knew slowly but surely the miles to Antigua were ticking down. Ben came back out on deck, sat in the bows chewing on a chocolate bar, watching the waves and the flag, and said, 'I'll have a go now.'

'Great.' The excitement of going faster than walking pace for the first time was starting to wear off, I needed to sleep. I'd been rowing hard for nearly four hours.

I left Ben to get on with it. I chose not to look at the speed when I settled down in the cabin, I didn't want to know. I woke up to the sound of screaming laughter, believe me, an unusual event on our boat.

BEN

I loved surf-rowing. I hadn't realized that rowing could be an adrenaline sport until now. I was doing 5 knots – roughly 5 mph – it may not sound much but compared to our average speed over the previous five days and given the fact we were on a rowing boat it felt positively galactic. I screamed every time we hit that speed: for the first time I was rowing *and* I was enjoying myself. This is what our journey was supposed to be about – we were actually crossing the ocean.

JAMES

I looked at the GPS – 5 knots. Ben was rowing, attacking the waves and loving every minute of it. We'd covered thirty-five miles in the last twelve hours, more than we'd done in the previous thirty-six. For the first time I was convinced we were going to make it.

BEN

In the absence of a postal service at sea, my family and Marina had written me several dozen letters to be opened at different stages of the race. Some were marked with distances, others with dates, and there were several for special occasions. Mummy had written the first one, I could tell by the large round letters of her handwriting. 'Just in case…' she had scrawled across the airmail envelope. Inside was a hanky.

I wept.

James and I had adapted to the watch system, each tailoring our own eating and sleeping habits around our shifts. I struggled most during the day, which often felt like an incessant battle against the elements. I cursed the unremitting sun burning at my exposed skin, and stealing the precious water from my body, forever threatening to bleed me dry of liquid and strength. To compound that, I also became paranoid about James analysing my rowing; keeping an eye on my progress.

Night-times, however, were when I came alive. I thrived under the moonlight. I'd often navigate by the stars, mesmerized by the sky peppered in pinholes of light that broke up the monotony of blackness. Brilliant shooting stars would leave a visible trail as they streaked across the sky. At night I'd row with my head crooked to the sky. I'd stare and stare and stare until my eyes hurt from straining. I had never really followed stars or constellations. The nearest I'd got was a school trip to the no longer London Planetarium, but out on the ocean I was interested. I could see all sorts of constellations, a hamburger, a fish, a bottle of wine, I could have sworn I saw a star dot to dot of Marina, but my nemesis was the plough. It appeared every night on the port side of the boat, just above the horizon, looking unmistakably like a big bright, shiny question mark. It plagued me, making me feel uneasy, constantly querying our journey.

The nights were also made a little easier by the provision of a snack bag. The snack bags had been packed by Marina on La Gomera and each one was a surprise. A good bag included four chocolate bars, a bag of nuts, and a packet of biscuits, a rotten bag had a packet of biltong and some energy bars. As with most things on the boat, spirits could be lifted or shattered with the rip of a bag.

At night I could row with peace of mind, I liked being invisible, free from James's scrutiny. Night-time also offered a break from the sun. I came to relish my skin losing the tautness that the sun brought with it, and there seemed to be a gentle breeze that accompanied the drop in temperature. This combination of factors lent the nights a serenity that even benefited my rowing – I tended to row faster. I was the best version of myself on the ocean, physically and mentally at my strongest.

Tuesday, 6 December 2005, 9 a.m.

1 *All Relative* (four-man boat), 473 miles

2 *Atlantic 4* (four-man boat), 408 miles

3 *Spirit of Cornwall*, 402 miles

4 *Atlantic Prince*, 371 miles

5 *Team C2*, 361 miles

6 *Mayabrit*, 355 miles

8 ***EDF*, 337 miles**

For nearly a week we had been alone on the vast ocean, when out of nowhere a light appeared on the horizon.

JAMES

'Big vessel, big vessel, big vessel: this is small rowing boat, small rowing boat, over.'

'Uh? What? What's happening?' I grumbled through a disorientated haze. It was the middle of the night, some time during my downtime. Was this Ben's funny way of waking me up for my shift on the oars by giving us radio 'handles'. If so it was very magnanimous of him to call me 'Big Vessel'. I opened my eyes. He wasn't rowing, but was crouched in the footwell of the cabin using the VHF radio – the first time we'd used it in ten days at sea.

BEN

'Attention unidentified large ship, we are *Spirit of EDF Energy*, a small ocean-rowing boat, do you see us, over?' I bleated into the VHF radio. There was no answer. The tiny speck of light continued its rapid approach towards our vulnerable craft, swiftly becoming a blinding mass of confusing lights, like a huge aquatic UFO.

JAMES

The tone of Ben's voice told me it was pretty close. I stuck my head out of the cabin; it was hard to tell how close it was or what bearing it was on but there was certainly no missing it with that many lights. 'Shit, we're going to get mowed down by a floating Christmas tree!' Thinking that wasn't the most constructive thing to say, I followed it up with, 'Shall we let off a flare?'

'I'll try them once more,' Ben replied, repeating his 'big vessel' call. 'Big vessel, big vessel, big vessel this is small rowing boat, small rowing boat, over!'

It was clearly an oil tanker, something we had been consistently warned about: huge, fast-moving and often on autopilot, with no-one on watch, obliviously pounding down a shipping lane. The best we could hope for was that their radar might be alarmed, so that if something came on to the screen it would alert them. Unfortunately our boat was so small that we wouldn't show up on their radar, hence the mild panic in Ben's voice. In theory we should have appeared, as every race boat was fitted with a Sea-me, a reflective device attached to the bows, which made us appear five times bigger than we were on another boat's radar screen. Our only previous use of the Sea-me had been to lean on it while we were having a pee overboard; unfortunately when I was relieving myself I had leant on it too hard, when unexpectedly the boat had rocked and it snapped. Although we managed to splint it with our fishing rod (that is to say, a piece of doweling with some string attached and a hook) the electrics inside were broken and the device was quickly renamed Pee-me', as that was the only thing it was good for.

BEN

Still no answer, and all the time the tanker was bearing down on our tiny boat with frightening speed. And then, out of nowhere:

'Don't worry, we are awake, we see you,' crackled the radio in a thick Russian accent. The ship was now just a hundred metres away from us as it steamed past at 20 knots, before disappearing over the horizon and leaving us once again with only each other for company.

My mood seemed to shift like the wind, not daily but hourly. One minute I would feel on top of the world, brimming with optimism, while the next I would be wallowing in self-pity and pessimism. We had resolved to call the girls a week into the race. I longed to call Marina and hear her voice, but it also scared me. I worried it might set me back psychologically. I still felt emotionally fragile and I was wary of upsetting that balance, 'Call her,' demanded James, handing me the phone.

I lay down in the tiny cabin, opened the small hatch and pointed the satellite phone upwards and tapped in her number, 'Hello?' I heard her sweet voice. My face lit up and a smile broke across my face for the first time since we'd left over a week ago. Angels sang. We chatted and laughed and once again I cried, but after hearing Marina the world seemed brighter. The best kind of tonic, talking to Marina had not only lifted my spirits but also strengthened my resolve.

Chapter Six

Depression: Stormy Weather

Friday, 9 December 2005, 9 a.m.

1 *All Relative* (four-man boat), 719 miles

2 *Spirit of Cornwall*, 558 miles

3 *Atlantic 4* (four-man boat), 553 miles

4 **EDF, 536 miles**

5 *Atlantic Prince*, 522 miles

6 *Team C2*, 520 miles

Woodvale press release:

Although the Atlantic Rowing Race 2005 is very much a race – and whereas in reality there isn't much spare time in-between the standard daily routine of rowing, sleeping and eating – it is amazing to see just how inventive the teams have become in finding ways to amuse themselves.

Single-handed rower Roz Savage from Boat No. 15 – *Sedna Solo* has been very productive and has been growing her own vegetables. Roz ran out of fresh food a few days ago so she implemented her seed-sprouting plan by putting chick peas and aduki beans in a seed sprouter, watering them twice a day and, hey presto, two days later she's got fresh crunchy bean sprouts. Apparently, the ancient Chinese mariners used to do the same on long voyages to avoid the scurvy.

While life in the Atlantic seems to have taken over all of our lives, it's hard to think that normal life continues on back at home. Phil Harris from Boat No. 4 – *Row4Life*, had a dose of reality today when he received some fantastic and exciting news. Phil's wife Nikki gave birth to twin sons, Joshua and Samuel, at Whipps Cross Hospital in Essex just after 10 a.m. this morning. On behalf of all the staff at Woodvale Events – many congratulations to Phil, Nikki and their families on this fantastic news. Who knows, Joshua and Samuel could follow in Dad's footsteps and be a potential Pairs team entry in a future ocean rowing race!

Posted 09/12/05 04:32:45 PM

JAMES

My dad called to say that we were the pair in second place. With the wind behind us we'd made great progress and our decision to take a southerly course seemed to be paying off. I never really doubted Ben's navigation! I got off the phone and stuck my head out of the cabin: 'Mate, we're up to second!' We took the opportunity to go all American for a few minutes, Ben yelling, 'Whooo! Yeah!' as we gave each other a high five – the ocean does funny things to your mind.

Ben's initial excitement didn't last long. When I came out of the cabin for my shift, he looked very down. 'What's up, buddy?' I asked, surprised at the drastic change in mood.

'I can't cope with the pressure of being second,' he replied.

'How can there be more pressure on us in second place than there was when we were in seventh?' I exclaimed in frustration.

'Because I don't know if I can keep this pace up.'

'But it's the same pace we were doing yesterday and you felt all right then. You should be pleased. We haven't changed anything to get into this position, and the course that you planned seems to be giving us the best weather.'

'I just don't want to race all the way there.'

'We haven't done anything different! Look, I was supposed to be the negative one on this boat; we're up to second place, enjoy it.'

I felt deflated by Ben's lack of enthusiasm. I was convinced that if we started doing well in the race he would become caught up in it and the chance to be the first boat to Antigua would spur him on. I needed his help. I was struggling trying to motivate us both and we needed to keep as high an average speed as possible, we hadn't

117

taken enough food for a leisurely crossing. Ben was never late out for a shift and never complained about the workload, but all the drive and motivation was down to me and I couldn't keep it up for another two months.

My mood dropped even further when the weather report came through on the satellite phone, forecasting a tropical storm in our area of latitude and longitude. The weather reports so far in the race might have come from Michael Fish for all their accuracy, often predicting north-easterly trade winds – winds that would blow us all the way to Antigua – that still hadn't made an appearance. Today, however, there was no doubt that the weather around us was changing.

The wind dropped and the atmosphere became charged. Our sensitivity to meteorological changes was becoming more acute the longer we spent at sea, and we soon learnt that the weather had almost total control over the speed of our progress. If the phrase 'calm before a storm' could be used at any time on our journey, it was now. Something major was on the way – and if a storm hit there would be no option but to put down the parachute anchor and sit it out.

I was adamant that we should make hay while the sun shone and suggested that we row together for most of the night, before the storm hit. As soon as we were forced to shelter in the cabin, we could then use that time to recover from the extra rowing.

Ben didn't want to do it; he believed that our shift system was the only thing keeping him going. I couldn't force him to row for most of the night, of course, so we stuck to our pattern.

BEN

The difference in our reasons for being on board *Spirit* and our strategies for getting to Antigua were something we debated endlessly. I could never get James to recognize the distinction between getting to Antigua as fast as we could, and winning the race. For me, getting across the ocean in as short a time as was physically possible was my sole objective. I was always happy to be in first place, but it made no difference to my commitment to the race, or my strategy on the oars. I gave my sessions

100 per cent all the time, there was nothing extra to give simply because we happened to be further along a journey that other people were undertaking separately. James couldn't accept that I couldn't push harder. And so we would begin again a disgreement we had been having since we first met back in the UK.

JAMES

The edge was taken off my frustration by the beauty of the night, with a still cloudless sky lit up by a full moon and a blanket of stars. For the first time so far in the race I actually enjoyed a night shift, and felt incredibly lucky to be out in the middle of nowhere, able to see all the constellations without the haze of London's pollution dimming their power.

I was basking beneath the stars when I heard a loud 'phoooff' beside the boat. Our close encounter with a tanker meant I was much more sensitive to anything out of the ordinary, and I immediately stopped rowing and looked around. No lights, no tanker, in fact nothing in sight.

I started rowing again, uneasily.

'Phoooff' – there it was again.

'Phoooff' – and again. I looked towards the noise and saw a pod of dolphins about six feet from the end of my oar.

Almost as soon as they appeared, they were gone, only to reappear with a 'phoooff', this time on the left-hand side of the boat. They were obviously checking out what kind of animal we were, and they can't have been too impressed because they dived under the boat a couple more times and got bored and disappeared. It was the first time I'd ever seen a dolphin and what a way to see them. Perhaps life out here wasn't so bad after all. I tried to tempt them back with some chunks of energy bar, with no luck (mind you, Ben and I were already bored with the energy bars, so I wasn't too surprised).

Saturday, 10 December 2005, 11 a.m.

1 *All Relative* (four-man boat), 802 miles

2 *Atlantic 4* (four-man boat), 620 miles

3 **EDF, 598 miles**

4 *Spirit of Cornwall*, 597 miles

5 *Team C2*, 576 miles

6 *Atlantic Prince*, 570 miles

The news got even better the next morning; we had taken the lead in the pairs race. We were now one mile ahead. Amazingly, after eleven days of hard rowing it was that close. Ben's enthusiasm was muted; he was clearly worried that I was going to flog us to death in order to keep the lead. I can understand his concern; I was definitely beginning to get caught up in the race. Having thought at the start that our chances of winning rested somewhere between no chance and absolutely no chance, it was now dawning on me that it was a possibility and I thought we should take a risk and see how fast we could go. I tried to reason with Ben; the quicker we went, the quicker we'd be in Antigua and he should look at it that way rather than thinking of it as racing.

My semantics weren't fooling him. I was going to have to be either more subtle or more forceful.

BEN

'We're in first place,' announced James with astonishment.

For three days we had followed the prevailing north-easterly winds, picking up speed all the time. At long last, James and I had started to settle into the rhythm and routine of daily life, and now to add to the buoyancy of our mood, we were also in the lead.

First place. First place. The words felt unfamiliar and strange. After all our struggles in La Gomera to get to the start line, it seemed inconceivable that we could actually be leading.

'Are you sure?' I asked incredulously.

James nodded with satisfaction.

How had we managed that, I wondered. To be frank, since the start of the race we'd been busking it. We weren't even sure we were heading in the right direction. We knew we had to head south before turning west in order to benefit from the prevailing winds and currents, but how *far* south was open to conjecture.

After the horrors and realities of the first week at sea, James and I had resigned ourselves to simply crossing the ocean. To finish, we had both agreed, was an achievement in itself – but against all odds we found ourselves in pole position, and it felt good.

I had never been in the lead before in anything, and I couldn't help but break into a big smile. I couldn't wait to tell Marina, but before I had a chance the sat phone beeped and a text message flashed on to the screen.

'YOU'RE IN FIRST PLACE, I'M SO PROUD,' read the message.

Once news of our position was absorbed (I agreed, being first couldn't be a bad thing) I reflected upon the consequences for me of this 'good news'. Our top position would be accompanied by James's plans to change tactics and that was utterly deflating. The moment we hit pole position James would, without fail, up the ante to try to get us to stay there. It was too much. I have always liked to be the outsider, it's given me something to prove and it has guaranteed less pressure on me because whatever I did I would always be better than expected. Up until hitting first place I had just assumed that my role as the underdog would remain secure. We wouldn't be first and I'd be the fall guy for us not winning. I had always accepted that. From the first time I asked James to be my partner, there was such a difference in our abilities it seemed only natural that James was always going to be the tough one and I'd be the handicap. After all, I'd made a career out of taking part whereas James is a professional winner. Once we were in first I felt I had to step up and perform and meet James's revised expectations.

There was also a problem outside the boat: the wind had shifted and the weather was about to deal us a heavy blow. It had been a long night and now we were beating into a strong headwind. Our speed had been reduced from a healthy 3.5 knots to a little under a knot. The westerly wind was picking up all the time, and rowing was becaming harder and harder and our progress less and less viable.

Sunday, 11 December 2005, 8 a.m.

1 *All Relative* (four-man boat), 815 miles

2 *Atlantic 4* (four-man boat), 644 miles

3 ***EDF*, 613 miles**

4 *Spirit of Cornwall*, 599 miles

5 *Team C2*, 597 miles

6 *Atlantic Prince*, 587 miles

JAMES

The weather was changing quickly. The sky filled with cloud and the wind began to pick up, coming at us from the side and making it increasingly difficult to stay on course. I was so frustrated: we'd just taken the lead, only to get stopped in our tracks. I became angry that we hadn't rowed two-up during the night, as it was clear we were going to have to stop if the wind carried on building like this.

The question was, at what point did we stop and put the anchor down? Although called an anchor it was in fact a huge sheet of nylon that worked like a parachute, attached to the boat by fifty metres of rope. As the boat gets blown backwards the sea anchor fills up with water in the same way a parachute fills with air, drastically decreasing the speed the boat gets blown backwards. Without it, we would be blown all the way back to La Gomera, undoing all the hard work we'd done so far.

The dilemma facing us, or more accurately facing me, as Ben would have been happy to stop straight away, was to establish at what point it would become pointless to keep fighting the conditions. To my mind, even if we were rowing and staying still, that would be better than being on the anchor and going slowly backwards. But using up so much valuable energy to go such a small distance could also be the wrong decision. It might be better to take the opportunity of getting some extra rest and be raring to go when the wind dropped.

We tried rowing together but that made little difference; it was becoming clear we had no choice, the wind was getting stronger and our speed was consistently less than 1 knot. There was also the chance that we'd damage vital equipment, since we had both already been knocked off our seats by waves slamming into the side of the boat. I didn't want to be the first boat to put the anchor down, but in my mind an even worse possibility was beginning to form: we could be the only boat affected by the wind, while the other crews raced ahead in glorious conditions.

BEN

Deploying the sea anchor wasn't something we were prepared to do readily, though I was much less concerned about the race than James. I didn't want to throw away our advantage, but more importantly, for me, each hour on the para-anchor was an extra hour at sea, an hour further away from Antigua.

The crux of the problem was that neither of us was really sure what sort of conditions warranted the deployment of the anchor. I had rather naively assumed that it would only be necessary in the event of giant storms. The weather we were experiencing wasn't in that category, since it was bright, sunny and hot, but it was practically impossible to row into what was now a strong headwind.

Our speed continued to decrease, until we were going at just 0.2 knots. We were effectively stationary, treading water.

'We have to put the anchor out,' I implored. For several hours we had fought against the elements, but I felt that we surely had to admit that they were beginning to overwhelm us. How I wished there was someone to tell us what to do. Neither of us had the benefit of experience and it was beginning to show. If we put the anchor down and got it wrong, we risked losing our hard-won position, but if we failed to put it down when we should, we risked burning ourselves out rather than conserving our energy reserves to take advantage of prevailing winds.

It was an agonizing debate, but the wind had continued to build and we eventually ceded to the weather. For the first time since our sea trials back in La Gomera, I unpacked the unfamiliar yellow chute, with its tangle of lines. I unfurled the little scrap of paper on which I had scribbled a diagram about its deployment and set about casting the long lines overboard.

As the lines went taut, the chute opened underwater and *Spirit* swung around in a slow arc like a pendulum, into the wind. It was the first time in nearly two weeks that our oars stopped moving. I collapsed into the cabin with a sigh of relief. We might have been on the anchor, drifting slowly away from our goal, but at least it was a chance to let my body recover and take a break from the gruelling regime.

JAMES

After our fumbled attempts to deploy the anchor last time in the calm waters of La Gomera harbour, which reminded me of nothing so much as messing around with a box of tangled Christmas tree lights, we figured 'more haste, less speed' and fed the lines out slowly. As it floated away from the boat like a giant jellyfish we felt it inflate; the boat stopped moving with the waves and turned directly into them as the anchor bit. Immediately we felt the difference; it was a rougher ride now, as the waves began to hit us head-on and roll through rather than pushing us along with them. Uncomfortable perhaps, but preferable to being blown backwards at anything up to 3 knots.

I found it impossible to relax, though. The frustration of not being able to row and the image of other boats making smooth progress tormented me. Our sat phone rang.

'Hello?'

'Is that James?'

'Yeah, who's this?' Surprisingly, you don't often get mystery phonecalls out in the middle of the Atlantic Ocean.

'It's Clint from *C2*; how are you getting on?'

'It's bloody horrible, isn't it?'

'I've certainly had more fun, but you guys are going well.'

'Not any more, we've just had to put our sea anchor down, it's doing my bloody head in. How about you?' I asked. I was on tenterhooks.

'Yeah, we've just put ours down as well.'

'You're not just saying that are you?' I asked hopefully.

'Would I do that?' he replied, laughing down the phone.

'Enjoy the storm, say hi to Chris.'

'Cheers.'

C2, the boat currently behind us in third place, contained a couple of ex-international rowers, Chris and Clint, who were every bit as competitive as me. It was clearly as frustrating for them as it was for me to have to put the sea anchor down, and to be frank it was great to know that another boat had been forced to stop. I wished I'd thought on my feet more and said that we were still trucking on; it would have done their heads in. Ah well, next time!

BEN

James and I both breathed a sigh of relief at *C2*'s news. Not only had we made the right decision, but it was unusual not to feel disadvantaged through lack of experience and preparation; after all, *C2* had called *us* for affirmation. The relief was only momentary, however, as the harsh realities of life on the anchor were about to become glaringly obvious.

'Right,' said James, appearing on the deck naked except for a scrubbing brush and a windscreen shield scraper, 'time for a spring clean!' and with that leapt into the rough water. I was astonished – not that he wanted to clean the hull, but that he was doing it in a brewing gale. It seemed a little foolhardy to brave such rough conditions now, not least because we had only been at sea for two weeks; it was a brand-new boat with a thick coat of anti-fouling paint. How many barnacles could have formed in such a short space of time?

JAMES

The presence of algae and barnacles on the bottom of the hull creates friction which slows down the run of the boat; not by much, but every 0.1 knots saved means less time at sea. Besides, we didn't have much else to do.

If rowing out into the ocean goes against everything you've been taught growing up, then jumping overboard nearly 1,000 miles from land is an even more alien concept. Before jumping in I made sure I had a pee in a bucket so there was no chance of peeing in the sea. I wasn't in a hurry to test the incredible sense of smell of any sharks in the area.

When I hopped in, the strength of the current caught me by surprise and with the boat anchored I rapidly found myself being pulled away from it. I lunged for the grab line which ran along the side of the boat and I just managed to get a hand on it. If I'd missed it there would have been little chance of swimming against the rough sea.

The anti-foul we'd painted on the bottom of the boat had done its job fairly well but there were still some critters hanging on, like me, for dear life. It took about twenty minutes to scrape them all off; it would have been quicker if we'd remembered to bring a face mask – as it was I had to feel the hull to check I hadn't left any hanging on. Job done, I wasn't upset to be out of the water. I'm not normally worried in the sea but there is something distinctly unsettling about swimming around naked knowing that there was nothing but miles of ocean beneath me, containing all manner of creatures. It felt like a cross between sitting on the edge of a plane waiting to do a parachute jump and the opening scene of *Jaws*.

BEN

While James scrubbed the boat in the dirty weather, I decided to use the time to download our emails, which involved a rather complex system of wiring and button-pressing on our laptop computer.

I rigged up our satellite phone, following the diagrams in my little book, and opened up the PC, which had been purchased especially for the trip. We had launched a website for the row, to which people could send in questions and where they could follow our progress, and with the aid of the computer we hoped to not only answer their questions but also send photographs to the web designers to be updated each day. Easier said than done. We had already been at sea for two weeks and we still hadn't had a chance to check our emails.

I wrote a brief note to Marina, attaching a photograph I had taken of James and me packed like sardines in a tin in the tiny cabin. It was only after I had beamed the email off that I realized I couldn't remember how to download our emails. I knew that there were hundreds awaiting our response from friends, family and strangers but I couldn't work out how to retrieve them. I conceded defeat and returned to the mind-numbing boredom of life aboard a boat going nowhere fast. I climbed back into the cabin and used James's absence as an opportunity to luxuriate in the now seemingly gargantuan space. I stretched my limbs with satisfaction and utilized every square inch of space, spreading my arms and legs across the cabin.

'CRUNCH,' I heard under my bony bottom.

'Shit,' I mumbled as I pulled myself up and lifted the mattress. I had carefully packed the laptop computer back into a waterproof bag to protect it from the elements. I had failed, however, to pack it into a Ben-proof bag and had subsequently rolled on to it.

I unzipped the watertight seal and pulled out the seemingly intact computer. It was only when I opened it that I discovered the cause of the cracking sound: the screen had shattered, rendering the computer useless. Any chance of retrieving or sending emails was now impossible. Bugger.

JAMES

After I had cleaned the bottom of the boat, Ben got to work cleaning the inside and cooking dinner: domestic bliss. I was very much looking forward to not having to wolf my food down and then row for two hours. As annoying as it was not to be moving, the prospect of getting more than ninety minutes' sleep in one go was damn appealing.

I don't know why I'd imagined us sitting outside enjoying the setting sun and a meal before heading into the cabin for a good night's sleep, because the reason we'd stopped was the arrival of a tropical storm. Almost as soon as the kettle had boiled for the meals the skies darkened, it started raining and we were forced into the cabin. It was the first time we'd both been in there together. Even the most enthusiastic estate agent would have trouble describing it as a double bedroom. The list of people I'd like to share a space that small with isn't that long (starting with my wife and then possibly Angelina Jolie) but nowhere on that list is a guy and definitely not one who hasn't washed properly for ten days.

Still, at this point spirits were high; it was a chance to rest and a chance to talk. Since the start of the race we'd had conversations, of course, but they had been mostly one-way as we tried our best to motivate each other through what had been a very tough time. A lot had been spoken about the course we would follow, our rowing and our position in the race and there had also been a few arguments – but there had been precious little in the way of casual chat because when one was rowing, the other was trying to rest.

One of the pros I had envisaged of undertaking this voyage with Ben was that, in situations like these, the fact that we didn't know each other would mean that there would be plenty to talk about. Admittedly the journey to Antigua wouldn't have taken so long if I'd gone with Steve Redgrave or Matt Pinsent but they hadn't been keen and I know more than enough about them already.

BEN

The Woodvale weather forecast arrived by text, warning us of an approaching low that would bring with it torrential rain and gale-force winds. Its ETA was midnight; we had just a few hours to batten down the hatches, and prepare to ride out the storm.

We waited for nightfall with trepidation, and decided to work out how best to cram ourselves into the tiny, cramped cabin.

'How shall we do it?' I puzzled, peering into the tiny space.

'Head to toe,' suggested James.

It seemed as good a plan as any; after all, we weren't exactly overwhelmed with choice.

We both squeezed into the cabin, James first and then me. I wedged myself into the corner next to the control panel, my knees scooped up under my chin. It was extremely cosy with our overlapping legs.

We both lay there for half an hour, just listening to the wind increase in strength. Waves crashed over the stern of the boat. We pitched and fell with each wave.

We chatted a little and listened to our iPods, and then spoke a little more. I volunteered to make up our evening meal and to keep our spirits up we allowed ourselves the luxury of two meals, one green and one orange, as well as a snack bag. James suggested we use the break to regain our strength, and food seemed an important component in our regeneration.

I struggled out of the tight confines of the cabin and on to the deck, where I had earlier prepared a Thermos flask of hot water. I dipped into the meal bins to fish out the four meals. Spray crashed over the deck as we were bounced around on the increasingly turbulent ocean.

I carefully filled each bag with its required dose of water. We had slowly become accustomed to the characteristics of each meal: the muesli was best with just a dash of water, leaving a thick, gloopy substance. The chilli con carne required the longest time to stew, or the beans were tooth-crackingly crunchy, while the shepherd's pie required an almost infinite supply of water to rehydrate, often needing four or five refills of water before it reached the required creamy consistency. It was tasty enough, but it did have the downside of producing the smelliest farts. Too much information, you might think, but imagine sleeping in a cupboard with a relative stranger, and you begin to see how delicate my choice of meal for the night was.

Each 'green', as they became known, developed its own personality and we each had our own preferences. My favourite was the spaghetti bolognese, followed by the Thai rice and then shepherd's pie if I was hungry, while James was fond of the shepherd's pie and the chicken noodle. But what really got our taste buds salivating were the 'orange' meals. I had sourced a selection of expedition foods from Norway, and while the bulk of our supplies was made up of the 'greens', I had packed eighty alternative meals for some variety.

James and I soon discovered that the Scandinavians have the best packet food in the world. Not only were the 'orange' meals twice the size, but they were infinitely tastier, the Cordon bleu of expedition foods. The sight of an orange packet would made both James and me go weak at the knees; fish pie, chicken curry… even the selection of mueslis were tastier than the greens; they reminded me of Marks and Spencer breakfast cereal.

JAMES

The daily unveiling of the snack bag *du jour* was one of the highlights of our punishing routine on board *Spirit*. Most of our energy came from the three meals, two mueslis, two desserts and 4–5 litres of sports drinks per day. But there was no substitute for the joys of chocolate at 2 a.m. in terms of taste, instant energy and morale. The problem was that we hadn't brought enough with us; we'd watched the other boats load up their food, and some crews had budgeted for as many as five bars a day each. When we arrived in the Canaries we didn't even have enough for one a day. I was in charge of sorting the diet, and although we had plenty of calories each day, I hadn't taken into account the psychological benefit of different foods and most athletes I know don't ram five chocolate bars down their throats every day. I conceded that this was going to be a totally different experience, however, so the supermarkets of La Gomera were raided for their chocolate. But despite our last-minute efforts, by the time we set off, the allowance was still less than two bars a day.

I'd read some scientific studies on diet in ultra-endurance races and the food cravings that people have. One that consistently cropped up was beef jerky and biltong as the body craves fat and salt under extreme conditions, so we had plenty of that on board. So far though, a craving for dried meat in the middle of the night hadn't come.

With the bags randomly packed by Marina we didn't know exactly what was going to be contained within them. When unveiled, contents were either cheered or roundly booed. Chocolate was always gratefully received and biltong got treated like a pantomime villain. Liquorice Allsorts got a cheer from me and a boo from Ben, and subsequently whenever they popped up they got an enormous cheer from me as I knew I'd get the whole bag. Pork scratchings (another good source of fat and protein) never got the reception I felt they deserved. Tonight though, the snack bag would be enjoyed even more because we didn't have to row all night to earn a delicious piece of chocolate.

BEN

We both sat in the cabin indulging in the glut of food and savouring the brief respite from the monotony of doing nothing. Our preparations had been dominated by urgent and life-threatening difficulties like securing a life-raft. We had not packed for a rainy day. It had never crossed my mind that we would need things to keep us entertained; after all, I had been reassured that if we weren't rowing we would invariably be sleeping, and while both of us were in severe need of rest, a generous coffin-sized cabin crammed with two six-foot-something men wasn't exactly conducive to a good night's sleep.

I tried unsuccessfully to relax and nod off, but not only did my bare limbs stick to the plastic mattress, we were completely unable to shift position without disturbing each other. The only practical solution was to sleep in a coffin-like position with arms folded over chest, but even this had a disadvantage. It meant that long legs were stretched out completely straight and wedged against the end of the cabin.

I dozed, listened to my iPod, moved, dozed, listened to the iPod, moved, and on it went until we were both maddeningly uncomfortable. The cabin had become stiflingly hot with both hatches closed, and each time we opened them for some air, a wave would inevitably break over the side and give us a soaking. It was hot, smelly, humid, uncomfortable and cramped.

We turned on the video-diary camera as a distraction and talked about life on board. We munched on chocolate and dozed some more.

It was about 3 a.m., and we had been stuck in the cabin for roughly ten hours, when James suggested we change positions. He felt too claustrophobic at the aft end and figured he would have more room the other way around. Slowly and awkwardly we swapped positions and I moved to the other end. Each of us had drawn an invisible line down the middle of the cabin and there ensued a silent battle for space, a little like the fight for the armrest on an aeroplane.

JAMES

The last thing I remembered was eating chocolate; I got woken by a huge crash and the boat shaking violently from the force of a wave. I obviously hadn't finished the bar before drifting off and had rolled on top of it; there was now a sticky, melted mess of chocolate all over me and the mattress and I tried to clean it up without disturbing Sleeping Beauty, who was snoring away next to me. This was a logistical nightmare in such a small space and with the only available wet wipes out on deck next to the 'toilet'.

I was wide awake, my body not used to being inactive for so long. The noise of the waves crashing into the boat was horrendous and the cabin was like a sauna, our two hot bodies so tightly constricted that condensation dripped steadily from the ceiling. With twelve hours of darkness ahead of us, there was still so much of the night left. What I thought was going to be a good night's sleep was turning into a nightmare and I needed the toilet. I squeezed past Rip Van Fogle and outside; the fresh air was a blessed relief (the wave that crashed over my head wasn't).

We had tried to persevere with sleeping head-to-toe but over the next couple of hours we tried every position. I think that spooning was even briefly suggested at one point, but fortunately there wasn't even room for that. Other packing deficiencies were fast becoming obvious, since one pillow was somewhat difficult to share when our heads were at opposite ends of the cabin.

BEN

Finally at around 4 a.m. I drifted off into a light sleep. Despite the hours spent lying in one place I had slept less on the sea anchor than when we had been rowing.

'Agggggghhhhhhhhh!' came a cry from James.

I jumped with a start, banging my head against the cabin ceiling just a few centimetres from my head. My heart was racing. James had cracked the hatch open to get some fresh air and with the resulting temperature drop had managed to fall asleep, just as a wave had broken, dousing him in a torrent of icy water.

I lay rigid, my stomach contorted with laughter, as I tried in vain to stifle my amusement. It was the first time I had laughed in days.

Monday, 12 December 2005, 8 a.m.

1 *All Relative* (four-man boat), 804 miles (–11 miles)

2 *Atlantic 4* (four-man boat), 628 miles (–16 miles)

3 **EDF, 605 miles (–8 miles)**

4 *Spirit of Cornwall*, 596 (–3 miles)

5 *Team C2*, 584 miles (–13 miles)

6 *Atlantic Prince*, 582 (–5 miles)

Woodvale press release:

The north-easterly winds that had been helping the boats make good progress towards their final destination changed direction last night and turned to a south-westerly, force 7 to 8. Boat No. 1, *Digicel Atlantic Challenge*, report being on their sea anchor for nearly 24 hours, as does virtually every other boat, with most competitors gaining shelter from the conditions in their cabins.

Liz O'Keeffe from Boat No. 33, *Row 4 Cancer*, describes the current weather: 'Weather rather savage overnight – gusting up to 50 knots, accompanied by big seas. Have been at sea anchor for 24 hrs and there seems to be no immediate promise of getting underway again. Both crew & boat are fine and coping well with the situation. We have mainly been surviving on the fantastic fruit cakes Richard's mother made for the trip. They are supposed to be kept until Christmas, but needs must!'

Chris Andrews & Clint Evans from Boat No. 8, *C2*, have been experiencing much the same conditions and, like everyone else, decided that their rowing progress no longer justified the effort and therefore deployed their sea anchor and retired to the cabin for the night. However, on emerging on to deck this morning they were met with a broken oar and then to their horror realized that the rope that attached their para-anchor to their boat was no longer tied on. Much to their relief a smaller line from the para-anchor that runs back to the boat in order to enable them to collapse the canopy was still attached, so they were able to recover this much-valued item of equipment and reattach it securely to the boat.

Other teams have used this non-rowing time as an excuse to do some much-needed boat maintenance. Yesterday afternoon, the girls from Boat No. 17, *Mission Atlantic*, armed with scourers and diving masks, jumped overboard to scrub the barnacles off the bottom of their boat. As the weather worsened, they returned to the boat to practise their Christmas carol singing.

The bad news is that this low pressure is not due to move away from the fleet until later tomorrow afternoon. Until then, the crews will continue to be on their sea anchors and progress will be very slow for at least the next 24 hours.

BEN

After what had seemed like an eternity, day broke. I had managed to sleep for little more than an hour in total, and my body ached from fatigue and cramp. I squeezed out of the hatch and looked for somewhere to sit. Anywhere was better than the cabin.

Now that we were no longer rowing the stark inhospitality of the boat's design became apparent; she was built for rowing and rowing alone. She was all sharp corners and hard surfaces. There was nowhere to sit or lie back, and in fact the rowing seats, with their sheepskin pads, were the comfiest place on the whole vessel. For weeks I had longed for a break from the rowing position and yet even while on the anchor I found myself perched on that same wretched seat.

According to the GPS we had lost nearly ten miles overnight. The little map of our progress showed a number of swirls and circles where the little *Spirit* had been spun back on herself in the storm, which had increased during the night.

The ocean had lost its aqua blue and taken on a murky black, I noticed as I peered overboard.

Monday, 12 December 2005

To: johncracknell@email.com
From: brucefogle@email.com

Hi John,
Julia and I spoke with a very positive-sounding Ben at 6:50 PM.

Their laptop is kaput (got sat upon) so that connection is probably permanently down. Ben wanted to know if any others had started rowing again. Frustrated at their loss of momentum and the reduction in the lead they were building up.

Desalinator failed but phone calls to 'Mr Desalinator' resulting in their repairing the unit. They're fully aware that technology failure is the greatest threat to their finishing the race. They're also fully aware that they were unprepared for the array of challenges they've met. Ben's quite literally staggered by how James drives himself. The result is that Ben does the same and, judging from his asking me if anyone's started rowing again, he's no longer looking to just row the Atlantic but now to do it as well as they physically can.

As ever
Bruce

BEN

As the endless tedium of the day stretched out before us our boredom was broken by two events. The first was the failure of the water maker and the second was the arrival of Lin aboard the support yacht *Aurora*. Until now, we had been using the water maker for an hour each afternoon, but stuck here on the anchor, our consumption had become vastly reduced and consequently this was the first time we had turned it on since we had stopped rowing. I turned the valve on the pipe and flicked the switch in the cabin. The machine roared into action, but nothing appeared. I waited and counted, thirty seconds, a minute, two minutes. Something was wrong; it had previously worked like clockwork, producing water in just a few seconds.

'James!' I hollered. This had been my worst-case scenario; I had dreaded the prospect of a water maker failure.

We fiddled and turned and switched and knocked, all to no avail.

'Are you sure the cog is open?' I asked.

'Of course it is,' James snapped back.

'Are you certain it shouldn't be horizontal?' I continued.

'Don't be fucking stupid,' he barked.

'Let's call Scott,' I suggested – the guy who had so helpfully fitted the water maker at the last minute, back in La Gomera. 'Do we have his number?'

We didn't. Damn.

The machine bore the number of its American manufacturers; it wasn't Scott's number, but it was a start. I dialled the number, and was given the number for their English distributor, who was subsequently able to give me Scott's mobile number. He was in the pub.

'Is the cog open?' was his first question.

'Which way is open?' I asked.

'Horizontal,' he replied.

I turned the cog, and in the blink of an eye the water started pouring out. What a twat, I thought, as I looked at James.

The crisis was over as quickly as it had started, but the temporary malfunction was sobering; without the water maker we were buggered, and we both knew it. Throughout my preparation for this voyage I had been convinced that we would be stymied by a technical difficulty. It would be a broken piece of equipment that would force us to withdraw from the race. This incident did nothing to allay my fears.

'There's a ship on the horizon!' shouted James, just as we were beginning to relax again. It was the *Aurora*. Lin was coming to check up on us.

For thirty minutes we watched, mesmerized, as the tiny ship grew on the horizon, her sails billowing in the wind. It was strange seeing another vessel. We hadn't seen one since our close encounter with the Russians.

'*Spirit of EDF*, this is yacht *Aurora*, over,' buzzed the radio.

They wanted to know whether our sea anchor was down, to gauge how close to us they could sail. I could just make out Lin's outline at the wheel, while a handful of crew busied around the deck.

'Hello,' I yelled above the din of the deafening wind. There was no reply as she circled us. James sat on the bow seat while I stood against the cabin, watching the yacht loop around us like a vulture toying with its prey.

'What are they doing?' I asked James.

He shrugged.

'Hello,' I hollered once again. This time Lin pulled a little closer and several of the crew waved. Lin remained motionless, her hands on the wheel.

'You know you're in first place,' called Lin, unable to keep the surprise and a touch of scepticism out of her voice.

'Great,' I beamed, 'and how are you?'

Her words were lost to the wind as she disappeared behind us. The wind was making it difficult and dangerous for *Aurora* to remain alongside. She circled us once again.

'What happened to your Sea-me?' shouted Lin, pointing to the broken mast that had been repaired with a wooden splint that had once been our fishing rod.

'James broke it while having a pee,' I answered.

There was no reply.

'We'll visit you again,' she screamed before disappearing off towards the horizon as quickly as she had come. And that was it; our little audience was over and we were alone once again.

'Thank god for that,' murmured James.

I was surprised not only by the brevity of the visit, but also by the indifference of *Aurora*'s crew. I had anticipated a warmer reception from our guardian ship and was disappointed by the frostiness of it when it finally came.

The rest of the day passed in a reverie of boredom, broken only intermittently by the comfort of food. According to the forecast, there was worse weather to come and we would be spending a second night on the sea anchor. I had found the previous night almost unbearable and the prospect of another was particularly daunting.

Once again as the sun dipped into the ocean, James and I jammed ourselves into the stifling cabin. I'm not usually preoccupied by personal space but now, confined to this tiny wooden box, I felt inhibited and claustrophobic.

I spent another sleepless night tossing and turning with each pitch and yawl of the boat. By now everything was damp again and the cabin was hot and humid, my clammy skin sticking to the mattress and peeling away each time I moved. Adding to our discomfort, James had managed to lie on one of our precious Milka bars, a 500g one. There was chocolate smeared everywhere, like Nutella it coated the mattress, our one and only sleeping bag, and the towels. Of all the things I would most come to regret in terms of our packing it was the failure to include a sheet for our mattress. Thanks to James's efforts we had one chocolate-encrusted sleeping bag, which was too hot for use during the daytime, and a plastic mattress to stick to or slide off. What I wouldn't have done for a cotton sheet.

In an effort to overcome boredom, we settled on playing 'Who am I?', at first allowing each other twenty questions, but eventually as many as we needed. James chose Brooklyn Beckham and Red Adair to my Paris Hilton and Mother Teresa.

I had been surprised how well *Spirit* had coped with the appalling weather. I had been nervous about riding out the gale-force winds in a boat I didn't really know. We had spent the best part of two weeks aboard, but she hadn't been really tested until now. I was nervous about the repair to the hole in the hull, and prayed she could cope in the massive seas.

I was impressed too by the sea anchor. We were still being blown backwards, but at just half a knot in the 50mph winds; it seemed astonishing that such a small canopy could hold us, but I was concerned too about the rope, which was chaffing dangerously against the side of the boat.

Tuesday, 13 December 2005, 9 a.m.

1 *All Relative* (four-man boat), 851 miles
2 *Atlantic 4* (four-man boat), 649 miles
3 **EDF, 611 miles**
4 *Atlantic Prince*, 601 miles
5 *Team C2*, 601 miles
6 *Spirit of Cornwall*, 599 miles

JAMES

Morning arrived and luckily the rain had passed, but the waves were still enormous and the boat was being thrown about like a rag doll. At least we were out of the cabin, though. Everything on deck was soaked but nothing had been damaged by the storm.

We turned the sat phone on just before midday, desperate to get the weather report; we were like a couple of old men gathering around a wireless. 'Please let it pass,' I said, 'I'd rather row all night than be in that cabin again; no offence, Ben.'

'Hey, you didn't have to sleep next to your feet,' he said, miffed.

'Yours aren't the nicest I've ever seen, buddy.'

BEEP BEEP. A text message came through on the sat phone; it was not good news. The storm was moving slowly and it looked like we were going to be here for another couple of days. There was no more housekeeping to be done on board, we had no books and the speakers for the iPod were out on deck; once again we were faced with the prospect of going back into the cabin to shelter from the storm. Damn, we really were going to have to talk to each other. It did, though, give the blisters on our hands and feet time to heal. I counted mine – forty-seven in all – and that was without getting Ben to count the ones on my ass, which, judging by how uncomfortable the seat had become over the last couple of days, may have seen me get a half-century.

We tried not to sleep during the day in order to be more tired at night, but it made little difference; it was just a case of coping with it. I was even starting to look forward to the two-hour shifts again just so I could have the cabin to myself. I got more sleep in two hours on my own than in twelve with Ben in there.

BEN

Once again James and I were up at the crack of dawn, desperate to escape the restrictions of the cabin that had come to feel like a prison cell. We were itching to get going. It was agonizing just staying put, wasting valuable time. Boredom had overcome lethargy, and we were now champing at the bit to lift the anchor and get under way. I relished the thought of returning to the oars and the prospect of proper sleep in a James-free cabin.

The wind had dropped, but we were racked with uncertainty about whether to take the sea anchor back out of the water. There was still a headwind, but the direction of the swell seemed to have turned slightly. The problem was exacerbated by the fact that our onboard compass appeared to be broken. We had purchased a special rowing compass designed to be read backwards in the rowing position, but with the anchor deployed and the nose of the boat automatically turned into the wind, both of us struggled to establish which way to hold the compass in order to gauge the true direction of the wind.

It sounds simple, but we were sometimes forced to calculate the double reciprocal. If the compass was held aloft in the direction of the boat, then you reversed that, but you then needed to reverse it back again to get the true bearing. Or did you? To make matters worse, the compass gave us a bearing that was fully 25 degrees out from that shown on our GPS.

James and I would spend what seemed like hours holding the compass aloft, puzzling over the mind-boggling contraption. I marvelled at the fact we had passed our Yachtmaster Ocean Theory, in which we had developed the art of navigating by the sun, moon and stars, and yet we were both utterly flummoxed by a common compass.

We had exhausted the few distractions we had been able to muster and so we resigned ourselves to lifting the anchor and seeing what happened. 'Trial and error' had been the overriding theme of the trip so far, so why stop now?

I hoisted the line into the boat, collapsing the underwater chute and hauling it on board, before retrieving the anchor's primary line. I carefully packed it away ready for redeployment while James pulled on the oars for the first time in days. It felt good to be on the move again. James struggled to pull the boat around on to the correct course. Our speed averaged a little over a knot, James was fighting a losing battle against the wind.

'We'll have to row together,' he strained.

I leapt into my seat and followed James's strokes. It was the first time we had rowed together since the day we had set off from La Gomera, and it felt strange. I had developed my own unique style according to the conditions, working around the waves, which rarely allowed both oars to be dipped into the water at the same time. It had worked perfectly well rowing alone, but now it was nigh on impossible to match James's strokes as waves crashed against us, breaking over the bow and soaking me as I struggled to keep up.

We had undoubtedly picked up speed by rowing together, but our progress was laboured and uncomfortable. My rowing was peppered with apologies as I crashed my handles into James's back. My throat became parched and my knees grazed as the handles scraped along my bare, salty skin.

For hour after hour we beat on into the wind, making little headway as we fought against the elements. It was hard going, worsened by the fact that the two days spent recovering on the anchor had given my bum, back and hands a chance to recover. Blisters had softened and cuts had healed, but now joints seized and skin cracked, as blisters were rubbed raw once again, forming new ones on top of existing sores.

I had longed to get under way in order to gain some respite from the conditions of the cabin, but this wasn't what I had expected. We had rowed two-up for nearly six hours and were in desperate need of a break and food. We resolved to put the anchor down once again to allow us to eat and have a short rest before continuing through the night. I had been aware at the outset that at night the wind had a tendency to drop, especially when the moon was full, and it seemed sensible to test the theory. We determined to use this lull to make up for lost speed.

James had become particularly preoccupied by our race position. The news of our lead had invaded every corner of his conscience and occupied his every waking thought. The sat phone had increasingly become an integral race tool, purveyor of valuable information about rival boats.

Wednesday, 14 December 2005, 8 a.m.

1 *All Relative* (four-man boat), 914 miles
2 *Atlantic 4* (four-man boat), 710 miles
3 **EDF, 663 miles**
4 *Team C2*, 650 miles
5 *Spirit of Cornwall*, 647 miles
6 *Atlantic Prince*, 646 miles

Thursday, 15 December 2005, 9 a.m.

1 *All Relative* (four-man boat), 994 miles
2 *Atlantic 4* (four-man boat), 725 miles
3 *Spirit of Cornwall*, 703 miles
4 **EDF, 701 miles**
5 *Atlantic Prince*, 692 miles
6 *Mayabrit*, 683 miles

Woodvale press release:

In stark contrast to the strong adverse winds and large swells of the weekend, yesterday brought flat calm seas, blisteringly hot temperatures and a light breeze but most importantly, blowing in the right direction. These surreal conditions provided the crews with the perfect opportunity for some much needed ocean grooming and personal hygiene.

Posted 15/12/05 10:41:09 AM

Friday, 16 December 2005 12 a.m.

1 *All Relative* (four-man boat), 1,069 miles
2 *Atlantic 4* (four-man boat), 767 miles
3 *Spirit of Cornwall*, 743 miles
4 *Mayabrit* (reading not taken)
5 **EDF, 737 miles**
6 *Atlantic Prince*, 717 miles

Woodvale press release:

As the weekend approaches, the racing fleet are hit by yet another low-pressure system – there seems to be a cycle appearing here!

At the front of the field, Boat No. 24 continues to run away from the rest of the fleet with a spectacular lead over second placed Boat No. 6 – *Atlantic 4* of over 300 miles. What are those Devon boys on!

Behind the two front boats, an interesting battle is developing for the podium positions in the Pairs Class and the lead boat changes daily. This week alone, Boat No. 10 – *Mayabrit*, Boat No. 9 – *Spirit of Cornwall*, Boat No. 30 – *Spirit of EDF Energy*, Boat No. 8 – *Team C2* and Boat No. 14 – *Atlantic Prince* have all been in first place for around 24 hours. This class is still very much open and it's going to be an incredibly exciting second half!

Posted 16/12/05 04:24:34 PM

BEN

For five days we had struggled onwards. The ocean felt like treacle. The wind had dropped completely and each stroke of the oars was laborious. Our speed had reduced to little more than a knot and morale was plummeting again.

Crossing the Atlantic necessitates a degree of calculation, an element of risk and a lot of luck. After two weeks at sea, and as many different routes as there were boats, the fleet had split and separated, with more than 300 miles of latitude between the most northerly and southerly boats. Justin Adkin and his cousins aboard *All Relative* were the most southerly crew and had forged ahead, leading the other four-man crew by some three hundred miles, while *Mayabrit* was the most northerly. James and I were somewhere in the middle of the pack.

Despite my best efforts and my 'nav' sessions in the Navy it had become apparent that neither James nor I was terribly proficient in ocean navigation. Route planning had not been particularly high on our agenda, and it was becoming clear just how huge an impact such a decision – whether to go north or south – could make. The weather had also continued to deteriorate, and we had been battling into heavy headwinds and sea for the best part of a week. The Atlantic had been whipped into a heady mix while the sky was littered with thunderclouds that broke over us, soaking us and further dampening what little enthusiasm we still possessed.

We simply hadn't packed for wet weather. James had categorically scoffed at my proposal to bring along waterproofs, on the grounds that it was unnecessary weight and that it was also 'unlikely to rain'. It wasn't the first time our lack of preparation had been exposed but it was probably one of the most gruelling examples. On our sea test James had produced a pair of Merrell shoes to row in, the same shoes that Justin of *All Relative* had – a ringing endorsement as far as my teammate was concerned. James had managed to acquire this specialist kit and so we'd tried it out. But, as with every pair of shoes in existence, they needed to be worn in. One brief session at sea did not count as breaking our footwear in and the result was a set of heavy blisters. I knew from bitter experience in that opening session that the shoes weren't worn-in enough and so rejected them in favour of my Converse trainers; not a natural choice you might think but the morning of the race had passed in such a blur it wasn't until we were well into the crossing that the full implications of my selection dawned on me. I didn't have any other shoes. I would be rowing the Atlantic in trainers. Of all the places to get blisters it hadn't been my feet I had been concerned about. If it had I certainly wouldn't have packed one pair of Converse trainers. Yet again, a piece of kit I didn't expect would play a fundamental part in our voyage.

The bonus of my less than strategic choice was that as we journeyed on my blisters subsided. James on the other hand, who had persevered with the Merrells, was suffering. By the time James realized that yet again lack of preparation was to be our downfall we could do nothing about it. We had both packed one pair of shoes each: the upshot of another Cracknell packing edict.

Onwards we fought into water with the consistency of glue, often rowing two-up in our battle against the elements.

'Where are the fricking trade winds?' I lamented. I was frustrated and angry. It wasn't fair. We had rowed and battled with all our might for our first place and now it was being stolen from us. Thick grey vertical streaks dotted the horizon, almost giving the impression of prison bars. How apt, I thought, as we rowed towards a particularly menacing cloud.

'It's going to be a heavy one,' I warned as we rowed towards the centre of the downpour.

It began to rain, initially just a few heavy drops that increased in frequency. The sky became darker as we were enveloped by the cloudburst. The horizon disappeared as visibility was reduced from a couple of miles to a matter of feet. It was ominously murky and the wind had picked up, but James and I rowed on.

The rain continued to increase in pace, those few fat drops becoming a cascade. Thunder cracked above our heads, deafening us with its loud bass. For five minutes we just sat in our seats, unable to row and mesmerized by the power of mother nature. I had never experienced rain like it, even in the Amazon. It was incredible. Coming to my senses, I leapt forward to turn on the bilge pump, but it simply couldn't keep up with the amount of rainfall; fully twelve inches of water had filled the footwell within a few minutes and James and I were forced to hand-bail our tiny boat.

And then as swiftly as we had been enveloped by the thunder burst, it was all over. Visibility returned, as did the bright Atlantic sun. All that remained was the cursed headwind.

We battled on for the rest of the day, until we could fight no longer. There was no great debate; this time we knew we had to deploy the anchor. We had been rowing two-up for hours now and we needed food, water and rest. The headwind had strengthened, as had the heavy swell that further impeded our progress. Worse still, the forecast was for another tropical storm.

Again with a heavy heart I unfurled the big yellow sea anchor and lowered it into the water. The *Spirit*'s nose turned into the wind and the boat fell silent once more. We had been assured that in the worst case we would use the anchor once during the whole race. Here we were on the anchor for the third time in less than three weeks. The weather forecast wasn't good. Tropical storm Edna was due to reach us the following evening, and at best we would be immobile for two days; at worst, four. Morale had reached an all-time low, and James in particular was finding our predicament hard to take.

JAMES

If it was a tough decision to put the sea anchor out in the first place, it was almost as hard to know when to pull it back in. The temptation, or to be more accurate *my* temptation, was to get going as soon as the wind dropped. The process of dragging the anchor in and putting the rope away took about fifteen minutes, but in my desperation to get going I tried this a few times before realizing how much the wind would have to subside before we could row off. It was very much my decision, since Ben seemed in no rush to get going again; he would never moan when I pulled the anchor out or put it in again, but he would also never say, 'Come on, let's give it a go'.

We pulled in the anchor for good at midnight two days later and set off. The conditions weren't ideal but at least we could get moving in the right direction. I thought it might be best to row together for a couple of hours and get a jump on everybody and then settle back into our routine. Ben thought that sounded OK but after two hours the conditions had worsened and the only way we could make progress was to row together. By 7 a.m. the strength of the wind was increasing and we were forced to drop anchor again.

This routine continued for the next three days: we would row and then have no choice but to stop for a few hours and then, with a change of wind, be able to row again. I don't know if we dropped the anchor too early or were too slow pulling it in again or whether we just had worse conditions than other crews, but over those few days no matter what we did, we slipped from first to fourth.

Mayabrit, a crew 200 miles to the north of us, did 100 miles in twenty-four hours whilst we drifted back nine miles. I could cope with being still when.everyone was caught by the storm, but being blown backwards while others travelled 100 miles in the right direction seemed totally unfair. In any race I'd competed in before if the conditions weren't equal the race was stopped; surely the same should apply? It didn't, of course, and I had to try to get my head around it. I couldn't control everything and it was beginning to dawn on me, finally, that the fastest crew wasn't necessarily going to win this race. There was going to be a hell of a lot of luck involved.

I was rowing with one arm, trying to keep the boat on course, when the weather report came through: another storm was on the way. Frustrated and exhausted – or at least, with one arm exhausted – we put the anchor down again.

Over the last week our progress had been slowed so much that if we maintained this average speed it would take us at least seventy days to reach Antigua. We had enough food on board for fifty. Tucking into chocolate treats and doubling our meal rations when we were anchored might have been good for our morale, but all of a sudden it became clear that it wasn't good for our supply levels. We had no option but to start rationing the food, which only served to make the days seem even longer. After a week of deadening boredom, the last remaining pleasure we had was being cut back.

BEN

At this rate we would run out of food completely a week from Antigua. As ill-prepared as we had been, food had never been a concern. In La Gomera we had been a laughing stock for the amount of food we were packing. We had carefully calculated that we would need two breakfast mueslis, three main meals, and one pudding each per day. This was then supplemented by protein and energy drinks as well as a snack bag of chocolate and nuts. But now, from a recommended daily allowance of 10,000 calories each, we were consuming around 6,000.

I had already been struggling to sate my hunger with the meagre portions, and we now faced the necessity of further cuts to our rations. If we didn't reduce our intake, however, we simply wouldn't make it.

'We'll have to cut out one breakfast cereal and one main meal while we're on the anchor,' I suggested. James rolled his eyes. He too had been having problems with the derisory portions, but had at least been able to eat the protein powders that I found so hard to digest.

JAMES

A text message came through from my Dad:

Mum and I just had our Christmas Party as ever too much fish pie, although I imagine that's the last thing you feel like!
All our love M&Dx

If only they knew what I'd have given for some fish pie. Luckily the GPS had been reading over 4 knots for virtually the whole of my two-hour shift, and there was nothing like easy speed to lift the soul and take your mind off being so hungry. The north-easterly trade winds had finally turned up and were currently blowing us towards Antigua.

After the last storm abated we stuck religiously to our direct bearing to the Caribbean rather than hitching a ride with the wind to the south and having the confidence that the trade winds would eventually come. So as we switched constantly between twiddling our thumbs and banging our heads against a fierce crosswind, other crews had gone due south, caught the wind and stolen a march on us. The further ahead they got, the darker my mood became.

With over three weeks of the race gone we'd hoped to be nearly halfway, but we hadn't even covered a third of the distance. The only half we'd achieved so far, in fact, was to have eaten half of our food. We had packed, or to be more accurate, I had packed, fifty days of rations, convinced that was the maximum time it should take us to get to Antigua. I hadn't counted on us having the worst weather on record for this time of year, resulting in seven of our twenty-one days so far at sea sat on the anchor; not going anywhere, but still eating.

We had no option but to ration our food for the remainder of the crossing, going from three meals a day to two and treating ourselves to a dessert every other day. We were doing the same shifts though, of course, burning up the same amount of calories but putting less fuel back into the engine – an equation that rationally could only result in a breakdown. I hoped that wouldn't happen before we reached Antigua.

Ben was complaining about being hungry all the time. I felt the same but made a conscious effort not to say it, not because of a macho desire not to show weakness but because I had planned our diet and it was on my insistence that we took no more than fifty days' worth of food. It was unfair that Ben had to live with the consequences of my poor decision-making. I knew that if I complained of being hungry, he wouldn't accept one of my desserts or a chocolate bar from my snack bag in the night. I'd made a promise to Ben that if he did what I asked on the oars then I would get him to Antigua in one piece, and clearly that wasn't going to happen if he didn't have enough energy. Admittedly we could have rowed less each day and burnt fewer calories, but for me at least that would have been worse than being hungry.

Biltong and pork scratchings, which in the first couple of weeks had been so poorly valued that they became fish food, were now precious delicacies. At 4 a.m. I tore open a bag of pork scratchings, scattering them all over the deck. Panic and horror gripped me as I saw vital calories being wasted, so I crawled around the deck picking up salt-water-soaked pork scratchings off the boat, like Steve McQueen in *Papillon* starving and locked in solitary confinement, scrabbling after a millipede in his cell.

For days we had coped with the lack of food by drinking more fluids to help take away the hunger pains.

BEN

I couldn't sleep as the boat was catapulted up and down by the ferocious waves, which for the first time on the whole trip had made me feel seasick. Alexis had called us late that night to check up on our morale, and seemed genuinely concerned with our state of mental health.

I had explained about our latest food crisis, to which he had answered rather cryptically, 'Have a look behind the padding in the camera case,' before ringing off. I had trudged out into the wind and rain to fish the yellow waterproof case from the forward hatch. I pulled the foam padding from the case to discover a large bag of mini Cadbury's milk-chocolate bars, carefully concealed in a hole hand-dug into the foam.

It lifted our spirits more than Alexis could have ever anticipated, reaffirming James's and my belief that he was more than the director/ producer of the TV programme; he was an integral and vital part of our team.

JAMES

I was missing home and called up Bev, who was going to a Christmas party that evening. I spoke to Croyde, who said, 'Hello, Daddy,' followed immediately by 'Chocolate, Mummy?' Bev came back on the phone and admitted that she'd had to bribe him to say hello. What was I doing out here?

We spent another three mind-numbing days on the sea anchor but there were crews far worse off than us: *Sun Latte* (the Kiwi entry) got attacked by a shark which had been caught up in the sea-anchor lines. Apparently it started thrashing around and then rammed the boat repeatedly while the crew hid in the cabin. The shark damaged the bottom of the boat, which caused a leak and forced them to abandon the race a few days later.

Saturday, 17 December 2005, 11 a.m.

1 *All Relative* (four-man boat), 1,141 miles

2 *Mayabrit*, 806 miles

3 *Atlantic 4* (four-man boat), 767 miles

4 *Spirit of Cornwall*, 745 miles

5 ***EDF*, 734 miles**

6 *Atlantic Prince*, 722 miles

We finally get to grip with our kit. *[Martin Pope, Camera Press London]*

Cruise Ship versus Rowing Boat. *[Alexis Girardet]*

Overleaf: We settle into a routine and try rowing naked – as recommended by many previous competitors. *[Alexis Girardet]*

Ben takes our picture inside the cabin. *[Ben Fogle]*

Christmas Day blues worsen with phone-calls to family back home.
[Twofour]

I photograph Ben after the capsize with one of the few pieces of equipment that is still working. *[Ben Fogle]*

We arrive in Antigua early on 19 January 2006. *[EDF Energy]*

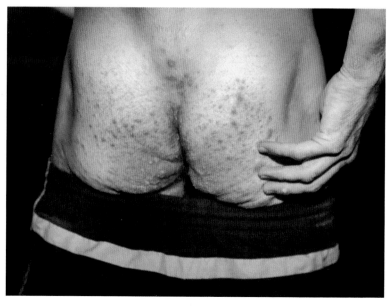

James's bottom after nearly 50 days at sea. *[Martin Pope, Camera Press London]*

The Cracknells. *[EDF Energy]*

The Fogles. *[Martin Pope, Camera Press London]*

Together through it all: we enjoy a moment of reflection, arm in arm at the finish line. *[EDF Energy]*

Sunday, 18 December 2005

1 *All Relative* (four-man boat), 1,146 miles

2 *Mayabrit*, 813 miles

3 *Atlantic 4* (four-man boat), 758 miles (–9 miles)

4 *Spirit of Cornwall*, 739 miles (–8 miles)

5 **EDF, 729 miles (–8 miles)**

6 *Atlantic Prince*, 714 miles (–8 miles)

BEN

The next day greeted us once again with skies painted grey with storms. I sat, luxuriating in moroseness, when something extraordinary happened. I felt the boat begin to list slightly before it returned to normal. It was a movement I hadn't experienced before.

I peered into the rough waters that surrounded our small boat. There was nothing.

Then, out of the corner of my eye, I caught a glimpse of a vast shadow moving through the water.

It was light, verging on white, I thought, as it circled our boat. I struggled to work out what it was. It was still a little too far away to calculate its size, but it looked very large.

'James!' I hollered into the cabin.

The shadow stopped circling and made a course for our tiny boat.

I watched, bewitched, as the shadow came closer and closer, eventually slipping alongside us. I stood there slack-jawed as the *Spirit* was dwarfed by this enormous silhouette. It must have measured thirty, maybe forty feet in length.

'James!' I cried again, with renewed excitement. The outline disappeared back into the gloom.

James appeared from his slumber to find me hopping around excitedly.

'There's a whale, a whale!' I reiterated, dancing about.

The outline reappeared, making a direct line for our boat once again. We both stood frozen to the spot, mesmerized by this oceanic apparition that moved with such measured grace. It was now just a few feet below the surface of the water, and I could clearly make out the barnacles hitched to its thick skin.

'It's going under us!' I cried, continuing my running commentary.

The boat began to move slightly as the whale lazily scratched its back along our keel. We were dwarfed by the mammoth beast, but I experienced neither fear nor alarm, just joy and wonder. It felt cathartic to be interacting with such a magnificent animal.

I had seen whales before. As a child I had been on a whale-watching trip with my sisters and my dad in British Columbia. We had observed them breach the water and I was completely amazed by them but they were a decent distance from us and I never got a true sense of their size. Then, when I was on Taransay, I had a different encounter. I had taken myself far from the group, up on to a bluff, and was on all fours throwing up after a bad batch of thistle wine. I had just wanted to escape so that I could be violently unwell without an audience. As I heaved and tried to draw breath I saw a basking shark below me in the bay. It was vast. I couldn't quite countenance that things like that existed in the ocean. I caught my breath and wondered at this majestic animal. Just he and I as far as the eye could see. Each encounter had taken me closer to phenomenal inhabitants of the oceans and here, miles from land and far from home, an enormous whale was right underneath me, occupying the same water.

Unbeknownst to me a very similar encounter was being played out with another boat, but their companion became caught in the lines. Yet my first reaction on hearing this wasn't 'that could have been us'. For reasons I still find inexplicable I felt slightly jealous of *Sun Latte*'s close encounter. (At this point I didn't realize this was going to put an end to their race.)

Having the whale swim alongside us was a humbling, strangely moving experience, as the vast creature continued its passage under our boat before breaking the surface of the water with an almighty 'whoosh' from its air hole. For thirty minutes it circled us, breaking the surface with its small fin every so often as if talking to us.

Even once it had disappeared I remained rooted to the deck, in the hope that it might return. It had been a welcome break from the monotony of life on board.

A smile stayed on my face for the rest of the day.

Chapter Seven

'Do They Know It's Christmas?'

BEN

The whale may have broken the monotony, but it didn't alleviate the hunger and James was dangerously depressed. He simply couldn't understand how we could be stormbound again. Stopping did not feature in his rules of racing and yet again we were slipping back in our position.

With less than half of our normal daily food allowance we had both become lethargic and despondent, moods made worse by the news that most of the other boats in the pack were under way once again. We lifted the anchor and dropped it again half a dozen times, beaten back again and again by the headwinds and seas that threatened to blow us back towards Africa. Once again we rowed two-up for hours on end, often just treading water and rarely making any tangible headway. It was like banging our head against a brick wall. All the while, *C2* and *Spirit of Cornwall* were making up distance. It drove James to despair.

JAMES

By mid-morning on 20 December the wind had shifted from a headwind to a crosswind and the weather report said that it was going to keep shifting round to a following wind (we'd had false reports like that before). We packed away the anchor for what we hoped was the last time, brooding over the fact that in previous races, crews had got across without ever having to use their anchor. We'd been at sea for three weeks and had spent a week going nowhere, but we had to look forward. We were moving again.

BEN

The arrival of a flying fish heralded the return of the north-easterly winds. Flying fish are extraordinary creatures. They somehow defy nature with their fragile wings and I often watched in wonder as schools of them skipped and sailed above the water.

Flying fish had been the cause of much amusement on board, particularly when they caught you off guard or at night. James seemed especially vulnerable to fishy attacks, screaming out whenever one smacked into him. The smaller ones were more of a nuisance, however, as they had a tendency to get stuck in inaccessible places, where they would slowly rot and, inevitably, stink in the hot, wet conditions. They also had an uncanny ability to disguise themselves as pieces of chocolate, particularly at night. I'd often break up my precious chocolate bar on the deck for easy access while rowing and on more than one occasion I picked up a tiny flying fish thinking it was a piece of Yorkie. It's not a nice experience, I can assure you.

This particular fish was larger than most, nearly a foot long, I estimated, as it flapped around the deck shedding its scales everywhere. I danced about trying to grab hold of it, but it kept slipping from my grasp before jumping back into the water, leaving a trail of slime behind it. A free dinner had got away, but with its flying visit had come the new winds we had been praying for, a strong north-easterly and a swell that would propel us towards Antigua directly on our course of 265 degrees. At last, we could make some headway.

The sky was once again streaked pink as the sun rose the next morning; yet another cloudy day. There had been little sun for three days now, and the dial on the solar-panel batteries was dangerously low.

We had begun to economize on our power usage. During the day we could use the GPS as it was fed directly from the solar panels, and it didn't draw much power away from the charging batteries at night, though we couldn't run the risk of losing any charge and were forced to row only using the compass. But the real problem with our lack of electricity was the water maker, which consumed a vast amount of power each time we used it. When we were on full power it could generate 30 litres of water an hour, but we had barely enough juice to run it for ten minutes.

JAMES

Despite our continuing problems with the amount of food on board, physiologically the importance of food pales into insignifance when compared to that of water. The most vital piece of equipment on board, bar none, was the desalinator. If the GPS failed we always had a compass, and on clear days the sun, moon and stars could all be used for navigation; and if the satellite phone broke then the luxury of calling home disappeared, but it wouldn't stop us crossing the Atlantic. If the precious desalinator stopped working, however, that was it: mission over.

After the worrying last-minute replacement of our old water maker back on La Gomera, we had settled on a larger, heavier model that would have made up to 25 litres rather than the original smaller, lighter model that made 5 litres of water per hour. Despite everyone reassuring us that we had made the right decision in La Gomera we failed to see the advantage of a heavier machine that made water much faster than we'd ever be able to drink it, which would result in us having to pull the excess weight along through the water. We would come to understand how right we were to have followed their advice.

Most boats had been ready to go days before ours, so there had been plenty of bored rowers wandering around La Gomera, passing judgement on our private race to get the *Spirit* into the water on time. There were some approving looks and positive comments as well as no shortage of helpful advice, but reactions to the desalinator had been pretty unequivocal: some looked as though they had smelt off milk, while others sucked breath in through their teeth and shook their heads, much like the plumber who had come to look at the leaking pipe in my kitchen days before I left for the Canaries.

We quickly developed a complex and tried to hide it away from visitors, like a couple of kids whose bikes still have stabilizers when all their mates are pulling wheelies down the road. When you're relying on solar power, the efficiency with which you use that energy is hugely important, and on top of the greater reliability the larger model offered, it produced our day's water in one hour rather than five. Although it needed more power when it was running than the smaller model, it was running for four hours less; in retrospect having to pull a few extra kilograms of water along seemed like a small price to pay.

The most common reason why unsupported crossings of the Atlantic fail is because the desalinator breaks down. We were about to set off with one not only that evoked pity from the other competitors, but that the organizers won't allow at all in the next race: not a great place to start. Luckily there was one of the larger models for sale on the island; the bad news was it was £3,100 and it would take a day to fit in the boat. Although we had eventually secured sponsorship we still hadn't covered the cost of buying the boat and entering the race, and none of the sponsors' money had come through yet. Ben and I were faced with a tough choice.

'What do you think, shall we change it?' Ben asked.

'We can adopt the ostrich technique and bury our heads in the sand, hoping everything will be OK, or we can say: look, this machine will work, don't listen to everybody else. It was built in Switzerland for Christ's sake! What we can't do is be out there,' I nodded at the sea, 'and say, "If only we'd gone for the other machine." We have to make a decision now.'

'It's so expensive and we've already had to buy an extra life-raft; and now this,' Ben sighed, shaking his head.

'How much would you pay for a glass of water if you had none?' I asked.

'Difficult to imagine, but if I was dying of thirst, then anything.'

'That's the position we have to put ourselves in, because this machine may help us avoid that situation. I think we should go for it. Shall we?' I half asked, half demanded.

'Yeah?'

'Yeah.'

The decision to change was tough, but actually buying it was proving to be tougher still. Ben's credit card got rejected, and my cheeky comments about a lavish lifestyle in Notting Hill that he couldn't afford backfired when I whacked my card down – and had it promptly rejected, too. Luckily for us Ben's dad had just arrived on the island and was quickly persuaded to purchase what he dryly observed as 'the most expensive drink of water I've ever bought'.

Despite the confidence we had in the new machine there were always a couple of seconds' anxiety before it kicked into life, with its simultaneously irritating yet reassuring sound of cutlery going round in a washing machine. Today was no exception. Ben turned the desalinator on to make water for the next 24 hours, and after the usual wait it fired up and began to clunk away merrily while fresh water squirted from the pipe.

Ten minutes later, I had been minding my own business, enjoying the silence, but couldn't work out what was different about the boat. Then it hit me: 'Shit, the desalinator's stopped.' As I figured out what was wrong, the hatch was flung open and Ben was there, his eyes wide with terror.

'Did you turn it off?' he asked hopefully. I shook my head; our worst nightmare was unfolding after all: a broken desalinator.

The cloud cover had been increasing over the last few days, yet most of my attention had been spent admiring the speed on the GPS, which for the first time in two weeks was making me smile rather than want to jump overboard. The voltmeter may have still indicated that there was some juice in the batteries, but if they ran down any further, the cloudy skies would make charging them markedly more difficult.

We decided to try the desalinator again; it started first time, and began spouting water. The atmosphere on board was tense; I carried on rowing and Ben carried on resting, but neither of us could do either properly with so many 'what if' scenarios going round our heads. This time it took less than ten minutes before our world was plunged into another sickening silence.

The batteries weren't totally flat, as the GPS was still working, but there clearly wasn't enough voltage to power the desalinator. We decided not to risk it again for now. Having not yet drunk all the water we'd made yesterday we decided to ration what we had left and try the desalinater tomorrow.

The next twenty-four hours were difficult despite our covering eighty-four miles, our best day in the race so far. There was real tension on the boat, both of us aware that our dream could be over if, as we feared, it wasn't just a case of low batteries but a fundamental problem with the desalinator. We didn't speak about it, instead choosing to handle the pressure in our own ways. For me the only way I could avoid thinking about what might happen when we tried the desalintor later was by trying to make the most of the great wind and catch up the crews ahead of us. I rowed harder than normal; probably not the most sensible thing to do with less food inside me and now less fluid too, but mentally it helped me to get through the day. After resting following a tough two-hour session on the oars, however, I woke up to see Ben going through the motions rather than working to move the boat.

BEN

I should have been positive and exhilarated given that the weather had finally changed in our favour, but instead, the new difficulties with our lack of food and water supplies meant that I became increasingly depressed and withdrawn. I did not want to be there. I'd had enough. I ached. I was sore. I was hungry, thirsty, depressed, tired and homesick. I longed to be with Marina. I stared at the picture of her on the beach in West Wittering with the dogs, and I cried for what I was missing, for what I had abandoned – lost, even. How I wished I could escape from this mess.

Until that point, I had very much kept my emotions to myself. I had felt it was important to remain positive and stoic around James and restrict my sadness to the cabin, shielded by the strip cloth that hung from the ceiling; but today was different. I had spent more than three weeks stifling my emotions and I wanted James to know how low I was.

'I'm feeling a bit down,' I said, as I rowed on. James sat behind me in silence, eating his chilli con carne, waiting for the start of his shift. With my admission hanging in the air, I continued driving on, trying to banish dark thoughts from my mind by escaping into a reverie of daydreams. I thought about Marina, and all the weekends we'd spent away; of the week we'd spent in Puttsborough during the summer; of swimming in the sea with the dogs, and of picnics on the beach…

'Can I ask you a question?' ventured James. I had stifled my personal feelings, but I knew James had been struggling too. Finally, I thought, a chance to open up and share the strain of what we had been going through, both physically and emotionally.

JAMES

For the first time on the row I was frustrated by the effort, or lack of it, that Ben was putting in. I'd been working so hard over the last few shifts and felt that all my effort was being wasted as Ben drifted along as if he was out for a Sunday morning stroll. It took the wind out of my sails and completely deflated any motivation I might have had for the next session. I had to ask Ben what he was doing; if he really thought he was giving his best I had to accept it and carry on doing mine, but if he was just cruising I might as well do the same; what was the point of me killing myself only for him to enjoy the view?

'Can I ask you an honest question?' I asked, sitting in the bow rowing position. I could only see his back.

'Yeah.' Ben's shoulders seemed to tense with anticipation.

BEN

'Why aren't you sweating?' James queried.

I was perplexed.

'You said you sweat when you exercise, but there's no perspiration on your face.'

Where was this going?, I wondered.

'Are you really rowing hard enough, or just going through the motions?' I was flabbergasted.

'Because if you really don't want to win the race…'

'JAMES,' I cut him short.

JAMES

'Don't take this the wrong way, but we said we would be totally honest with each other. I don't mind what your answer is but I need to know, do you think you're doing enough? Do you think you're giving it your best?'

Ben slammed the oars down and started ranting. 'How can you ask me that? I've done everything you've said since we started this race and never complained' (I bit my tongue at that one). 'I'm having my worst day, I've been crying in the cabin between shifts and now you ask me that.'

There was nothing I could say. Well, I could have said sorry, but I didn't feel as though I'd done anything wrong. I'd asked an honest question and truly wouldn't have minded what answer he gave. I just wanted to know if there was any point in me flogging my guts out every shift. With previous crewmates we'd always be completely frank, take criticism and answer tough questions, although admittedly we hadn't been hungry, sleep-deprived and running out of water.

BEN

We both sat in stony silence, absorbing what had just happened. I had admitted the fragility of my mind in a moment of weakness, and James's response had been to berate me for not trying hard enough. Of all the reactions I had prepared myself for, I hadn't expected this.

I wanted to jump up and scream my head off. I wanted to yell and holler. I wanted to jump overboard.

'I can't believe you could be so insensitive,' I said, throwing down the oars. 'Is that supposed to make me feel better?' I asked, wondering if this was Cracknell's warped form of tough love. What was the point?, I mused. The competition was forming a rift between us. James's obsession was becoming a problem.

JAMES

Ben went into the cabin without another word and I said nothing else. At least we had two hours to think about what had happened. This was our first serious argument on board, and although that was always going to happen some time, how we responded now would determine how the rest of the trip would go. At least it gave us something other than the desalinator to think about for a while.

Ben came out for his next shift and sat down. 'I'm sorry, I'm really struggling today. I'm missing home and worried the desalinator is going to fail us, and I just can't believe you asked me that.'

'I'm sorry buddy, I asked for my sake. I didn't want to keep working my ass off if you weren't interested in how fast we were going. It wasn't the right time when we're so hungry and thirsty; let's try and make some water in a few hours and hopefully things will look better.'

The time came to turn the desalinator on. It kicked into life but sounded weak from the beginning, lasting only five minutes before grinding to a halt. This time, however, the silence was interrupted by a 'beep-beep': the GPS had cut out, too. The batteries were totally flat. We were in serious trouble, very low on water and facing a night of navigation without GPS. The argument was forgotten, as was our position in the race. We had more important things to worry about. We were facing the possibility that we had run the batteries so low they wouldn't recharge, it was that or the desalinator was broken beyond repair and draining the batteries. If either scenario was true, we wouldn't be able to make any more water.

We agreed to row through the night on one litre of water every twelve hours each while sticking to a bearing of 265 degrees on the compass and praying for a sunny day to charge the batteries. Thankfully the wind was with us during the night and the distance we covered went some way to make up for being so tired, hungry and thirsty.

I spoke to Bev in the morning. She'd been at a Christmas party the night before and was off to my parents' house the next day for Christmas. Our regime was the same day and night and dates were totally irrelevant but it was going to be horrible being out here at Christmas, knowing all my family would be meeting up to eat, drink and enjoy each other's company. It was bad enough not being there, but our lack of food and water made me miss the celebrations and excesses even more.

BEN

For two days we cooked our food in salt water and restricted ourselves to just two litres each. We turned on the water maker each evening, and for five tantalizing minutes it would run, before shutting down, leaving us with just a few meagre litres. Water occupied our every waking moment. It was all we thought and dreamt about. My mouth was permanently parched, my throat dry and with every pull of the oars I pictured a tantalizing, ice-cold glass of water.

Slowly but predictably I began to lose my marbles as I became increasingly dehydrated. With our salty snack-bag food augmenting the process I became irrational and emotional. We were, quite literally, killing ourselves.

We had four litres of water to last us two days, an impossible situation, but we simply weren't prepared to break into the ballast and incur a time penalty. We didn't deserve to lose our hard-earned lead just because of a bottle of water. The ballast had been a contentious issue from the beginning. According to Woodvale, the 150 litres of water stored under the deck are integral to the design of the boat, ensuring it rights itself in the unlikely event of a capsize. Most boats carry some form of ballast – historically, ships had carried timber or even stone for this purpose – but in our case, the organizers had concluded that fresh water would be far more useful, in the event of emergency.

The problem was that in past years, race competitors had dumped the ballast soon after setting off, reasoning that the added weight compromised speed. Woodvale had resolved to stamp this out by incurring a penalty for each of the 5-litre bottles found to have a broken seal: four hours' time penalty for the first bottle used, twelve hours' for the second and a whole lost place in the final rankings for each bottle thereafter.

While their rules may have ensured the overall integrity of the race, it severely compromised our sanity. We simply weren't prepared to throw away four weeks of hard rowing for the sake of a bottle of water, but did we have a choice?

JAMES

I was angry and frustrated by a ballast rule that many of the crews had thought both dangerous and unnecessary. If a crew has lugged 150kg of water for thousands of miles, it should be up to them whether they drink it or not.

Despite being desperate for water we decided to wait until lunchtime to try the desalinator again. The sky was still cloudy but the GPS had come back to life briefly so the batteries must be charging. Would it be enough? According to the GPS we had somehow covered sixty-seven miles despite our problems, and the progress was reflected in our race position – we were up to second. Normally on receipt of such good news we'd cheer and allow ourselves a few minutes of self-congratulation. More accurately *I'd* shout and be happy, and then immediately get frustrated that we hadn't made more ground up on the boat ahead, whereas Ben would cheer but then become worried because of the extra pressure he felt in being amongst the leading group. This time our celebrations were muted; our race position was irrelevant since without water we were never going to make it across to Antigua. If we turned the desalinator on and nothing happened, we were very low on options.

The voltmeter was showing a reasonable charge and we decided now was as good a time as any. As I flicked the switch, two things happened: the needle on the voltmeter leapt to the left indicating no charge, and the GPS shut down again. Ben was distraught; his premonition that our crossing would have to be abandoned due to a technical failure was coming true. My faith in technology must be stronger, though. I was convinced a couple of sunny days was all we needed to fully charge the batteries and that there couldn't be anything seriously wrong with the desalinator. We'd spent a whole day and a heap of money switching to this model for its bullet-proof reliability, and I wasn't giving up hope yet.

Although it had been cloudy for the last few days, the sun had been breaking through and the batteries should have been charging more than they were. It was time to break the habit of a lifetime and hit the instruction manual.

BEN

We pored over our various instruction manuals, and discovered that the solar panel had been installed with a flow restrictor in order to run it into two batteries. We reasoned that if we could remove the restrictor and one battery, we stood a far greater chance of fully charging the other battery.

We unscrewed the unit from the wall and peered into the dizzying maze of wires and cables. How I wished I had paid more attention in electronics at school, rather than flirting with a nice girl in my class called Catherine.

JAMES

My DIY skills lean more towards the destructive than constructive end of the spectrum. I wouldn't have attempted a rewiring job at home, but stuck out in the middle of nowhere we had no alternative but to do things we normally wouldn't. Trying to keep positive and negative wires apart, concentrating on not losing the tiny screw while being bent over double in a stinking hot cabin, was making the task almost impossible. After half an hour of sweating and swearing I felt I'd made a pretty decent fist of it, even passing the rule-of-thumb 'Test of Success' by having no spare parts left at the end. All we could do now was to pray for sunshine and leave the battery at least twenty-four hours to fully recharge, drawing a tiny bit of power to use the GPS to check our position every few hours.

I tried to switch on the GPS and nothing happened. The charge in the batteries had crept up (although from our earlier experience that wasn't evidence of any real power) and should have easily been enough to work the navigation system. I thought my DIY had gone too smoothly, but clearly I must have dislodged some other wires. I tested the running light and it still worked, so at least the whole circuit wasn't down. Hopefully it was just a case of finding the dodgy connection.

I checked the fuse on the GPS praying it would be an easy solution, but obviously it wasn't. I was going to have to take the panel off again. The temperature hadn't increased but sweat was pouring down my face while Ben's eyes were boring into me from the rowing position, adding to the pressure I already felt under. Having passed the Yachtmaster Ocean

Theory course we shouldn't (in theory) need the GPS but I desperately wanted it to work, as much as anything to give us a sign that not everything was going wrong with our crossing.

I unscrewed the panel and played a game of Snakes and Ladders with the wires, following each one and pushing in every loose-looking connection. I could have sworn my mouth couldn't have got any drier than it had been for the last day but for those twenty minutes, I don't remember swallowing once. Instead I had to keep peeling my tongue from the roof of my mouth, as the likelihood of no water or GPS was increasing by the minute.

I'd started working through every connection for the third time when the GPS went 'Beep-beep' – it was rebooting! Relief flooded through both of us. The lack of water was starting to affect us physically and emotionally – our argument had shown we weren't thinking clearly and there was still a strained atmosphere on board – but the joy of getting something back that two hours previously we hadn't even worried about losing was fantastic. Although we were still without water the mood was far more positive and we were filled with a fresh belief that maybe not everything was against us.

The sunset echoed our newfound hope, the sun slipping into the sea and illuminating clouds that were glowing a beautiful red and, more importantly, thinning out. It was Christmas Eve tomorrow and we were hoping for clear blue skies but before then we had another night surviving on just one litre of water. Thankfully the urge to drink at night was vastly reduced, replaced by a desire for chocolate, but I couldn't generate the necessary saliva to eat more than half a Yorkie.

All night the same thought had been going round my head: 'What if the batteries don't recharge?' I realized we were going to have to start drinking our ballast water before we tried the desalinator again. The combination of lack of water and twelve hours' rowing a day was taking its toll.

Ben suggested stopping rowing and waiting for the batteries to recharge so that we could conserve energy, sweat less and therefore need less food and water. I thought that if we weren't rowing we'd sit around and feel even more hungry and thirsty, and if everything was charging we would have wasted a valuable day's food going nowhere. We were making such good progress and I was convinced we could reclaim the lead that night, and although the race position was inconsequential compared to the need for water, I desperately wanted to be in first place if we did choose to dip into the ballast. If we ended up getting a time penalty, I at least wanted to prove that we were the fastest crew.

It was a horrible night's rowing, constantly thinking about the charge in the battery and checking the sky for clouds. Whenever they covered up the stars, my heart sank. There was nothing we could do but wait, but that was becoming harder and harder. I was starting to break down emotionally; just thinking about the earlier conversation I'd had with Bev had tears rolling down my face as I was rowing along. We desperately needed water, not only to drink but also to fill us up and trick our bodies into believing we weren't that hungry.

My shift ended just before dawn and I headed into the cabin with the sky full of clouds, trying not to think of the consequences of another overcast day. An hour later I got woken up by sunlight pouring through the hatch in the roof. This was more like it; I looked at the voltmeter and it was definitely moving in the right direction. I opened the hatch to share with Ben the sense of optimism I'd woken up with. I was greeted by a broken man; his shoulders were hunched, he was sobbing and from beneath his sunglasses I could see tears tumbling down his cheeks. He looked like I had felt during the night. We were going to have to look after each other today otherwise we weren't going to get through it.

'The battery's charging, buddy. It looks like we're going to get loads of sun today,' I chirped out of the cabin.

I got a teary 'Hmm' as a response.

BEN

We had both become emotionally unhinged, breaking down in front of one another. I couldn't cope with the pressure, and began to seriously worry about my mental health. I didn't want to call home, nor speak to Marina. I didn't want to tell them about our suffering, after all, what could they do to help us, thousands of miles away? We had done everything we could do and now it was just a waiting game, but I didn't know which would come first, the water maker or madness.

'I can't cope,' I cried to James, 'I can't do this any more.'

'Call Marina,' he demanded. 'You've got to call her, man, what will she think if she finds out you didn't call her when you needed her most?'

JAMES

The BBC had installed a solar panel and battery separate to our system to power their cameras, and it was now busy charging our sat phone. I told Ben he should phone Marina and talk to someone who unconditionally loved him about how low he was feeling. He refused, so when he'd disappeared inside I phoned Marina myself, asking her to call back in a couple of hours when he was next on shift. Admittedly my actions didn't come under our rule of total honesty, but they were necessary under the circumstances.

BEN

When the phone rang I closed the door to the cabin and extended the plastic aerial. 'I'm going mad,' I bleated into the phone. 'I don't know what to do,' I said, before breaking down into uncontrollable sobbing. This wasn't me. Where was this coming from, I wondered, as I wailed down the phone. I didn't want Marina to know this side of me. I was strong, full of resolve and stoic. My surest asset was my strength, but now it had gone, evaporated by the sun.

Why was Marina remaining so composed?, I thought, as I wept uncontrollably. I hadn't wanted to call her for fear of upsetting her. It was nearly Christmas, a time of festive frivolity, not suicidal boyfriends.

Where I was irrational and emotive, Marina remained logical and poised.

'Use the ballast,' she reasoned, 'you NEED water.'

'But we'll have a time penalty,' I sobbed back.

'So what?' she snapped. 'Since when were you so concerned about the race? Who cares about a stupid race position?' she continued with a hint of exasperation in her voice. 'Open the ballast,' she reiterated, lovingly blunt.

I could see her point, but my thirst-addled mind was still telling me otherwise. I decided to call my father, the king of reasoned logic.

'Open the ballast, Ben,' he said, before I could say a word.

'You're not thinking rationally,' he added, 'you're dangerously dehydrated and you'll do yourself some permanent damage unless you rehydrate.'

The Cracknell/Fogle grapevine had been red hot, and James had received the same advice. We both understood the rationale, but it had become a matter of pride.

JAMES

Rowing under the bright sun, I felt confident that everything would work out, although I was acutely aware that in no time at all I could be feeling as bad as Ben. Just after noon a text came through on the sat phone: we were in the lead by 0.8 miles. I read it and burst into tears. They were not tears of joy or sadness, it was unlike any emotion I'd ever experienced; we'd achieved the target I'd set the night before but we were still no nearer to solving our biggest problem. I wanted to get into the lead so that if the desalinator did end our race, at least we would have been winning at the time. Making sure we got into the lead had held my emotions together until this point and now they all came tumbling out.

I've won big races before; I didn't even break down in tears on the Olympic podium (I left that to Matt Pinsent), so it wasn't the fact that we were leading that caused the outpouring. Whatever the reason, I couldn't do anything to stop myself; for ten minutes I had to stop rowing as it all flooded out. The strength of my emotions terrified me; I just wanted to get off of this boat.

We both knew there wasn't enough water to see us through until the battery had charged. We were going to have to start drinking the ballast, unless we tried an option which we'd spoken about and hadn't wanted to resort to: the BBC battery. It wasn't as big as ours but it charged very quickly and might have been able to power the desalinator for thirty minutes. It would give us ten litres of water, a reservoir compared to what we'd been living off for the last few days. The only problem was that it was going to take electronic skills that neither of us possessed and there was a risk we might blow the circuit. This meant Ben wasn't keen, as the battery was currently charging the phone, our sole link to the outside and the only thing keeping him sane. He was terrified about losing the ability to charge it, but I didn't want to start drinking the ballast until we'd exhausted every option.

Finally we agreed – at least, I don't *think* I bullied him into the decision – that we were both so thirsty that it was worth a go. The light in the cabin was going to have to be sacrificed for the cause. I cut, then stripped, the wires which connected the light to a plug that in turn went into the cigarette-lighter socket (a socket that was powered by the BBC battery). Carefully, I wired the positive and negative ends directly to the desalinator. This took half an hour, over which time the anticipation grew and when the time came to push the plug in the socket we'd somehow convinced ourselves it would work. I pushed it in…

Nothing. Our heads dropped. The last chance had gone.

I stuck my head inside the cabin. 'Ben, I've shorted the battery, we've lost all power from it now.' He didn't reply, instead just shaking his head. It was probably taking all his self-control to avoid saying, 'I knew we shouldn't have done that,' a comment that in our fragile states would have only created another bitter argument.

'We've got no option, buddy, it's time to crack open the hatch and grab some water,' I said. As much as it was going to hurt, we'd waited long enough. We were leading the race and whatever happened afterwards, at least we were the quickest crew up until that point, and in my mind that made it easier to break the seal on that first bottle. Neither of us knew how much of a punishment for drinking the ballast we would face at that point, and I for one didn't want to know; we had lasted as long as we could, and probably longer than we should have done.

BEN

With tears streaming down our cheeks we cracked open the plywood cover and pulled out one of the precious five-litre bottles. We placed the bottle on the deck and stared at it. The security tape had been damaged in the storms, but its fluid content remained intact and tantalizingly close.

'It's just four hours, that's just fifteen miles,' I reasoned.

James stared at the bottle, his eyes red from tears and torment.

'Fuck it,' he relented, 'open it.'

I picked off the security tape and unscrewed the lid and handed it to James who held it aloft before moving it to his lips and taking a sip. Tears streamed down his cheeks. What a waste of water, I thought, as I watched his tears splash on the deck.

JAMES

I was gutted. I wanted to win the race and it was obviously going to be close all the way; after 1,078 miles of hard slog there was only 0.8 miles between the first two crews, and any penalty was going to have a massive impact. I kept telling myself, 'We've got no choice, we've got no choice.'

Opening the ballast wasn't like discovering an oasis in the desert, diving in and drinking your fill. We only drew one 5-litre bottle out, two and a half litres each: just enough to see us through until we tried the battery, but still ten litres less than we had each been living on every day earlier in the race.

As the sun set, I couldn't resist having a sneaky look at the voltmeter. The charge was as high as I could ever remember it being, but was it enough? Now that we were going to be operating on one battery, if it wasn't fully charged the desalinator would eat up the electricity in no time at all.

'I reckon we're gonna have to let it charge for another twenty-four hours,' I half said, half asked. Ben was still coming to terms with losing the ability to charge the sat phone, not to mention the cameras, and just nodded. 'Let's see if we can make the water last until this time tomorrow,' I said. 'If we do, the time penalty can't be that significant.'

'OK, but I reserve the right to take more out if I'm desperate,' said Ben.

'Fair enough, but I'm not going to,' was my defiant response. I wasn't sure whether my sharp reply was directed to Ben or myself. In less than twenty-four hours, we'd know whether our crossing was going to be aborted because of a lack of water.

BEN

Another night passed, and the sun reappeared, but we needed two full days of uninterrupted charging. Without water, our mental states continued to deteriorate rapidly. My body rejected the salty food, and the snacks made me too thirsty. Not only were we dehydrated but because we didn't have enough saliva to eat properly we were also going hungry. I was going mad. I began hallucinating and my head pounded with headaches. My wee was brown.

The much-needed sun was beneficial to the solar panel but it sucked what little liquid we had left from our shrivelled bodies. It was 6 p.m., we had been continuing to row despite our severely dehydrated condition and we were both reaching our bodies' limits. We had another twenty-four hours until we could run the water maker again; we couldn't last that long and we both knew it.

We'd bitten the bullet and dipped into the ballast, but we'd decided to open just one bottle. We had two and a half litres each to last us through until tomorrow. We rowed on morosely, rueful and ashamed at our 'weakness'; we were still dangerously dehydrated and exhausted. In a scanning of the horizon I spotted a sail on the horizon. I wasn't even sure was real: it was *Sula*, the second support yacht – she had been trying to find us for several days now.

I called them on the VHF and relayed our coordinates, and they were soon alongside us as we rowed on into the headwind.

'You're in first place,' they shouted.

I rowed on in silence. Tears welled in my eyes. I didn't need this now.

'How are you doing?' they added.

'Not great,' I answered, 'I've had better days.'

'Stick in there boys, you're doing great,' they cried before disappearing.

Christmas Day arrived, three times. I had been scheduled to give a short phone interview with BBC's *Breakfast News* at 6 a.m. It was the last thing I felt like doing, as I felt about as festive as a llama.

'Happy Christmas,' I sulked down the phone.

'How's everything out there?' chirped the presenter.

'Well, we've got no water or electrics, but other than that we're holding up,' I replied, sounding for all the world like Harry Enfield's ungrateful teenager Kevin.

'And are you rowing naked?' he chuckled.

I remained silent. Here we were, teetering on the edge of a life-or-death situation in the middle of the Atlantic Ocean, slowly going crazy and he was asking about naked bums.

'No,' I replied curtly.

'Did Father Christmas come?' he asked.

'No, because our navigation light doesn't work, as WE DON'T HAVE ANY POWER.'

'And what are you hoping for this year?' he continued, oblivious to my mood.

'All I want this Christmas is a glass of water,' I answered without pause.

As morning broke, the sun began its relentless, merciless climb, sapping our energy and our spirits, yet still the battery was only half charged. The situation was about as far from a usual Christmas as it was possible to imagine. I had only ever missed one other family Christmas, and that was when I was living on Taransay for the BBC series *Castaway 2000*.

Fogle Christmases always follow the same structure. The family all gather at my parents' house in Arundel: aunts, uncles, grannies, cousins and friends all converging on West Sussex for the festive period. With anything up to six dogs it can be a somewhat chaotic time, but great fun, walking along Climping beach with the dogs running in and out of the surf. Marina and I still hadn't spent a Christmas together and this year would be no exception.

JAMES

As the sun went down, so did my spirits. I didn't feel depressed, just incredibly selfish and sad for being out here and away from my family at Christmas. I urgently had to apologize for doing the race. It couldn't wait.

'Hey, baby, it's me,' I said when Bev answered. Judging by the background noise, I could tell she was in the car, driving to my parents' house for Christmas Day. I wasn't going to be there.

'Hi, darling, how's it going!' She sounded happy and excited; Bev loves big family events. Tears started streaming down my face.

'Not so good, beautiful.' My voice started to break.

'Oh baby, what's wrong?' She sounded concerned.

I knew it would be better not to say anything and to avoid worrying her, but I had to tell her how I was feeling and I wanted to apologize.

'Its horrible, baby, I'm so thirsty and hungry, we're running so low on water, I'm so sorry for being out here.' I was sobbing now.

'Oh, baby, don't be sorry, we're OK back here.' Her voice sounded anxious and slightly amused at the state I'd got myself in.

'I'm sorry, so sorry. I'll call you later.' I couldn't say anything else, and instead felt a strong urge to apologize to my dad, too. The conversation started off along similar lines and ended with me not only apologizing for being out here, but for all the times he'd had to bail me out of things I'd rushed into without thinking of the consequences. Those calls exorcised some of the weird emotions I was suffering from, but despite my best efforts to reassure them I was all right, I must have left Dad and Bev worried about me.

Ben and I wished each other 'Happy Christmas'; they were just words, with no real feeing – both of us would rather have been anywhere else. The sun rose into a clear blue sky for the second day running. If the battery hadn't charged by tonight then it was never going to. We agreed to row until mid-afternoon stop, call home, try to celebrate Christmas and then switch on the desalinator.

BEN

James opened his letter from Beverley and wept openly as he read it. I decided to call my family. My mother answered the phone. I'd promised I'd try to remain calm and composed, but it all became too much for me, and I once again broke down and shed tears I couldn't afford to waste. I spoke to my sister Emily, over in the UK visiting from her home in Dubai, and then to my other sister, Tamara. Each time I managed a short 'Merry Chris–' before breaking into tears. Life couldn't have been bleaker.

JAMES

The irony of being more hungry and thirsty on Christmas Day than we've ever been was not lost on us. With our biggest Christmas wish being a drink of water, for once in our lives we were given a glimpse of Christmas for a large percentage of the world's population.

I had a letter from Bev, one from my parents and a couple of small presents. I opened my letters first. Apart from Bev's 'Low point letter', they were the only ones I had brought with me for the trip. It was strange hearing the voices of the people I love, as their words talked me through what they would be doing on Christmas Day. Yet again, tears were streaming down my face. Meanwhile Ben was on phone to Marina, sobbing away. It must have been a strange sight, two half-naked skinny guys in Santa hats crying their eyes out on a boat in the middle of the Atlantic.

BEN

My mother had packed us a small Christmas kit, which consisted of two Father Christmas hats, a string of tinsel and a Christmas horn. Reluctantly, we put the Christmas hats on, and I strung out the tinsel. I still didn't feel very festive in the 35 degree heat. I opened up a present from one of the other boats, *Gurkha Spirit*: they had given us a small packet of Jaffa cakes, which we polished off in seconds. My mother gave us each a dog tag, while James's parents gave us a keyring each. It was utterly surreal.

JAMES

A reindeer keyring. Not the most useful gift, I thought – it must be edible, I reasoned, so I took a bite. It was made of rubber. 'I thought you might like it and I knew how paranoid you were about weight,' was my mum's response when I asked her, when I got back on dry land, what she thought I might do with it. Bev had given me a two-inch square M&S Christmas cake; my mouth tried its best to water as I opened it. I could see Ben in my peripheral vision looking longingly at the cake. I debated whether to pretend I hadn't seen his puppy dog expression, but my conscience got the better of me and I broke it in half and gave him a piece – the joys of teamwork. My last present was from Matt Dawson and Joanne, his girlfriend; they must have expected I'd have time on my hands, sending me a 'Magic Foam Cock'. It wasn't that magic after all – it just increased in size tenfold when put in a glass of water – great.

BEN

I was going insane. 'HELP ME,' I scrawled in my diary. It was unbearable waiting for the sun to set so that we could test out the water maker. We were on edge all day. If it didn't work, then we were in serious trouble. Even if we were to consume all of the ballast on board, it would last us only a few days. The single alternative was to be rescued by *Sula*, or the 'boat of shame' as James referred to it, and to scuttle the *Spirit*.

To make matters worse, we received a text from Lin aboard the *Aurora*.

'Please call *Aurora* immediately, we have a problem,' it said. What was wrong?, I wondered as I typed in their satellite number. I broke into a cold sweat with anxiety. Was everything OK? Had someone been hurt?

'We have a slight problem,' announced Lin in her best teacher's voice. 'We have a photograph,' she continued, 'taken by *Sula*, which clearly shows a T-shirt on top of your Sea-me. We're concerned that it's acting as wind assistance.'

'You mean a sail?' I asked, seeking clarification.

'Yes,' she replied.

'You think that a T-shirt held by one side and into a headwind could be considered a sail?' I asked again, incredulous.

'In *Sula's* opinion, yes,' she answered.

'So how exactly do you expect us to dry our clothes?' I continued.

'On the deck, like everyone else,' she said.

'And my pants, can I dry them up there?' I pressed.

'No, they would also act as wind assistance.'

Things weren't going well.

Time passed agonizingly slowly. When I was a child I had longed for Christmas to last this long. We continued on our rowing shifts until 6.30 p.m. and we could wait no more. It was time to test the battery.

We opened the stopcock, and James flicked the water maker power button. It roared into action. It sounded strong, but it had done precisely that so many times previously, only to conk out.

JAMES

I looked at the voltmeter. It hadn't moved. So far, so good. But we needed it to run for an hour to give us the water we were so desperate for. Would it last that long? Ben was rowing, so at least he had something to focus on; I was stuck in the cabin unable to do anything except stare at the voltmeter, waiting at any moment for the battery to fail.

BEN

Fresh water began to trickle from the narrow pipe, which we had placed reverently into the jerry can. I rowed on, the water maker resonating through my feet; I could feel every vibration though my body. I felt sick with nerves as the machine whirred on and I watched the water-line rise up in the can.

Ten minutes passed and the machine buzzed on. Twenty minutes. I could see James through the window, staring at the voltage dial. Thirty minutes, and still it turned over.

James appeared through the hatch. His face was expressionless.

'It's still on full,' he stated, lifting the pipe from the full container and turning the machine off. 'We've just made twenty litres of water.'

We were both silent as we digested the news.

'WE HAVE WATER!' I screamed at the top of my lungs. 'WATER, WATER, WATER, WATER, WATER,' I ranted hysterically.

James leapt from the hatch and dive-bombed the ocean.

It was a moment of pure elation, an unadulterated, full-proof, no-holds-barred high. All the misery of the last few days seemed to disappear as I held the liquid to my lips and sated my water-starved body.

JAMES

It's difficult to describe the seismic shift in our emotions from the wrecks we had been only an hour previously, to the re-energized idiots leaping around the boat. I rowed with a grin on my face into the setting sun with the Red Hot Chili Peppers singing 'Californication' on the iPod.

'...The sun may rise in the East
At least it settles in the final location.'

For the first time in days, our final location was once more a possibility.

Chapter Eight

Hitting Zeta

JAMES

In spite of our surviving on two-thirds rations, our physical recovery from the extreme dehydration we had experienced over Christmas had been quicker than I had expected. It was the mental recuperation that was taking time. I had been shocked by the strength of our emotions and the dramatic mood swings we had both experienced during those terrible dehydrated days. We had scared our loved ones, scared ourselves – at one point I had even contemplated jumping overboard – and seen sides of each other that even our best friends and families hadn't witnessed.

Those feelings of vulnerability and helplessness continued to haunt me. I realized there was very little we could do if something went wrong. Up until that point, the worst thing I had been able to imagine happening was that we might fail to complete the crossing. I now knew how naive I'd been.

The routine which had formed the backbone of our voyage thus far – the clockwork cycle of rowing, cooking, and charting our daily progress – had returned to normal straight away. The process of making water was never the same, though; the desalinator had proved its value to us and we had no option but to trust it, but it was like dating a diva: when it was good it was fantastic, but when it played up we were nervous wrecks.

When we were struggling without water our position in the race wasn't our highest priority, so coming out of our 'drought', our ranking was a massive surprise. I wanted to keep rowing hard as much for my sanity as my race position, thinking I'd feel worse sitting around doing nothing than I would if I was rowing. Amazingly, I managed to convince Ben of this as well.

On Christmas Eve we led the race by just 0.8 miles (after some 963 miles of racing). At that point we'd been living on two litres of water a day for three whole days. Our emotions were shot and we both felt incredibly weak. And yet amazingly, by Boxing Day we had a lead of twenty-two miles and by 28 December, we were fully seventy-six miles ahead of the nearest boat, C2. I wasn't sure how; we hadn't increased our pace, and if anything we were going slower than usual as our bodies struggled to recover from the dehydration.

Our bodies seemed to be recovering OK but I wasn't convinced about our minds. Before we left there were warnings to look out for partly submerged containers that would rupture the boat if you ran into them. We never saw one. But at about 10.30 a.m. I was convinced my eyes were deceiving me when an inflatable crocodile lilo with red handles floated past. I stopped rowing, stared at it in disbelief for a few seconds before standing up and checking the horizon for a cruise liner I assumed it must have fallen off. There was nothing in sight. I sat back down and watched it drift off into the distance still not believing my eyes weren't playing tricks on me.

Despite my precarious state of mind our rowing was looking good. All we had to do now was to go the same speed as the crew behind and we would win. Easier said than done; we had no idea why we had recently increased our speed relative to the other boats, and if we could find speed from nowhere, then so could they. Maybe we had got lucky with the weather, or maybe we were just 'party poopers' and hadn't stopped to celebrate Christmas like the others. Either way, we did stand a good chance of holding on to our lead for a while, as the crews in second and third places were travelling along the same bearing, almost directly behind us. In theory, we would all be similarly affected by changes in the weather. If previous race history was anything to go by, the leading crew often gets the rub of the green with the weather. As far as I was concerned, after the Christmas from hell, all was rosy in the Fogle/Cracknell household.

But Ben was worried about our race position; earlier in the race he'd said that the better we were doing, the more pressure he felt under. I could understand his concern if we'd done something unsustainable to get there; if, in order to hold on to the lead, we had to keep pushing and pushing. But the truth was that we hadn't deviated from our routine; in fact we knew there was more speed to come because against all the odds, we had taken the lead when we had been at our weakest.

Now that we had a fairly significant lead, Ben was scared I was going to suggest we try to break the opposition by pushing really hard for a few days. He must have known me better than I thought, that's exactly what I wanted to do; but I was sure that he wouldn't want to change the shift system in order to make that happen. The two-hour system had become his foundation, something to get him through the day, and clearly I needed to find another way of motivating Ben to keep the pace going. His goal was Antigua; I reasoned that if I could make that goal seem closer, it might lift Ben's spirits and make him less worried about his body breaking down and therefore be prepared to give that little bit extra.

My weapon of choice was a spreadsheet. Dad would have been so proud that the accountancy gene had passed from father to son after all. Using a pencil and paper I drew up a sheet for three different arrival dates: a realistic one (24 January), an optimistic one (22 January) and an ambitious one (20 January). Each date could be achieved by sustaining an average daily mileage (53.7 miles, 57.7 miles and 62.4 miles respectively) so I entered those figures into the spreadsheet along with the number of miles left and, as the days went by, a record of how far ahead or behind schedule we were. Bearing in mind our average daily mileage in the race so far was 37.3 miles (although that includes the time we were sat still during the storms) all three targets were tough, but I hoped that, since racing the opposition clearly didn't interest Ben, fixed arrival dates and a mileage countdown would persuade him to give just that tiny bit extra each shift.

Every night at 7 p.m. I'd read out the mileage for the previous twenty-four hours. It seemed to be working. The results were greeted with far more enthusiasm than our race position ever was. We were on a roll, as we quickly established a new average of 67.7 miles and were twenty miles ahead of our most ambitious arrival date after the first four days of introducing the spreadsheet.

BEN

Our recovery from the days without water was faster and more comprehensive than either of us dared hope. But as we found renewed strength in our rehydrated bodies a new enemy lurked in the corners of the boat. Unlike the desalinator it wasn't a bolt from the blue, it was a very familiar nemesis. It was James's competitive streak and it was at its most insatiable when we were doing amazing speeds and impressive distances. Nothing spurred James on like extending our lead and it filled me with dread. How would he respond to this latest change in our fortunes?

I can honestly say I didn't see the spreadsheet coming. There was something extremely incongruous about drawing up a spreadsheet at sea – which James constructed from scratch – drawing the boxes, filling them in and correcting them by hand. What came as a bit of a surprise is that it did motivate me, although I knew that it was more for him than for me. It was an oceanic equivalent of a revision timetable and it worked because the distance we covered each day became more tangible and it really helped psychologically to have a number of arrival dates. Our estimated arrival date in Antigua had been an enormous question mark. No-one knew, or was able to pinpoint our arrival time. I remember one satellite phone conversation when I learnt that 14 February had been posted as our probable arrival date (based on our average speeds up until the date the ETA was put online). I hadn't been shocked or disappointed by that, I just didn't believe it. Every sailing person, every oceanographer and every meteorologist had assured me that we would get faster in the second half and so I dismissed their projections. So there was something truly reassuring about the spreadsheet and its basis in fact. It wasn't about what we *could do*, it was about what we *had done*. There are many responses to the kind of intangibility we faced on the Atlantic; my assumption had always been that we would arrive on 19 January – it was simply a gut instinct. Of all the responses to that uncertainty a spreadsheet hadn't featured on my list of options.

JAMES

Most people who've crossed the Atlantic seem to have a tanker story. Oil tankers are like bullets: there is one out there with your name on it. Our run-in with a tanker back in the first week of the race hadn't been as exciting as some stories that we'd heard – it hadn't actually passed that close, we hadn't fired off any flares and we didn't capsize – but a comedy Russian accent had at least made up for the lack of danger in any future retellings of the anecdote.

Of course, nobody told us that there might be two tankers out there with your name on them.

Although the battery was charging again and the desalinator was working well, we were being careful not to overload it, so I was listening to music through headphones rather than the speakers. I rowed along smoothly, trapped in a happy bubble, enjoying the chilled-out tunes of Jack Johnson.

After our previous encounter with a tanker I had taken to looking over my shoulder every few minutes during the next few shifts, but days later I reverted to not really bothering. In over a month we'd seen one tanker and one yacht and even that was the official race support vessel that had come looking for us. It wasn't exactly the M25 out there.

I don't know what made me turn round – I certainly hadn't heard anything other than Jack singing in my ear. But there it was: a tanker just 100 metres away from us. I'm not talking about a Channel ferry here; it was the whole of Canary Wharf, bearing down on us at 30 knots. Luckily it was going across our track; if it had been heading for us, we would have been dead. I stopped rowing and stupidly called Ben. 'Buddy, you'll want to see this. Get out here.'

Ben was out on deck in time to see the stern of the ship in line with our bows. I like to think we wouldn't have hit it if I'd carried on rowing, its speed taking it past our crossing point before we'd have got there, but Ben's face said it all. 'How the fuck did you let it get so close?' he stammered.

BEN

'Ben,' I heard James call from his shift. I clambered out of the cabin and I could not believe my eyes. It was colossal. It was a supertanker and it was far too close for comfort. When I spent my weekends down on the Solent training as a junior officer in the Navy, boats under motor and boats under sail were separated by a crystal clear hierarchy. In the Navy we called a yachtsman a 'wafi', a 'Wind-Assisted Fucking Idiot'. Well if wind-powered sailors were 'wafis' where do two semi-naked men in a flat-pack rowing boat fit into the rules of the road? It was fairly plain that we were the lowest of the low, with our relatively easy manoeuvrability and flexibility, but our ability to change direction quickly didn't necessarily mean we could always get out of the way.

As I stared, agog at the immensity of tanker disappearing behind our stern I recalled an outing I'd had as a member of the OTC to Hayling Island. The naval facility has an extraordinary boating lake upon which captains can learn to predict the huge stopping distances these vessels demand. The lake is populated by exact scale models of tankers. A supertanker takes an inordinate period of time to stop – up to three miles when travelling at full steam – which was something I was acutely aware of as our latest problem bore down upon us. The boats on the lake had mirrored those incredibly long stopping times. It had been strange to see grown men concentrating so hard on what to all intents and purposes had looked like dodgems, but I know I hoped whoever was in charge of this vessel had practised their emergency stops.

JAMES

Despite having a policy of total honesty on board, I thought it best to put Ben's mind at ease with a little white lie. I wouldn't want to row with somebody who didn't notice a floating skyscraper in broad daylight. 'I saw it about twenty minutes ago but I thought we'd pass further away than that. I just underestimated its speed.'

'We've got to keep a good lookout, there is no way they can see us, especially with our Sea-me broken.' He was absolutely right, of course.

'Shall we call them up?' I asked. Ben ducked back into the cabin.

'Big vessel, big vessel, big vessel this is small Atlantic rowing boat, small Atlantic rowing boat, over.' Nothing.

He tried again. 'Big vessel, big vessel, big vessel this is small Atlantic rowing boat, small Atlantic rowing boat, over.' Again, nothing.

He tried once more and got no response. They must have been on autopilot, in which case if they had been heading for us, we would have stood no chance.

I spent the last fifteen minutes of my shift twisting my head like an owl and apologizing to Ben. In the cabin I looked at the chart; sure enough we were smack in the middle of the New York to Cape Town shipping lane. I comforted myself that if we'd had to abandon ship and be rescued by the next tanker, of all the ports in the world to end up, Cape Town wasn't bad.

I wrote down the latitudes of the shipping lanes we were going to cross from here to Antigua and stuck them next to the GPS. We'd ridden our luck with tankers and I hoped that was the one with our name on it after all. I didn't fancy getting closer than that.

When we had run out of water, I'd made a promise that if we managed to get the desalinator working again, I would make sure I enjoyed the rest of the journey. The time for moaning and whinging about life on board had to stop; it was hard, uncomfortable and isolated but we knew all that when we signed up, and indeed that was one of reasons why I agreed to do the race in the first place. I wanted to test myself away from the comforts of home, to see if I could cope with life at sea and everything the Atlantic could throw at me.

I was determined to enjoy life on board; every time I wished I was at home I told myself that after being back a few days I'd appreciate our simple life. No emails, no mobile phones, no work to do and nobody hassling me, all I had to do was get up, row for a couple of hours, have something to eat and then rest. Paradise.

I was even starting to enjoy the night shifts. At times it resembled a light show, bright stars lighting up the sky and phosphorescence turning the sea luminous green around the oars when they entered the water. Violent lightning squalls associated with the trade winds gave spectacular light shows, like a Jean-Michel Jarre concert without the music. They were small in diameter and fast-moving, and often there were two or three in sight at any one time. The squalls were less entertaining when overhead but as they approached from behind we were faced with the choice of diving into the cabin for ten minutes to avoid getting a soaking from the violent downpours, or rowing on and surfing the stronger winds, telling ourselves to enjoy the cool shower.

The excitement didn't end with bright lights; there were flying fish to contend with. They leap out of the sea, spread their fins and glide in the air before diving back into the water, unless they collide with a small rowing boat. They varied in size from a couple of inches up to about eight inches.

It was a surprise the first time one leapt on to the boat, flapping around as it gulped for air, but that was nothing compared to the shock of being knocked off my seat when one flew into the side of my head in the middle of the night. The first thing I knew about it was when I found myself lying on the deck next to a flying fish who appeared equally stunned, but who was finding it considerably more difficult to breathe.

Thursday, 29 December 2005

1 *All Relative* (four-man boat), 2,068 miles
2 *Atlantic 4* (four-man boat), 1,411 miles
3 ***EDF*, 1,354 miles**
4 *Team C2*, 1,301 miles
4 *Spirit of Cornwall*, 1,260 miles
5 *Mayabrit*, 1,168 miles
6 *Scandlines*, 1,167 miles

Woodvale press release:

The start of the fifth week of the Atlantic Rowing Race 2005 and as snow covers the majority of the UK, a stark contrast from the weather conditions currently facing the 26 competing boats, speeds and mileages steadily begin to increase as the trade winds kick in!

Single-handed rower Chris Martin from Boat No. 5 – *Pacific Pete* reports winds gusting 30 knots and waves over 20 feet high. At first these conditions seemed quite daunting but it didn't take Chris long to perfect the art of surfing down these huge waves to increase boat speed. At one point, the GPS on board *Pacific Pete* recorded a top speed of 15.3 knots – not bad at all!

Posted 29/12/05 1:40:00 PM

BEN

It was 29 December, 2005 was almost at an end, and the weather was about to take another turn At last the sun had reappeared, basking our thirsty solar panel in its powerful rays. The wind had also dropped, and for the first time on the journey there was silence. Stony silence. For weeks now, the wind had been an ever-present din, whistling around our ears, often stealing words and even music in its hullabaloo, but today there was nothing: no wind, no waves, just the creaking of the oars and the sliding of the seat as it raced up and down the salty rails.

It was sweltering under the blazing Atlantic sun, its powerful rays reflecting off the water, stinging us with the intensity of its heat. Sweat streamed down my face and body, draining my body of fluid and stinging my eyes. My sunglasses filled with salty fluid and even my legs dripped with sweat. The problem now, however, wasn't so much the rowing time, but the downtime. Without the once ubiquitous wind, the cabin had become a sauna.

JAMES

We quickly learnt that we had to get as much sleep as possible during the night. The sun's ferocious rays during the day were good for the boat's energy levels, but not for ours. The oppressive heat drained us when we were rowing and made it impossible to rest properly. The cabin was like an oven; the baking sun cooked the outside and there was no air, since the top hatch had to remain shut to avoid a soaking from the big seas.

We'd made life worse for ourselves by forgetting to bring a sheet, which forced us to lie on a clammy rubber mattress. This was just about bearable in the first few weeks but since Christmas the temperature had risen considerably and getting any decent rest (especially during the day) was almost impossible. Within five minutes of lying down we would find ourselves sliding round in a pool of communal sweat.

When the sun was up the maximum time either of us could spend in the cabin was about fifteen minutes but we really were caught between the devil and the deep blue sea. If we went outside and rested on deck we might find a cooling breeze, but we would also get dehydrated by the sun for good measure. The race rules were clear in stating that crews weren't allowed to erect any shade, in case it was used as a sail; the only option was to roast in the cabin, or let the sun top up your tan while it sapped you of precious energy.

Rowing for two hours in the heat of the day no longer seemed the best option. It was almost impossible to keep drinking at the rate we were losing fluid while rowing; the need to stop every few minutes pretty much defeated the object of the exercise. By comparison rowing at night was a dream, not so hot that you sweated all the time, but not cold enough to make you dread going outside for a 2 a.m. shift. I suggested doing shorter rowing stints during the day, which wouldn't have been so draining, but 'Two hours on, two hours off' Fogle (I'm going to pay for that to be engraved on his headstone) wanted to stick to the routine, despite looking like death after each of his afternoon sessions.

BEN

We pushed on in the blazing sunshine and I felt my body weakening by the hour. It was simply impossible to keep up with the loss of liquid. My urine had turned chocolate brown, and I began to feel lethargic and weak.

As the sun set over the calm waters, I prayed the moon would bring with it some light winds to give me respite from the scorching temperatures, but the stuffy heat continued to hold us in its miserable grasp, as sweat poured from my heat-addled body. I felt light-headed and clammy and it was difficult to breathe in the heavy air. Every so often I'd break out in a cold sweat that covered me in goose bumps, even though it was still more than a hundred degrees.

I struggled on through the night as my body succumbed to a bout of diarrhoea and vomiting.

I have never liked to show weakness, and decided to keep my ill-health to myself, although the weak stomach was hard to conceal, particularly when one had to go in a bucket just a foot behind James.

'Bloody hell!' he exclaimed, as I released my bowels into the bucket with a thunderous whoosh. 'Are you OK, mate?'

'I'm fine,' I uttered with embarrassment. 'The heat sometimes does that to me,' I added by way of explanation.

As I started my 2 a.m. shift that night, I felt the punishment of the last few days of intense heat begin to take its toll. My rowing had slowed down to a snail's pace, and my head began to spin. I retched on an empty stomach and sweat continued to stream down my face.

The sea was deathly calm, as my vision began to wax and wane. The stars above my head seemed to fall. The heat was oppressive as I fought to hold my eyes open and I was overcome with dizziness.

I felt myself collapsing, but couldn't muster the strength to prevent it. My heavy lids drooped and I disappeared into darkness as my body fell backwards, the oars dropping from my hands, my head falling heavily on to the deck. I had fainted.

I don't know exactly how long I was out for before my eyes flickered open, but it was minutes rather than seconds. I felt a dull pain in my shoulder and elbow where my body had fallen on the awkward deck. I hauled myself up and vomited over the side. It didn't take a doctor to work out I was suffering from heat stroke.

I sat back on the rowing seat and emptied a packet of rehydration fluid into my water bottle. My head throbbed with pain and I felt weak and wobbly. I still had twenty minutes on the oars until James's shift and I felt bad about cutting James's valuable sleep time, so I resigned myself to soldier on until his shift.

JAMES

December the 30th was not a great night for either of us; the wind had dropped in the evening and the boat speed with it, but when I got the dreaded rallying call, 'Ten minutes to go, dude,' I was shocked to see we were doing less than 1.5 knots.

'You OK, buddy?' I asked when I got out on deck. There wasn't much of a following wind but there was no reason that I could see for the speed to be that slow.

'I had a bad shift; I fainted and fell off the seat. I woke up leaning over the side of the boat.'

'Jesus, how are you feeling now?' I asked.

'I feel better, I've been sick a couple of times and I've got a runny tummy.'

I love it that even under such extreme circumstances, Ben couldn't bring himself to say he had the shits: that's good breeding.

What was wrong with him? I ran through the possibilities in my head. It couldn't be food poisoning; we didn't have the most hygienic cooking conditions in the world, but we'd had the same germs and the same diet for over a month now. The upset stomach could have been a result of too many sports drinks, but in the heat of the day it was almost impossible to replace the fluid and minerals we were losing.

BEN

I tried to focus on the familiar silhouette of James getting ready for his shift. I could just make out the features of his face as he peered into the light of the GPS to check on our speed and progress, a ritual of his, which inevitably had the habit of making me nervous and apprehensive.

'What's going on?' he exclaimed as he appeared from the hatch. 'We're only doing a knot,' he continued.

'I'm not feeling great,' I answered. 'I fainted.'

'You what?' he stared at me. 'Why didn't you wake me up?'

I shrugged my shoulders.

'You idiot, you could have cost us our position,' he shouted, grabbing the oars from my hands.

I was confused. I didn't want sympathy or even empathy, but I hadn't expected this reaction.

'How long ago did you pass out?' he demanded.

I explained that it had been about a quarter of an hour ago, and that I didn't want to disturb him from his valuable sleep.

'I can't believe it!' he shouted angrily.

'Sorry,' I whispered, confused.

'You should be,' he answered.

I was shocked. I had never had heat stroke before, and given the extreme elements that we were exposing ourselves to, surely it was a very real possibility?

JAMES

Heat stroke! The idiot had heat stroke! I'd been right to worry about the shift length; two hours was too long to row in that heat, especially without a hat. No wonder he'd looked like death.

'Drink some isotonic drink, eat something and get some rest,' I told him. I resisted mentioning the hat, the amount of fluid he should have drunk and being more flexible with the shifts. This was no time for 'I told you so'.

'I'll be OK for my next shift,' he said defiantly. Ben never wanted to do less than his share and I admired him for that. A bit more competitiveness would have been even better, but I couldn't fault his commitment. He would have got up two hours later and tried to battle through but it would have slowed his recovery. If he was going to get through the day tomorrow, he needed to rest and recover tonight.

'No, you rest, I'll row for three or four hours then wake you up for a short shift if you really feel like it. It's important you refuel now,' I responded.

'Honestly, I feel OK now.'

'No, Ben. Look, you think I'm pushing us too hard during the day. I promised to get you to Antigua without breaking down. If you carry on rowing tonight you won't get through tomorrow.' I gave him no option but to take the rest. I then had four hours to relieve my frustration on the oar handles. Before leaving we had stressed the importance of looking after ourselves. Apart from equipment failure, self-inflicted health problems would be the most likely reason for us not making it across.

The sun rose signalling another long day at the oars, and its focus seemed to be solely on our boat. The solar panels might have been loving it, but we certainly weren't. Ben was out on deck eating breakfast.

'You feeling better?' I asked.

'Yes, much, thanks.' He certainly sounded cheery enough.

'You've got to look after yourself, you know.' It wasn't subtle or a particularly nice thing to say but I needed to show how serious it could have been. Heat stroke can be debilitating for a long time, especially coming on the back of so many days with so little water.

'I'm not an athlete. I don't know how much I'm supposed to drink!' he shouted.

'You don't have to be a sportsman to know that when it's as hot as it was yesterday you need to drink more than normal and that when it's that sunny it's best to wear a hat. I suggested doing shorter shifts when you were struggling because of the heat and you didn't want to know.' I was firm but also fair; I didn't want to create any unnecessary tension.

'I'm not going to agree that I should stop, you'll have to tell me.'

'Why should I have to tell you what to do? You know your body better than me.'

'Because I'm too stubborn to stop,' he pouted.

'Being stubborn is not some badge of honour.' I was a fine one to talk. 'We're in a team and all that is important is that we give everything, but in the right way. There is no point in being a hero during the day and then doing nothing during the night. We need to be on top form from here until we get to Antigua. There is nothing wrong in saying you want to cut the shifts or that you feel shit and are going to have to miss a session. We have to be honest with each other. Christ, after all we've been through we're not going to start passing judgement on each other.'

With my Gettysburg Address over, Ben looked neither offended nor in agreement with what I'd said. Instead he put his hat on and said, 'OK, shall I do a ninety-minute shift then?'

The heat wasn't the only thing affecting the length of the rowing shift; our bums were really starting to feel the effects of spending twelve hours a day in the same position on an uncomfortable seat. I had been trying various lotions and potions on my undercarriage since the first week in an attempt to reduce friction and to try to prevent spots, sores and, even worse, boils developing. Sorting the latter out would be a two-man job and despite everything we'd been through, we weren't that close yet.

The only mirror we had on board was from our emergency grab bag, designed to reflect light as a way of attracting attention. It was not for reflecting an image of my bum back to my face. It was too small, so I only ever really got a good look at the underside of my thigh or crown jewels (thankfully the latter seemed to be in decent shape). The same couldn't be said for my ass, and I didn't need a mirror to tell me that. It felt like the surface of the moon when I ran my hand over it and we still had a month to go. At this rate, it was going to be the bit of my body that let me down first.

Something had to be done. I had to be able to sit down and although I hadn't talked to Ben intimately about his bum, I imagined it was in a similar state to mine. If we couldn't sit, we weren't going to get anywhere.

Our seat pads consisted of cut-up camping mats stuck on a wooden rowing seat with sheepskin on top. That might sound quite cosy, but the mats had been compressed so much over the last few weeks that they now gave no protection at all. We needed something softer.

The only soft thing on board was our mattress, which presented us with a tricky decision. Did we cut up the mattress to make the seat more comfortable? Rowing would be easier, but sleeping on what would now effectively be a plywood bed would make getting a good rest almost impossible. Perhaps we should just hope that our bums toughened up? In the end there was no choice; we could sleep all we wanted, but that wasn't going to get us any closer to Antigua.

The decision made, I attacked the mattress with a pair of scissors and proceeded to put together a makeshift seat. It was a huge improvement, but unfortunately it did not relieve all the problems. Time for plan B.

Much had been made of Ben and me doing a lot of the journey in the nude, and it's fair to say that we hadn't stopped this line of enquiry, since it generated interest at a time when we were desperately in need of sponsors in order to make the start line. Up until now I hadn't felt the need to go naked; the chafing from the salt water hadn't been as bad as I had expected and during early experiments with nude rowing, I'd found that the lack of support led to certain parts of my body being crushed – body parts that I usually try to keep away from moving machinery.

But my ass was very sore and it was time to try something different. With a fresh piece of sheepskin and extra padding the seat looked like an inviting, freshly made hotel bed. Now was the time to experiment seriously with naked rowing. It felt marginally better but was as much a change as a solution. I was just going to have to grit my teeth and get my bum through the journey any way I could, even if that involved making sure I applied suntan lotion to places the sun don't shine.

A sore bum didn't only reduce the quality of my rowing; it also had an effect on the set-up of the rowing position itself. It was impossible to be comfortable for much more than a few minutes and so I was constantly wriggling, shifting my weight and putting extra stress on the seat. This meant the thin metal axles that connected the seat to the runners (fixed along the entire length of the boat) were under particular pressure. Factor in the rocking motion of the sea and the fact that we were at the oars twenty-four hours a day, and there was hardly ever an even weight distribution going through the seat.

Two weeks earlier an axle had snapped and we were now using our only spare. Ben had been worried when it had sheared, confirming in his mind that equipment failure was going to ruin our crossing. I tried to convince him that that particular axle must have had a weak point, since in fifteen years of rowing I'd never had one break on me before. This was only partially true; they rarely snap, but these axles were longer and thinner than usual and therefore much weaker. I thought we'd be lucky to get across without another breaking.

I was in the cabin on the satellite phone to my dad when I saw Ben stop rowing; he looked down at the seat and put his head in his hands.

I knew instantly what had happened. I ended the call and headed out of the cabin. 'James we've got a problem with the seat,' said Ben. He sounded like someone who'd come home to find his house had been burgled.

'OK, I'll take a look at it,' I said. Since the first axle snapped I'd been trying to think of a way of splinting the metal, but I hadn't managed to come up with a design that was strong enough to hold our weight, rotate sufficiently and cope with the movement of the boat and a wriggling ass. We were either going to have to row without a seat, or find a solution.

Ben was no use right now, sitting in the bow with his head in his hands, crying. Although we still had one working rowing position, we both knew it was only a matter of time before that axle broke as well. For Ben this seemed to have been the last straw: having overcome homesickness, storms, battery problems, the desalinator failure, the broken GPS and two near misses with supertankers, he couldn't take any more. I had to come up with something fast, something which, at the very least, might convince Ben that we still had every chance of completing the crossing. The boat and equipment were my area of responsibility and the onus was on me to solve the problem.

The only metal on board strong enough to splint the axle was another axle. I sawed up the axle that had broken earlier into six pieces and splinted them around the break in the second axle using insulating tape. By splinting the break in every direction it shouldn't, in theory, be able to move, despite only being held together by tape. Ben didn't look convinced by my bodged job, but as I finished taping I thought it might hold. I clipped the axle back to the underside of the seat and sat on it.

There was no sound of grinding metal. The splint must have held, so I slid up and down. It worked. The colour flooded back into Ben's face and he practically offered to have my children.

I wasn't sure how long the repaired axle would stand up to the stresses it was going to be placed under, but it wasn't required yet. One rowing position was still made up of its original components and Ben and I rarely rowed together. But for Ben, knowing we had a solution (no matter how temporary) was a huge relief and the confidence gained from solving a tricky situation gave me real belief that we could cope with most things that might be thrown at us.

Nonetheless, it was difficult to get away from the fact that, despite sorting out the seat Ben was still preoccupied by potential equipment failure whilst I was concerned with boat speed. The trade winds that had been blowing us towards the Caribbean for the last week had died away. A tropical storm – Zeta – was coming and although north of us it was affecting the weather in our area. What the hell was a tropical storm doing here at this time of year? They should have all been and gone before we even started the race.

The spreadsheets which had been such a motivating force when the miles were flying past were now having the opposite effect. Having been over thirty miles ahead of the ambitious target we were now 132 miles – two days – behind that and thirty-nine miles behind the easiest target. We slowed from doing eighty miles a day to barely doing thirty. Fortunately we weren't the only crew affected, and still had a lead of seventy-two miles.

The wind normally changed when the sun went down. I was convinced I'd wake up for my first night shift to find the wind had picked up and was blowing us in the right direction. I was half right: the wind had got up but it was blowing from the side. It was not strong enough to stop us from moving but when I came out on deck Ben was rowing with one arm to keep us on the right bearing. I wasn't looking forward to the next two hours.

Shift after shift I kept telling myself, 'The wind is going to change, the wind is going to change'; our speed and my head had both dropped. I was struggling to cope with our slow progress and rowing with one arm was so frustrating and alien to me that it was doing my head in. I tried to console myself by saying the other boats all faced similar problems.

The next weather report said Zeta had moved south and was now on a similar bearing to us, moving at the same speed. The good news was we weren't going to get battered by another storm but the bad news was the helpful weather systems to the east of us (the trade winds we so desperately wanted) were going to be blocked by this huge depression. We were going to go nowhere fast for a few days and we couldn't afford another storm delay – having already rationed ourselves, any further decrease in our daily food allowance would mean our calorie intake would be so low we'd have to reduce the number of hours a day we rowed, something I couldn't even bring myself to think about.

I was doing the early-evening shift. The winds were most changeable in the last hours of sunlight. Was it my imagination or were they shifting round to the west? I could now row with two oars and row straight – it was definitely shifting. Both the flag over the cabin and the speed on the GPS confirmed it. I might have been able to use both oars but the speed had dropped – we were going into a headwind. It wasn't strong enough to stop us but it made it incredibly hard work and difficult to keep the boat straight.

I watched Ben trying to row into the wind, struggling to keep it on track and barely doing 1 knot. For the hundredth time I cursed Ben for not learning to row properly before doing this race. Keeping a boat on the right course is as much about technique as it is about strength. It was infuriating as he could have done something about it, but if I was honest we'd both let each other down in the build-up to the race and it was just frustration getting on top of me.

The wind had picked up. Soon we'd have no option but to put the sea anchor down and break the promise we'd made when we pulled it out the last time that we weren't going to use it again.

At midnight we dropped anchor, good news for my bum, which was grateful for a longer break from rowing but bad news for my stomach. If we'd been moving I could have had that night's supply of chocolate from the snack bag. No mileage meant no snacks, we had to conserve food and if we weren't rowing we didn't need any. I checked the wind every hour, hoping that there was a change in direction and we could get going again. It didn't change.

Ben didn't bother to check; he seemed to sleep blissfully through most of the night while I was going out of my mind. He probably figured there was no point in him checking because he knew I'd be constantly doing it, desperate to get going again.

My only salvation was a belief that others were in a similar position. The next morning I was anxious to know if that was the case. I went out on deck to phone my dad. He loved following the race on the internet and whenever I called he had a mountain of stats at the ready. Today they weren't ones I wanted to hear. *C2* had halved our lead overnight – clearly they weren't being affected in the same way as us. I couldn't believe the injustice of it, the crew in the lead was supposed to get the best weather. We'd earned it, for fuck's sake. I couldn't believe Zeta was hitting us worse than everybody else.

The same rules should apply to Atlantic rowing that exists in MOTO GP (Motorcycle World Championship). If it rains during a race that started in the dry the rider who is winning the race can decide when it ends. Not surprisingly they normally decide that as soon as it starts raining. I wanted everybody else to put their sea anchors down as well. Unfortunately it didn't work like that and I had to get used to it, although that was unlikely to happen now if it I hadn't come to terms with it over the previous five weeks.

Later that morning the wind dropped and we could get going again, but after only one shift we had to stop. I went mad shouting and swearing at the wind and throwing the oars around. Ben retreated into the cabin and left me to it. He was seriously worried about how the race was eating me up.

Down went the anchor again and we decided to use the time to do some housekeeping. The boat desperately needed cleaning inside and out, we had to do a stock-take to find out exactly how much food we had left and weight needed to be repositioned around the boat so that it ran level.

I've not found every cloud to have a silver lining but Zeta certainly had one. Our stock-take gave us as big a surprise as Nick Leeson gave Barings Bank, but ours was good news; we found an extra 100 meals we didn't know about. Or to be more accurate 100 meals that Ben had forgotten about. He was in charge of packing the food on board while I was underneath mending the hole in the bottom. However, this was no time to squabble. It was time to eat. We boiled a kettle and wolfed down two meals each; we could start eating properly again. With enough food for four meals a day, we were going to live like kings; well, kings on dehydrated food.

I was leaning against the cabin enjoying the feeling of a full stomach when I heard Ben mumble 'Oh,' whilst rummaging around in the bow cabin.

'What have you found?' I asked, hoping it was a bag full of chocolate bars.

'Nothing much.'

'Go on what is it, you're not keeping an extra bag of snacks from me are you?'

'No, it's not that good news, I'm afraid. I think it will make you either laugh or cry,' he said cryptically.

'What?'

He turned round holding what looked like a bag of rubbish and threw it to me.

'You're joking!'

Inside the bag were hundreds of pieces of green foil, needless corners of the muesli bags Marina had cut off in an attempt to save a little bit of weight. For the last five weeks every third bag would leak where it had been snipped. We'd suffered leaking bags of cereal at 4 a.m. for nothing. We looked at each other and burst out laughing, it seemed to sum up everything about our trip so far – good intentions but poor execution.

The great discovery and the high spirits that accompanied it did not deter me from wanting to get going. I couldn't stand being sat still any longer. The competitive spirit which had served me so well throughout my Olympic career was now threatening to drive me mad.

Chapter Nine

Capsize

8 January 2006, 5.08 PM
Woodvale press release:

Today (Sunday 08 January 2006) four men from Devon triumphantly crossed the finish line of the Atlantic Rowing Race 2005 in first place. Boat No. 24 – *All Relative* was crewed by four relations from Beer in Devon – brothers Justin Adkin and Robert Adkin and cousins Martin Adkin and James Green. Tonight will be a double celebration for the crew as Martin Adkin, who at the tender age of 19 is the youngest person ever to row the Atlantic Ocean, turned 20 yesterday.

JAMES

'All things must pass.'

This is my definitive memory of third-form English. I may have got the year wrong, but not the quote: it was written on the classroom whiteboard in permanent marker, not, as you might think, by our teacher but by a rebellious sixth-former from a previous year. To his credit – and the caretaker's annoyance – our English teacher insisted on leaving the quote left up there. Perhaps he needed some reassurance that his Friday afternoons spent guiding thirty kids through *Lord of the Flies* would eventually end; or perhaps he just appreciated the presence of a thought-provoking piece of graffiti which I would later discover was Solomon's wisdom as opposed to a schoolboy's or George Harrison's. Either way, I've always liked to think that the sixth-former was a smokescreen and that the teacher actually wrote it himself. That quote has helped me in a number of situations over the years and the thought that it was written by a spotty seventeen-year-old kind of ruins it.

In the twenty years since first seeing the quote I have never thought of it as often or relied on it as much as I did in the Atlantic. I used it to get me through the grinding two-hour rowing sessions, and I used it to believe we'd eventually get to Antigua; it gave me hope that each night would end when we were locked in the cabin sheltering from a storm and, more recently, that Zeta would pass through and we'd be on our way again.

Eventually Zeta did change course and headed north, leaving the way clear for the trade winds to blow through again and allow us to make up for lost time. The race was back on, but later that day we were given a stark reminder that our real opponent in this race was the ocean itself.

BEN

'Digicel capsized and sank during an incident last night. The boys were picked up by a cargo ship and are on their way to Cartagena in Spain,' read the text on the Iridium satellite phone.

I was lost for words. CAPSIZED. I repeated the word, trying the syllables in a new and strange order. They felt wrong. It tasted bad. No-one had ever mentioned the 'C' word. As far as I knew the boats were made to right themselves, and no-one had ever suggested that a capsize was a real possibility. SINK. This was even worse, a word I had only ever used in conjunction with a toothbrush or a bar of soap, not one I wanted to hear in the middle of the Atlantic.

Night had fallen and I was on the oars. There was no moonlight and the sky was black and forbidding, the sea was whipped into a confused frenzy. It was particularly rough because the wind had been held up behind a high weather system for about a week and it was now making the most of having the freedom to blow across the Atlantic. It made conditions very peculiar. Something didn't feel right, and I felt more vulnerable than ever.

'How could Digicel sink?' I asked James, who just shrugged his shoulders. I couldn't work out whether James was pleased that one of his chief opponents was out of the race, or genuinely shocked to hear the news. As always, he kept his feelings close to his chest.

I rowed on, the waves propelling us along at a healthy 3.5 knots, sometimes even exceeding 4. It felt good to be making such quick progress after days spent trawling along at a snail's pace. It felt like we were finally getting somewhere, but the sense of vulnerability lingered. I couldn't shake the notion that we were very exposed. The news had triggered a new set of worries for my already fret-addled mind. If *Digicel* could capsize and sink, then so could we, I reasoned.

I tried to imagine their feelings. What must it have been like splashing around in the water in the pitch black, their shattered boat strewn around them? And now they were aboard a cargo ship on their way to Spain. I imagined them wrapped in blankets, sipping on cups of tea. Would they be relieved or disappointed?, I wondered. There was a part of me that envied them, getting out of this angry ocean and returning to the safety of land and their loved ones.

JAMES

I was gutted for Gearoid Towey, one of the guys on board *Digicel*. We'd trained together at the same rowing club for a couple of years and had both competed at the last two Olympics, him for Ireland and me for Britain. *Digicel* had been considered the pre-race favourites because of their obvious rowing pedigree; the boat they were using had won the race in 2001 and they were incredibly well organized. Early in the race they were amongst the leading boats but after the first week they had slipped back and were some 600 miles behind us when they capsized.

It may have been us being over-sensitive after hearing the news, but Ben and I both agreed that it felt like the wind was gaining strength. It was going to be another night of big seas: great for our boat speed, but with a heightened risk of something going wrong. Ben was deeply concerned about the devastating effect the wave had had on the Irish boys. I tried to explain that some of the irreparable damage their boat suffered might have been down to the fact that their boat wasn't brand spanking new like ours. Our boat was bought straight from the race organizers, and had coped with the seas we had experienced thus far incredibly well. The most important thing was to be confident but not blasé or foolhardy in the large waves. If at any time we felt the sea was too big we had the option of using our drogue to drag in the water and slow the boat down. A drogue works in the same way as a sea anchor, a small parachute about the size of a bucket that fills up with water as the boat drags it through the sea, therefore slowing the progress of the boat. The big difference is that whereas the sea anchor stops you getting blown off course during a storm, a drogue is used when the conditions are too fast and for safety reasons you want to reduce speed. It is attached by a rope to the stern of the boat and acts as a brake. And yet to me the possibility of capsizing wasn't half as bad as the prospect of deliberately slowing our progress if we deployed it. The drogue stayed in the boat.

The news had shaken both of us up but it had had a more profound effect upon Ben than me. He still wasn't totally confident in the big seas, whereas I'd managed to convince myself that if we kept the boat square to the waves, we'd be OK. At night that was becoming increasingly difficult to do, however. Over the last day or so conditions had worsened and we had been hit by smaller, fast-moving waves coming at us from the side – waves that weren't necessarily dangerous themselves, but which either knocked us off our seats or kicked the boat sideways and off-line just as bigger waves were bearing down on us. So far we'd got away with it, but hearing about the Irish boys reiterated that it would take only one wave to do the damage, and our luck wouldn't last for ever.

Throughout the race something that surprised me constantly was how quickly things that had been worrying us one minute were completely forgotten the next. Within an hour of hearing about the Irish capsize, we were racing down the face of a wave trying to get the best speed possible.

The seas were bigger than ever, with waves consistently reaching thirty feet in height. These weren't the towering vertical waves a surfer powers down as he thunders into Hawaii's North Shore; 'our' waves were more like pyramids, with high peaks but solid, wide bases. It might sound obvious, but a wave only breaks when the bottom of the wave starts to move slower than the top, so that the wall of water effectively falls over itself. In Hawaii this process is almost instant: the waves are moving through deep water and then hit a reef, which slows the base of the wave, forcing it to stand up and then come crashing down with incredible force.

In the middle of the Atlantic there is no reef and the ocean bed is thousands of metres below, so even the biggest waves generally roll straight through. But that isn't to say they aren't dangerous; these are enormous lumps of water, containing huge amounts of energy. They still 'break' but for a slightly different reason, the crest overtaking the base through the force of the wind alone. The effect might not be as visually dramatic as a classic Hawaiian wave, but powering down the face of a 30-foot pyramid of white water in a 7-metre boat, it certainly feels it.

Faced with such raw power, you have a choice to make. The force of the wave can be harnessed, but it can be very dangerous. If the boat is at a slight angle, you lay yourself open to being violently kicked sideways, but with the boat straight on to the wave nothing should go wrong; the water will either roll harmlessly through or, if you're lucky, push the boat forwards with it. With a clean following wind, individual waves were easy to spot from a long way off. I started paying close attention to them when they were 50–60 metres away, trying to judge where they were going to break. If the wave rolled through and broke later then there was no ride, just a waste of effort; if it broke too early we'd get a good soaking and a rough ride for a few seconds. But if a wave looked like it was going to break just after passing the boat, that was the one to go for; I'd make sure I was square on and as it approached, row like mad for a few strokes to get the speed up, catch the wave and then enjoy the ride, shipping the oars and using the rudder to make sure we went in a straight line.

When we caught a wave it was fantastic, the boat carried for a hundred metres or more on a roaring bed of white water. It was worth a soaking to see the speed on the GPS rise to levels we couldn't have dreamt of doing under our own stream. I remember shouting like a madman as I got a new boat record of 10 knots – hardly Donald Campbell's *Bluebird*, but I was mighty proud of it. Every big wave sped us closer to Antigua and increased our chances in the race; and yet when Ben came out for his shift I noticed that, before getting on the oars, he dug a life jacket out of the bow cabin and put it next to his rowing position. Perhaps he hadn't totally forgotten about the dramatic end to *Digicel*'s crossing after all.

BEN

It was nearly midnight and I was aching for the end of my shift and a welcome rest. The waves were now propelling us at an average speed of 4 knots and all around I could make out the white peaks of breaking waves as I rowed on into the blackness. It's amazing how quickly one's eyes adjusted to the darkness, predicting each jolt and jerk of the boat as she lurched through the waves. For several weeks now we had rowed without the little navigation light. We had found it blinded our night vision, and besides its purpose was to make us visible to other shipping, and we hadn't seen a vessel for weeks.

I became aware of a vast wave building behind the boat, its white hat looming above the hatch. It was just a few feet from breaking so I dug the oars into the angry water and pulled with all my strength to edge us away from the wave before it broke on top of us.

The *Spirit* edged forward as the wave enveloped the stern, picking her up and catapulting her like a sling shot. I threw myself into the brace position, raising the oars into the air and away from the water. Like a bullet, we shot through the fierce surf. A wall of water formed on either side of the gunnels, several feet high. It felt almost as if we were *in* the wave as we raced forward: 4.5 knots, 6 knots, 8 knots, 10 knots, 12.5 knots, 14.1 knots... we were travelling at tremendous speed. I wondered if I was dreaming – and then as quickly as we had reached our terminal velocity, the wave dropped us and our speed fell to just 2 knots.

Everything was silent out there in the middle of the black ocean, the only evidence of the wave's passing a lone snack bag floating around the deck in the water that had washed over the gunnels.

'Whaaaahooooooo!' I screamed belatedly. 'Whaaaaaahooooo! Fourteen knots, dude, fourteen bloody knots!'

'Whaaaaaoooo!' I bellowed again in a roar of approval. 'Another!' I shouted at the sea, 'Give me another one, man!' I felt like the king of the ocean, like Neptune, taming the waves and harnessing the surf. I was on top of the world and *Digicel*'s capsize was confined to a remote corner of my mind.

JAMES

I got woken up by two horrible screaming noises and the sound of water rushing by my head. I couldn't work out what was going on, and by the time I stuck my head out of the cabin, things had calmed down. 'Fourteen knots dude!' he said with a big smile on his face. The first scream had been from water on deck being forced out of the scuppers as we stormed down the face of the wave; the second was Ben expressing his delight at having smashed my boat record. With only 6mm of plywood separating the sea from the cabin, when we stormed down the face of the wave it felt and sounded like we were going over Niagara Falls in a barrel.

We'd made good use of the big seas and strong winds and had clocked up eighty-four miles, our greatest distance in twenty-four hours so far. We were delighted until the race report came through informing us that *C2* had taken some five miles out of us over the same period. I couldn't believe it; I knew we were still forty miles in the lead and that even if they managed to make up five miles every twenty-four hours – something they hadn't done consistently so far in the race – for the remaining 800 miles, at the speeds we were doing they would struggle to catch us. And yet we were travelling the fastest we'd ever gone, and they were still taking distance out of us. Until that point I'd managed to convince myself that when the conditions were with us, we were the fastest crew in the race. That clearly wasn't the case and I didn't enjoy the realization. Ben got frustrated when the wind halted our progress but he couldn't comprehend my frustration at losing a few miles when we'd covered over eighty in a day. To him we were that much closer to Antigua and it didn't matter that somebody else was getting there quicker.

The only way I could see of increasing our speed was to change the shift system. Earlier in the race I wanted to try ninety minutes on/one hour off during the night so we would have half an hour overlap where we rowed together and thus gain extra boat speed. Ben wasn't keen then and his enthusiasm for the idea hadn't increased so there was no point in pushing the issue; in the big following seas, rowing two-up wouldn't have made that much difference. It was as important to be well rested so that we were alert and able to position the boat correctly on each wave.

I decided to row harder in my shifts to try to make a little bit of difference. I knew that Woodvale's race website was updated every couple of hours, so every time I finished a shift I'd call Dad to check on our progress. After putting the phone down for the fourth time that day I realized I was driving myself mad and (if I hadn't done so already) starting to drive Ben mad with me. I needed to focus on what I could control and that was our boat speed; it was no use worrying about other crews with 800 miles to go.

I tried to think of all the good things that were slowly coming into reach: seeing land for the first time, arriving in Antigua, the joy of seeing Bev and Croyde and all the food and drink I'd be able to consume. These were all reasons to be cheerful and with every hour they came closer and closer. But much as I tried to ignore it, a voice inside my head kept saying, 'Yes, but how much better will it feel if you're the first boat home?'

As a compromise, to appease my competitiveness, Ben agreed that if the race was close with 300 miles to go, he would row whatever shift system I thought would give us the best chance of winning; until then I agreed that we'd stick with two hours on and off. I 'cold turkeyed' on the race updates and tried to enjoy life on our little boat.

BEN

Throughout our adventure James was keener than me to take the plunge when it came to ocean swimming. I had felt since the outset that the sheer force of the Atlantic was something to be treated with great respect and so unlike James I was rather more tentative about the kinds of weather conditions I felt were conducive to going for a swim. The only time I went in was when we weren't rowing and the weather was calm. I certainly wasn't going to dive in during a storm – it just seemed reckless. I didn't understand why James would risk so much in bad weather. I couldn't jump in to save him and I wouldn't have been able to row to him had I needed to. It all seemed a little bit pointless for the sake of a barnacle and the physics of it just didn't work. All of this meant that we were some weeks into the race before I braved the water.

When I did eventually swim I was first struck by the very high salt content of the water. I don't think I'd ever tasted such salty water. Normally when you swim in seawater it's relatively close to land, which means that the water has been diluted by rivers and rainfall so the salt is not as concentrated as it is out in the ocean.

But once I overcame the salty taste and feel of the water I luxuriated in being outside our tiny boat. It was wonderfully liberating to be able to stretch out fully and to kick out my arms and legs after the constriction of the boat, but above all it was about seeing *Spirit* from the water: she looked surprisingly large and there was something reassuring about her physical presence.

All you see from inside the boat is the bulkhead and the rowing boat: the same view, with the same colour palette day after day. After just a few minutes in the sea I realized what I found so exhilarating gazing back at the boat: its colourfulness. There was very little colour on the boat and because of the last-minute repairs we had undertaken she looked like a boat under construction still. But outside, the vibrancy of the red of the Vodafone logo and the green of the Glenlivet icon with the turquoise of the boat and the blue of the water were a startling contrast to the monotone of the perspective from inside *Spirit*. From outside the boat by swimming around it your view could actually change; a welcome respite from a boundless horizon. I do like my big spaces and huge skies. This is true of all my favourite places – the Hebrides, the Pacific islands – I relish the enormous vistas. But nevertheless, it was a relief to be able to escape that vastness even for a few minutes.

It was revelling in these simple joys that made life on board such a memorable experience. But as we approached the final third I had no conception of quite how unforgettable this journey was going to become.

My shifts came and went, as our tiny boat steadily picked up speed in increasingly rough conditions. Averaging almost 4.5 knots we covered nearly fifty miles in a single night and once again Antigua was within our grasp.

The wind kept up all night and we made amazing progress. It was hard work as much because of the level of concentration required to make sure the boat was in the right place on the wave as from the physical stress of rowing. I was enjoying it but looking forward to daylight, which would make it easier to see the approaching waves.

'It's ten to seven, dude,' I hollered to James at 6.40 a.m. James was scheduled to have a telephone interview with Radio 4's *Today* programme at 7 a.m., and I soon saw the little hatch flung open, the familiar antenna of the satellite phone pointing skywards. I heard odd words carried on the wind, but as always, the wind drowned out most of the conversation – a blessing that afforded both of us some privacy during our phone calls home.

'Wave!' I screamed as a vast wall of water rose above the cabin and collapsed over the hatch.

James snatched it shut just in the nick of time. Every so often I heard snippets of his conversation through the front hatch, which James had opened slightly to let some air into the stifling, airless cabin. 'No, I'm not opening it,' I heard.

JAMES

The *Today* programme had been following our progress throughout the race, and the interview was the most positive one I'd given (apparently just after the start of the race I sounded like I was about to slit my wrists). I was asked what it felt like to be into the last ten days at sea and in the lead; I told the presenter that this race had taught us that anything can happen and we were taking nothing for granted, citing the experience of the Irish boys. Off air I asked him to check how far we were in the lead; he told us we'd pulled out another six miles overnight and were now leading by forty-eight miles. Fantastic news.

BEN

'Mate, you won't believe it,' shouted James five minutes later. 'We're back in first place, and we took eight miles off *C2* overnight,' he said excitedly. 'You're doing so well, mate,' he added. I smiled with pride. He had often praised our progress, but always with the plural, royal *we*. This was the first time he had singled me out and complimented me directly.

I knew I had been rowing hard, and I'd longed for his approval. I puffed out my chest with satisfaction. James was always generous with his enthusiasm and motivation but he was prudent with his compliments. When you received one, you most certainly deserved it.

It was still dark. We were working to GMT, even though we had crossed several time zones, and consequently the sun wasn't rising till nearly 9 a.m. by our watches. We had at least three hours of darkness to go before daybreak and as always I had the sunrise shift, the last of the night spells. The ocean had continued to build, with an ever-increasing wind that was gusting at nearly 40 knots. The swell had grown and conditions were becoming increasingly frenzied. I began to feel vulnerable again, and the dreaded 'C' word returned to my thoughts. If we can just make it to daybreak, I thought, it will be easier to read the waves and prepare for the breakers. I rowed on, worried by the deteriorating weather, and I thought of Marina, back at home. I longed to be with her and away from this intimidating ocean. As I rowed, a barely perceptible blue hue appeared on the skyline.

The swell was gathering, and the breaking waves were becoming ever more frequent. 'Come on, sun,' I thought, willing day to break. Something wasn't right.

JAMES

I looked at Ben rowing away outside; I could only half see him in the dawn light, but he looked exhausted. We'd both put in a lot of effort overnight. I thought about going out early for my next shift, re-energized as I was by the news of our progress, but the effect didn't seem to last that long; as I lay there contemplating whether to head outside or not I could feel myself drifting back to sleep and slowly began to doze off. I was due on in thirty minutes; Ben would be OK until then.

BEN

I watched as a vast wave gathered behind the boat, soaring above the cabin, a wall of white water towering over our tiny boat. Once again I dug the oars in to propel us forward, but the wave was too big. For a moment it felt like we were moving backwards as we were sucked into the belly of the wave, the horizon disappearing as the churning surf enveloped the stern of the boat. I felt the aft lift, as a torrent of water crashed over the boat and I felt myself falling backwards. I was aware of the boat collapsing on top of me. I struggled to pull my feet from the stirrups to no avail. The world went black. I felt a weight on top of me and then a rush of cold water as my body was brutally submerged into the bottomless Atlantic Ocean. My feet were sucked from my shoes as I clung on to the oars for dear life, but then they too were dragged from my clasp. My mind went blank as I tumbled through the surf, spun around roughly like clothes in a washing machine.

I was somewhere underwater, but which way was up? Everything was midnight black. I panicked as I grabbed the water, desperate for something to clutch on to. There was nothing. No boat, just inky cold water.

I had been under water for a seeming eternity and had started to panic. It felt as though my lungs were collapsing and I struggled to find which way to swim. I felt my hand break the surface as my body burst from the depths of the ocean. 'Paaaaaaah,' I gasped as my body screamed for air.

'James!' I cried. There was no sign of him, nor the boat. I was in the middle of the ocean without a life jacket, being tossed around in the surf like a rag doll. I spun around in the water, gripped by panic.

There was the boat, a black upturned hull. 'James!' I screamed again. Nothing. Nothing in life had prepared me for this. No amount of planning could have readied me. What the hell now? The boat seemed an incomprensible distance away. How could I be so far from it? Who would ever find me out here, hundreds of miles from the nearest boat, let alone land? I had to get back on to that boat.

My mind was numb with shock, but somehow I made it back to the upturned hull, and clung to the grab line on the side of the boat. There was still no sign of James. Why wasn't the *Spirit* righting herself? I fretted, as I hauled myself up on to her keel.

'What's that doing there?' I thought incongruously at the sight of a large barnacle also clinging to the bottom of the boat. I could feel the boat listing. Slowly but surely the boat began to turn on top of me. I clutched on to the grab line as I collapsed back into the water, the boat springing upright. I clung on, silent and in shock.

JAMES

CRASH!

I heard and felt it at the same time. I don't know when I realized I wasn't dreaming and that something was really wrong. The noise sounded like part of a dream, but the bang on my head told me it wasn't. I opened my eyes; my face was pressed against the small hatch on the roof of the cabin, and it was pitch black. I could hear water rushing in through the door behind me. Almost as soon as I realized I was lying on the ceiling and that the boat must be upside down, I felt myself falling again as the boat began to re-right. It was the second time the water ballast had saved us.

I remember thinking, 'Shit, we've capsized, the boat's broken, our race is over, we're upside down, where's Ben. Shit, where's Ben?' It normally took a Houdini-style manoeuvre for me to extricate myself from the cabin, but somehow I was on deck in a couple of seconds. The boat was listing at 45 degrees and there was just enough daylight to see around. Ben was nowhere to be seen.

BEN

'Ben, Ben, Ben!' I heard James's cry. He was alive. Thank god.

'I'm here, I'm here!' I squeaked, still clutching to the grab line.

'FUCK!' I heard him shout, 'FUUUCK!'

All around us the ocean was strewn with debris, loose equipment swept from the deck. After five weeks at sea we had become complacent and had long stopped lashing things down; we could only stand back and watch as all our worldly possessions drifted away into the rolling ocean.

JAMES

I grabbed the throw line and scanned the water, littered with equipment. 'Ben! Ben!' I shouted, panicking that I couldn't see him.

'I'm here,' came a weak reply from the water. I still couldn't see him. I moved towards the voice and he was hanging off the grab line. I reached for his hand and pulled him on to the deck.

'You OK?' The look of terror in his eyes told me the answer. 'Are you hurt?'

'No I'm OK. You?'

'It wasn't the best way to wake up but, yeah, I'm all right.'

Ben seemed alright, so I turned my attention to our belongings that were drifting further away. I scanned them to see what we needed, catching sight of the sea anchor and our large water containers. Were they too far away? Could I swim and get them and still get back to the boat? I stood on the side of the boat about to dive in, but decided it wasn't worth the risk; the seas were too big and the current was just too strong: there was no guarantee I'd make it back.

I turned back to Ben; he was still shivering, his arms wrapped around his knees in the bows of the boat. I stuck my head in the cabin to try to find a dry top for him to put on. The cabin looked like a house that had been burgled; literally turned upside down, and plunged underwater for good measure. Staring at the contents of the cabin floating in the water, I didn't know where to start with the clean-up. I managed to find Ben's half-wet fleece and chucked it to him.

'It was huge, James, there was nothing I could do, there was nothing I could do.' He was shaking, crying and going into shock.

'It's OK, buddy, neither of us is hurt and the boat is still floating. We'll get out of this.' I was really worried about him. Passing a sea survival course is one thing but coping with a real situation is another.

BEN

'I knew you shouldn't have been rowing,' exclaimed James. 'You were far too tired,' he added inexplicably. Since when was James such an expert on my state of mind? Was he blaming me? Was this another of James's half-camouflaged accusations? Why was he blaming ME for nature's work? A wave had just pitch-poled us, and James had the audacity to blame me! I was too shocked to reply.

I huddled in the front of the boat, clutching my knees and shaking with fright. I was hyperventilating and quivering like a jelly. I couldn't talk and tears streamed down my cheeks, unchecked. I wasn't scared, frightened or even sad, I was just in deep, deep shock. I pulled my fleece over my head.

'Shit, we've lost so much stuff,' lamented James as he emptied the cabin of water, dumping all the remaining, drenched equipment on to the bare deck.

JAMES

I looked for the sat phone and found it on the floor underneath two feet of water. Not surprisingly, it didn't work. I opened the hatch under the mattress that contained the spare phone and batteries for the torches; it was full of water, but the small waterproof bag seemed to have protected the phone. My cold hands took an eternity to open the bag, but finally I pulled the phone out and turned it on; it had one bar of charge.

Who should we call? I was more concerned about Ben than informing the race organizers about what had happened so I just put a brief call into Lin to say that we'd capsized and were OK but not to tell anybody as we'd let them know. She told me we weren't the only ones who'd capsized and that she was over 700 miles away with some of the boats at the back of the fleet. I didn't want to worry Ben's family about the state he was in so I called Alexis. He knew the boat almost as well as we did and having worked with Ben on numerous occasions knew him better than most. 'Alexis, it's James.'

'Hey, James, how are you doing?'

'Not good. We've capsized and Ben is in shock.' Bang! Not the most subtle way of breaking the news, but I didn't know how long the battery would last.

'Are you both OK?' he asked, seeming concerned rather than shocked.

'Physically we're fine, but Ben is pretty shaken up.'

'Can you carry on? Have you called for help?' he asked.

'No, you're the first person we've called and we haven't fired the EPIRB yet.' Until then pressing the panic button and asking to be rescued hadn't even occurred to me. We were still on the boat and weren't sinking; why call for help?

'Alexis, can you tell our families what's happened and that we're OK?'

Ben shouted from the other end of the boat, 'No, don't, I don't want my family to know!' I assumed our families would hear about it somehow and I wanted them to know we were all right, but Ben seemed so adamant that I went along with it.

'Alexis, change of plan: don't tell our families, we'll call them, OK?' I quickly added. 'Alexis? Alexis?' The phone had run out of charge; we couldn't call anybody else until we'd recharged the phone.

I checked the boat to see if there was any obvious structural damage. Both seats were still there and, amazingly, none of the oars had snapped. Ben's shoes were still strapped into the footplate; he must have been literally ripped out of his seat. No wonder he was in shock – but it did mean we were still able to row the boat.

I crawled into the cabin and grabbed our only remaining chart; typically it was the unlaminated one that had remained on board and it was soaking wet. I remember checking our latitude and longitude during the night, and roughly plotted our position: we were over 150 miles from the nearest shipping lane; one of the Woodvale support yachts was some 700 miles to the west of our position, no doubt enjoying a rum punch at the finish in Antigua, while the other was even further away to the east watching over the main body of the fleet. 'Do you want to fire the EPIRB?' I asked Ben, knowing I couldn't stop him if he really wanted to.

I hadn't been through the experience that he had. The ride in the cabin had been bad enough but that was nothing compared to seeing a giant wave bearing down on you and then getting catapulted overboard. I would have understood if he had wanted to bail out, but I can't pretend that I wouldn't have been frustrated by the decision.

'I don't know, I'm not sure if I can go on,' was his answer.

'I've had a look on the chart, we're 150 miles from a shipping lane and the support yachts are even further away. If we do want to be rescued, it is going to take a while for anyone to reach us. Why don't I clean up the cabin and you grab some rest, and I'll row us out of here?' He nodded in agreement. My mind was already refocusing on racing; it must have been my way of coping. I thought I'd share my thoughts out loud, on the grounds that it would help Ben if I appeared to be in control of the situation even if I didn't feel it.

'In the *Today* interview, the guy said we'd taken six miles out of all the other boats last night. That gives us two hours to clean everything up and get going again before we've lost any ground.' He didn't even nod this time.

I set to work on the cabin; it was half full of water and in a total mess. If only I'd shut the main hatch airtight, no water would have got in, but then I wouldn't have been able to get any sleep because it would have been too hot. At least the top hatch had been shut properly; if it hadn't been, the boat would have stayed capsized and I would have been trapped in the cabin. I shuddered at the thought. I'd probably have been able to get out but we would have had no option but to abandon ship and sink the boat when we got rescued. Compared to the Irish boys on *Digicel*, we had come out of it well.

I emptied the contents of the cabin on to the deck; anything that looked like it hadn't survived the dunking, I ditched overboard. The primary sat phone and both iPods were dead, our torches and spare batteries were of no use, and if we ever managed to get going again life was going to be pretty unpleasant on board. The manuals for the desalinator, GPS and radio were all soaked through but it was worth drying them out. I hadn't dared to check the electrics yet. With everything outside I started bailing out the cabin with a drinks bottle. Bottle after bottle came out before the water level eventually started dropping. The main battery had been completely submerged. I prayed it could take it. I'd got most of the water out but it was far from a dry environment. I put the mattress back in, repacked the cabin and ordered Ben inside for a lie-down.

BEN

'The cameras are all knackered,' he stated. Not only had we lost the sea anchor and drogue, but our clothes, towels, flasks, journals and more significantly, it seemed, our electrics.

'Where's the satellite phone?' he said, before fishing the unit out of the full bilge, waterlogged beyond repair.

'Where's the spare Iridium?' he asked. I had carefully packed it in a waterproof aquapac and sealed it away inside the cabin. Miraculously that, along with a small emergency video camera also stashed in an underwater pack, had survived the crash.

'What about the water maker?' I panicked. It had been struggling in the damp conditions already, and now it had been fully submerged upside down in the corrosive salt water.

Once again we opened the stopcock and flicked the switch on the control panel; it wheezed and coughed, waxed and waned, spluttered and then came to a shuddering halt. I thought that the water maker had had it, and without it, so had we. The drought of Christmas day rushed back into my mind. Until a few moments ago, it had seemed like a distant memory.

Life was about to become very different on board. For the first time in the race we were truly alone. It was just James and me against the sea. For me the race was over and now it was a battle for self-preservation.

JAMES

I tried the electrics; the running light worked, so we had power – all was not lost. I turned the GPS on but nothing happened. I decided to row using the compass for a couple of hours. I knew our heading, turned the boat around and rowed off on a bearing of 268 degrees. It was still less than ninety minutes since we'd capsized.

As I rowed, it quickly became clear that the boat didn't feel the same; it was badly listing to the left and I resolved to check everything in a couple of hours. Right now I just wanted to keep moving; it was important to prove to ourselves that we were OK and could still make it to Antigua and that we didn't need to be rescued. By the time I was finishing my stint, I could see Ben moving around in the cabin.

Ben opened the cabin hatch. He didn't seem to be in the same state of intense shock but he looked far from happy. 'The spare phone won't charge,' he said, simply.

'Bollocks, you're joking, the power's working?'

'It's not that; the charger doesn't fit.' He looked totally despondent as he said this. With the primary phone broken and unable to charge the spare there was now no way of contacting anyone. We were totally isolated and we had no way of telling our families that we were all right. Having been able to call us almost anytime, they had now lost all communication and we'd told Alexis not to tell anybody what had happened.

'I wish I hadn't said that Alexis shouldn't tell anyone,' he said.

'Me too, although I'm sure he will tell them. The reason we called him was because he's great in these situations. He'll do the right thing,' I said, as reassuringly as I could.

'I guess,' Ben mumbled.

'The best thing is to keep moving,' I said. 'That way our tracking beacon will show the distance we've covered and people will know we're OK.' I hope I sounded more positive than I felt. I wasn't even sure that our Argos beacon was working.

Ben said that he was OK to row. I wanted to check the boat because it was leaning so badly, worried we might have put a hole in it. I checked all the hatches that housed the food; only one of the eight had let any water in, so that wasn't the cause of the problem, and the hatch storing the ballast in the bottom of the boat had remained watertight. I couldn't for the life of me work out why the boat was listing. It was time to check the hull for holes.

I couldn't ask Ben to get back into the water – he'd only just about recovered from his last unscheduled dip – so I clambered over the side, making sure I was securely attached to the grab line, and spent the next fifteen minutes feeling the underside of the boat. I couldn't find any obvious hole, and meanwhile Ben had checked the bow cabin and verified that that hadn't been compromised either.

There was only one place left that water could be, and that was beneath the false floor in the cabin, underneath the mattress. I emptied the cabin for the second time that morning and smashed a small hole in the plywood, but that space was dry as well. It was a mystery; I couldn't find any water or any hole yet the boat was still listing, making rowing really uncomfortable. The only option was to try to balance the boat. I shoved the 40kg life-raft over to the right-hand side, which seemed to level things out, but it made moving about on deck even more of an obstacle course.

It was time to check the electrics and see what did and didn't work. We knew there was at least some power and I really hoped that the GPS would dry out and come back to life, but it didn't; an absolute disaster. We still had our hand-held GPS though, which meant we'd have to plot our position and rely solely on the compass, but we would have to remember to allow for the compass declination – that is, the difference between true north and magnetic north in the bearing to any given location – and cross our fingers that the hand-held batteries would last, as the spares had 'drowned' in the capsize.

We tried the VHF radio. Despite the aerial being snapped off when the boat went upside down, the wires were intact. It worked or at least the large cackle of static that was there before we capsized was still there now. Ben tried calling all shipping but as the radio only had a range of 5–10 miles the chances of any being that close were pretty remote, so we weren't 100 per cent sure if it worked or not.

We'd left the most important bit of kit until the end: the infamous desalinator. We were still too far from Antigua to rely on our water ballast alone, and we could only hope that having had a couple of hours to dry out, the desalinator would work. Ben flicked the switch: there were a couple of seconds of silence that felt like an eternity, before the grating noise kicked in. If that temperamental bit of kit survived then there was hope for the GPS being resurrected after all.

The BBC's equipment hadn't fared so well; the 'waterproof' camera had flooded, while the internal camera and the hand-held camera didn't seem to approve of a salt-water bath and had bitten the dust. We were left with the small emergency camera that had been protected by a waterproof bag and, luckily, Alexis had put some spare batteries with it, despite me telling him not to because (a) we wouldn't need them and (b) it would only mean extra weight.

I thought we'd come out ahead on the electrical front, so now it was time to see what we'd lost off deck. The big items were conspicuous by their absence: we'd lost the sea anchor, so if the wind changed direction we would be blown backwards at a rate of knots. I tried to make a joke out of it.

'At least we won't have to put the bloody thing out again.' That got a flicker of a smile. The drogue had gone too, though this wasn't a big loss since we'd never used it. (Ironically, the perfect time to have used it would have been last night, racing along in the big swell.) The big water container had gone; we could cope without it, but it made life more complicated. We'd lost our 'poo bucket' so the washing bucket was relegated to that job, but then the concept of washing clothes had become redundant since nearly all our shorts and T-shirts had been washed overboard with the towels. I was left with just one pair of shorts to nurse my sore ass to Antigua.

BEN

Our boat was being tossed around in the water. We had lost the drogue and the sea anchor and were now at the full mercy of the ocean. It seemed incomprehensible that we had capsized. What now? I wondered. We couldn't go on in these conditions, in this state!

'Do you want to go on,' asked James, more of a statement than a question. I nodded. 'Right, we have two hours to get the boat ready; more than that and we'll lose our position,' he added.

I was astonished. We had just capsized, I had nearly drowned and we had lost half of our equipment and James was still preoccupied with the race! He had become obsessed, fanatical even.

We were all alone in the middle of the Atlantic, 800 miles from land with only a hand-held GPS which just gives a position – our onboard GPS system had been reassuringly comprehensive, more like sat nav in a car, giving directions as well; but no VHF, nor any means of communicating with the outside world. We knew that the Argos tracking beacon was still working, as it flashed its little red LED every ninety seconds.

I was in shock, and terrified that another wave would capsize us again. The swell had gathered, and every so often a rogue wave would break over the boat, swamping it with water. Like a driver getting back into a car after a nasty accident, I climbed into the seat and took the oars in each hand. My pulse quickened as once again the waves propelled us along the angry ocean.

Every now and then I'd panic as a wave formed at the stern of the boat and I'd scrunch my eyes closed, waiting for the impact, only to be soaked by its salty spray as the boat diffused the waves.

James had been remarkably cool throughout the whole episode. I had been impressed by his calm, rational thinking. We hadn't sunk, and we were both safe; for James, it was simply a case of picking ourselves up and dusting ourselves down, while I had been quite prepared to set off our EPIRB and abandon the race. It was only James's remarkable composure that got me through.

JAMES

I made some lunch as Ben rowed. I'd looked for a life jacket for him but couldn't find one. They must have gone overboard as well. He was rowing away fairly steadily. Unlike most of the equipment that was designed to take a soaking the stove had passed the test. I had a kettle of boiling water and was looking for the Thermos flasks to keep the water warm for the rst of the day, when I realized the flasks must have made a bid for freedom in the capsize. It really was like being burgled; we didn't know what was missing until we went to use it. We were faced with two options: either to boil water three or four times a day, or make a few meals up at a time and eat them cold later. We decided eating cold meals was easier;

they might not taste as nice but they wouldn't kill us and they hardly tasted great to start with.

While I was munching through my cold and imaginatively named spiced rice I asked Ben what had happened.

'It was a huge wave, it just came out of nowhere and flipped us.'

'I remember looking out of the cabin and seeing you looking really tired,' I said. 'I was going to come out and take over a few minutes early. I wish I had.'

'Are you saying it's my fault?' Ben demanded.

'No, I didn't mean it like that. It's just that you looked tired and I felt pretty fresh. We'd both rowed really hard last night,' I explained.

'There was nothing you could have done,' he pouted.

'I'm not saying there was, I just wished I'd come out, that's all. How did it flip us?'

'It just picked the boat up and pitch-poled us.'

'What, we went stern over bow?' I couldn't believe it. I assumed we hadn't been square on to the wave and had been rolled over sideways; it hadn't occurred to me that we'd capsized like that. No wonder Ben was so shaken up; it must have been horrific to see the wave bearing down and the stern of the boat come flying up towards him. 'Man, we were lucky to escape with such little damage. How are you feeling about having no comms?' I knew this would be the hardest thing for Ben.

'I just wish I'd been able to tell them I'm OK, they will be so worried.' He was getting upset. 'I was so stupid to think I could do this, what was I thinking?'

'Hey, we got flipped by a big wave, from what you said it would have done the same to anyone. If we can't do it, then nobody else behind us can,' I said, 'because we're leading the bloody race. One of the reasons we both signed up for this was to see what it was like to be isolated in the middle of nowhere. Well now we are: I can't go back in the cabin and call home if I'm down and you can't call Marina, it's just you and me. This could have happened three weeks ago and at the pace we've been going we've got less than ten days left. Once we're on dry land and look back on this part of the race, we'll be glad we lost the comfort blanket of being able to call home.' I'd almost managed to convince myself.

'I don't want them to worry,' he repeated.

'Well if we get our little dot motoring across their computer screens, they won't worry! Now row harder,' I said jokingly, although we both knew it was true. (And if a side-effect of capsizing was increased boat speed, I wasn't going to complain.)

My mood plummeted in the afternoon. Maybe the reality of what had happened was sinking in. I went into the cabin and stared at the roof. It was so close to my face and now, more than ever, it felt like a coffin. I didn't want to spend another night in here. Bev's other letter – the one to be opened only at my lowest point – had survived the ordeal along with my passport and diary in a small waterproof bag. If there was ever a time for opening such a letter, it was now. I'd avoided doing this so many times: the very first night on board; when we were stuck in the cabin sheltering from the storms; when we ran out of water; when Zeta stopped us dead... and now we'd capsized. There was very little else that could go wrong and I hadn't felt this low since the first couple of nights at sea.

I opened the letter. It said all the things that I wished she'd been able to say before I left: that she was proud of me, that she was glad we were married and would be waiting on the beach for me in Antigua waving, with Croyde. I could hear her voice reading it to me, making the words real and their effect incredibly emotional. I'd only read two lines before tears were rolling down my cheeks and I was sobbing by the end of the first page. It ended with two impossible requests: to call her day or night if I needed to, and to get my sexy ass to Antigua. We had no phone and my ass right now was as far from sexy as it was humanly possible to be.

It was night-time again. I was glad to take the first shift, not wanting to spend one second longer in the cabin than I had to. There were still plenty of waves around but the sea wasn't as big as the previous night. For the first time in the race, my two hours on the oars ended before I wanted them to. Ben came out for his shift, I sat out on deck and ate another cold rehydrated meal. He was nervous about the waves and I was in no rush to head inside.

I was worried that Ben had lost his confidence in the sea. If he had, we were more likely to get caught out because it is important to be confident, dominate and take on the conditions. Once more I looked for a life jacket for him but I had to accept that they must have gone for a swim.

I told him he was doing a great job and he'd be fine. Despite not wanting to go into the cabin, I had to rest. I couldn't sleep, though; the thin plywood amplified the noise of the water rushing against the boat and I kept thinking I was trapped underwater in a wooden box. The cabin was as hot and damp as ever, the wood was soaked and there was still some water sloshing around in the bottom. It was like being in a damp sauna but the top hatch had to remain closed as waves were breaking over the roof. After everything that had happened, the last thing I needed was a salt-water bath, especially without a towel.

'Dude, ten minutes to go!' My rallying cry from Ben. I was out of that cabin almost as he finished saying it. I wasn't eager to get back on the oars, just glad to be the hell out of that cabin. Ben, on the other hand, finished his shift and went straight inside. Twenty minutes later he came flying out naked, pushed past me and went up to the bows shouting, 'Fuck, no, no, fuck, fuck it, no, fuck!'

'What's wrong?' I asked. It couldn't be a bad dream, he'd only just gone inside.

'The cabin's full of water again,' he moaned, 'a wave crashed through, everything is soaked.' I was glad he couldn't see the smirk on my face; it wasn't funny but it was a laugh or cry situation. I chose the former, whereas Ben had chosen to go off-piste and rant. I don't know why I was smiling, it was horrible in there last time and it was going to be even worse now.

Ben either calmed down or got cold; either way, he dragged his naked ass back inside. I could see and feel him moving around the cabin as he tried to clean up the mess in the dark. We changed shifts without saying a word but when I came back out on deck at 4 a.m. he was a different person.

'I'm sorry about before,' he said.

'Don't worry about it, man, it's been a tough day,' I replied, just glad to see he was feeling more positive.

'You're right,' he said, always a good start to a conversation. 'We need to go as quickly as possible so everyone knows we're OK.' Now he was talking my language. 'We're going to stop and dry everything out tomorrow, we've got plenty of food, the water maker works and the boat still feels like it's going fast. We're going to get there and get there first.'

'Jesus, I wish we'd capsized a few weeks ago!' I said.

Chapter Ten

Falling Apart

Friday, 13 January 2006

1 *Atlantic 4* (four-man boat), 2,376 miles

2 ***EDF*, 2,326 miles**

3 *Team C2*, 2,245 miles

4 *Spirit of Cornwall*, 2,128 miles

JAMES

Unbelievably we got through Friday the 13th without any further disasters. The last twenty-four hours had been fantastic, the boat flying along with the wind right behind us. Despite plenty of waves looming the sea was very consistent and we were able to get the most out of it.

Calculating our daily mileage wasn't as simple now that the boat's GPS wasn't working. Fortunately the emergency hand-held version was holding up well though, so we had an accurate position without having to resort to navigating by the stars. Despite having been taught how to do so, I wasn't confident that the information had sunk in any deeper than had been necessary to pass the exam, though we might still have been able to work out how to use a sextant – if we'd had one on board, that is.

Even without the GPS, it was still relatively straightforward to work out our daily mileage; it just involved a few more stages and plenty of scope for human error. When the GPS was functioning it had just been a case of looking at the screen. By noting that at 7 p.m. Greenwich Mean Time (GMT) on 4 January we had 1,091 miles left to Antigua, for example, we could check our position at 7 p.m. GMT the following day, see that we had 1,063 miles left and by a simple act of subtraction work out that we'd travelled twenty-eight miles.

Now we had to manually record our latitude and longitude at 7 p.m. GMT and then do so again at 7 p.m. twenty-four hours later. These points had to be accurately plotted on a chart and the distance between them measured using the chart's scale to find out our daily mileage. Admittedly it's just elementary graph plotting – NASA won't be on the phone any time soon begging us to go and work for them – but basing our calculations on a soggy chart that covered the whole Atlantic, without a ruler, made it more challenging and definitely less accurate.

Despite having been at sea for over six weeks, we still found it hard to guess how fast the boat was going. Sometimes I thought we were flying along, only to look at the speed on the GPS and find that we were doing just 2 knots. Other times I'd be swearing at how heavy the boat felt and yet we'd be going over 4 knots. The difference was down to the strong currents in the Atlantic and the lack of landmarks to gauge our speed against, of course (unless you counted a whale or the odd pod of dolphins). Today though, the currents must have been in our favour: according to the charts, we'd clocked well over 100 miles on Friday the 13th even after allowing for significant human error.

In real terms we probably rowed even further than that, as our calculations assumed that the boat travelled in a straight line, a big assumption when the GPS was guiding us but almost dangerous now we were steering from just the compass. For the last 1,000 miles we'd been holding a bearing of 268. According to the way point we'd programmed into the GPS, that should, in theory, have taken us right through the middle of the mile-long finish line off the southernmost point of Antigua. Up until the capsize, we'd always tried our best to make sure that the GPS bearing was as close to 268 as we could make it but now, with no screen to help us, we were forced to rely on the compass.

Every time we read the compass, we had been taught to allow for declination. For us this boiled down to subtracting 15 degrees from what the compass was reading in order to get our true bearing, so suddenly we were going to have to get used to rowing on a heading of 283 degrees; not complicated, I know, but I lost count of the number of times I forgot and rowed along on 268 before remembering.

If that wasn't enough for our tiny brains to cope with, we couldn't see the compass at night; its battery had run out and the spare was ruined in the capsize. Every ten minutes we were forced to stop and check we were still on the right bearing by shining a very temperamental head-torch on the compass. Neither of these problems had a positive effect on our course; if a policeman had asked us to walk the line, we'd definitely have lost the keys to our car.

Our progress over the last few days had been fantastic and according to my nerdy spreadsheet we had a great chance of getting there before 20 January, which had been our 'unrealistic' arrival date. The possibility of pulling up in Antigua ahead of schedule – one night less on the boat and one night extra in the Caribbean – was a thought to cherish. Ever since setting off I'd visualized our arrival in Antigua: rowing into a lagoon full of bright turquoise water, grounding the boat on the golden sand, jumping out of the boat into warm, knee-high water and running up the beach into the arms of Bev and Croyde. Ben had already ruined this image by reminding me that we were arriving in English Harbour, a marina like many others in the Caribbean filled by expensive yachts, where we would be directed towards a mooring point for our boat. So, not the golden beach arrival I was hoping for.

Now, however, there might not be anyone there to greet us anyway. When I had last spoken to Bev, they had booked flights out to Antigua and a hotel room for 20 January. If we pitched up on the 18th or 19th there would be nobody there to meet us and, given that we would be arriving with only one pair of shorts, no money and no hotel booked, we'd have to spend another night on the bloody boat while we waited for our families to arrive. I tried to reassure myself that my dad would have developed intricate spreadsheets to cover every conceivable arrival date.

Perhaps it's not surprising that I was worried about arriving into Antigua early, because so far every time we had believed we were going to get to the finish, our boat seemed to punish us. Despite leaving Friday the 13th behind, I couldn't quite shake the feeling that bad luck was heading our way again.

Right on cue, the desalinator broke. Ever since our 'Eskimo roll' it hadn't been producing water as quickly, but as it was still working and had had a chance to dry out, I was convinced that although it wasn't fully operative it would see us through to the finish. But on the morning of 14 January it cut out after making just under five litres. When we checked, the battery still had plenty of power, the pressure in the pump was fine and the filter clean. There might have been a problem with the wiring, or perhaps a twisted hose was restricting the flow of water, but it was difficult to get a good view because the desalinator filled up the hatch it was housed in. Ben gamely reached in to check the hoses.

'Shit!' he yelped, pulling his hand out and blowing on his fingers.

'What's wrong?' I asked. The memory of Christmas without water was still disturbingly fresh in both our minds.

'It's boiling hot. It must have shorted itself out.'

'Shall we let it cool down and try again?' I asked. Taking it apart was beyond my technical capability and with electrical equipment I tend to abide by two rules: 'If in doubt, turn it off and on again' – it works for computers, so it should work for everything else – and 'Time is a great healer'. Most things tend to recover if you leave them long enough.

'OK, let's try it again in the afternoon,' Ben sighed, cutting a forlorn figure as he went back into the cabin, shaking his head.

From the outset, Ben's biggest worry (and he had a few) was that our crossing would be cut short by a technical failure. Since Christmas, the desalinator had more than lived up to his fears of a technical gremlin that was going to let us down. Ben had a love–hate relationship with it, whereas I had adopted a more *laissez-faire* approach. He loved the fact we got 30 litres of water out of it in an hour, but loathed having to rely on it to survive; he hated the way it sounded when it was working, but if it went quiet even for just a few seconds, whether he was rowing, resting or cooking, his head would pop up and stare at the desalinator like a startled meerkat until the grating noise started up once more.

I knew Ben would be worrying for the next few hours until we tried it again, and that if the same thing happened he was going to get down and negative. A broken desalinator and a manic-depressive crewmate wouldn't make for an enjoyable last week.

We rowed on for a few hours, both of us clearly anxious. For almost the entire journey there had been a problem for us to worry about. Was the gearing too heavy? How were we going to make water? Was there enough food on board, or should we cut rations again? Are the seats going to last the distance? Are we going to capsize? Are we ever going to get there? How accurate is our navigation without GPS? The frustrating thing was that neither of us ever seemed to know any of the answers.

It was time to try the desalinator again. For ten minutes it clunked away, before slowly becoming quieter and quieter. The slower the water trickled out of the tube, the tenser Ben got. Then it stopped completely.

'The pump's red hot and there's no pressure,' Ben said, sounding resigned to the fact that it wasn't going to work.

'Have we still got the manual?' I asked.

'It got soaked in the capsize but it's in the cabin,' he answered.

'Do you want to have a look through that and see if there is anything we've missed?' I suggested, thinking that it would at least give him something to focus on, to stop him from driving himself into a nervous breakdown.

He came out of the cabin quarter of an hour later clutching the soggy manual looking like Tom Hanks holding his imaginary friend Wilson in *Cast Away*. 'I've worked out why it's getting so hot: we haven't got the cooling system installed. I think it's optional and there probably wasn't room for it anyway.'

'But it hasn't overheated for six weeks. Why should it start now?' I said, addressing the question as much to myself as to Ben.

'I don't know,' he sighed.

'What does the manual say about the lack of pressure?' I asked. 'That's probably what's causing the pump to overheat.'

'It might be, we have a couple of options. We can take the filter out and give it a clean, or remove the top of the machine and bleed it of air like a radiator.' Ben didn't sound totally convinced by either of those possibilities, but at least we still had options.

'I don't think the filter needs cleaning; it says they last six months before they need changing and it's only done six weeks. Are you really sure it's worth risking taking the system apart?' I wanted to be certain this wasn't going to end its life prematurely. I was in favour of letting it die gradually, giving us every last bit of its water-making life.

'It's been totally underwater. That can't be good for it,' he countered.

'Fair point. Is there anything else we can do first? Double-check the hoses and electrical connections or something?' I asked. Ben nodded.

Then I had a thought. 'It's been slowing down for a few days now. Maybe it's something as simple as a blockage in the inlet pipe? It's got to be worth a look,' I suggested, desperately hoping that was the case and that we could avoid taking the machine apart. I jumped into the water and felt around the surface of the hull for the machine's water inlet. I found it but despite sacrificing a toothbrush to get right up into the pipe, there didn't seem to be anything blocking it. As ever, there was no simple solution.

Meanwhile Ben had checked all the hoses, and found them to be clear. He turned the desalinator on, and again it started up straight away before soon grinding to a halt. I was torn as to whether we should take it apart or keep it running until it stopped; at least it was making water. If we took it apart, there was a risk that we might get nothing at all. Unlike the situation at Christmas the risk now wasn't life-threatening, because barring storms and delays, we had enough emergency water to see us to the finish line; but neither of us was keen to incur the risk of more time penalties.

If we didn't try to do something, I knew that a partially working desalinator was going to eat away at Ben, so it was probably better to get the situation sorted one way or the other. I wanted Ben to be free to focus on the rowing as I believed that in spite of the capsize, we might still be in the lead and the thought of getting to Antigua first was the only thing

231

keeping me going. To have been through what we had, coming into Antigua first would be fantastic but to achieve that goal I needed Ben's mind to be on the quality of his rowing, not on the desalinator.

We decided to go for it. Ben carefully took the filter out, cleaned it with the last of our fresh water and replaced it, before unscrewing the top of the machine to let air out of the system. Ben followed the instructions to the letter but when it was reassembled and he flicked the switch, nothing happened. 'There must be an air leak somewhere,' I suggested helpfully. Ben tightened everything up and tried again: nothing. His chin slumped to his chest as if the life had been sucked out of him. We left the machine running for fifteen minutes – the maximum the manual said it would need to equalize again – but nothing happened.

We were now out of water again, with a broken desalinator. Of course at this point I should have said, 'Well, there's no option now; let's get a couple of bottles out of the ballast and get our asses to Antigua first.' But instead I said petulantly, 'If it had been up to me, I wouldn't have touched it.' That may have been true, but I had agreed with our plan and therefore lost any right to say that. I regretted saying it as soon as it came out but despite straight away saying, 'I'm sorry, I didn't mean that, we'll just have to dig into the ballast,' it was too late; I could see Ben was about to erupt.

BEN

'You decide everything!' I screamed.

It was true. I don't think I'd call it bullying but James is very forceful in his manner, and I was coerced. I felt that it was easier to make him happy than to make me happy. The outcome might have been the same – arriving in Antigua as soon as possible – but the goals were completely different.

JAMES

Weeks of pent up anger – at me, at the desalinator, at life on board full stop – burst out in my direction. 'We always do what you want! Every decision we make is what you want to do!' he shouted. That wasn't true. If it had been up to me, we'd have rowed more and rested less, or at least played around with the shifts, but I knew that was Ben's bedrock, so I hardly ever suggested any changes. We hadn't disagreed on anything else; we'd discussed our course but never deviated, and I'd got pissed off when, after three weeks at sea, he still couldn't remember which way to point the rudder to steer left (to the left, funnily enough) but I struggled to think of any really contentious issue; unless he held me responsible for how long we had waited before dipping into the ballast at Christmas. That would have been a fair enough accusation, but he hadn't said anything at the time, and now certainly wasn't the right moment to bring it up.

I believe that it's really important to keep arguments to the point you're arguing about. I'd be lying if I said I always manage to do that, but I do try to avoid saying, 'You always....,' as it is guaranteed to make the situation worse. Ben was clearly looking for an argument; whether it was just to vent his frustration or because he had an issue with me, I wasn't sure.

'You agreed to try to mend it. How dare you say otherwise!' he shouted.

'I'm not saying that. I apologized. I shouldn't have said that, but don't make sweeping statements, unless you want to make things worse,' I replied, trying to sound calm.

'Why? If it's not this, it will be something else; you can't decide everything.' He was pouting now and I had a glimpse of what it will be like to have a teenage son, but I also knew that my single-minded determination (combined with a stubborn streak) can make me come across like a bully.

'Don't push it, Ben.' I was determined not to rise to it and make it personal. I'd really enjoyed Ben's company and didn't want either of us to say anything that would tarnish that or make the last week on board difficult. I carried on rowing and Ben went into the cabin.

I took my frustration out on the oars. Normally, Ben would have either ranted to the camera in the cabin or spoken to Marina, but those were no longer options. I wondered how we were going to get back on track.

BEN

The cabin was the most natural place to retreat to after an argument. It was the only private space on the boat and it had witnessed James and

233

me in every conceivable emotional state. It was the tiny space in which we admitted our true feelings to ourselves and allowed them expression, which seemed terribly appropriate given that it was about the same size as a church confessional box!

However, by day 43 the boat was disgusting and neither of us wanted to be in the cabin. It was soggy and smelly. We couldn't dry it out fully after the capsize and we had never cleaned it, so anything that wasn't damp was chocolate-encrusted. This, combined with the fact we hadn't washed for over a month guaranteed that if an object wasn't squishy or chocolatey it was crispy with human debris. We had reached a nadir in terms of how disgusting it was. So although I sought refuge from our fight in the cabin I realized very quickly that I had to get back out and clear the air – no argument could be worth the punishment of a prolonged session in the cabin.

With earlier rows there had been more options as to how to blow off steam. I could phone Marina, turn up my music or be lulled by the voice of Griff Rhys Jones reading *To the Baltic with Bob*, a talking book I had found strangely reassuring throughout the preceding days. Our lack of communication made me increasingly paranoid about what our friends and family thought had happened to us. It had been at my insistence that James had told Alexis not to tell anyone about the capsize and as the days went on I became more and more convinced that our silence would be having a devastating effect on our loved ones. Before our capsize I had been speaking to Marina pretty much every day, and for days now she would have heard nothing. Surely they would think we were dead? James reassured me that the movement of our tracking device would be enough to satisfy them, but I wasn't so sure. I was agonized that my family were already grieving for me and I felt dreadful once again about what this race was costing those I cared about. But whilst my anxiety for those back home continued unabated, life on board *Spirit* actually became even more straightforward. We could no longer tell anyone else what was on our minds. We had to communicate our fears to each other.

JAMES

Fortunately, we didn't have to make a decision about when to use the emergency water – there was no option since it was all we had – but we needed to agree how much of it we were going to drink. With 145 litres of water on board and only 320 miles left to Antigua there was plenty of water (unless a storm delayed us); the question was: did we ration it? The more we drank the bigger the time penalty we were going to be handed on arrival. We had already received a one-hour penalty at Christmas for drinking five litres of water. That may sound like nothing over a 3,000-mile, fifty-day race but at the time it would have been enough to relegate us from first to second place. The penalties ramped up quickly after this: the next five litres consumed would mean a six-hour penalty, the following twelve hours – and if we drank any more after that, we would lose one whole position in the race.

The problem was that the decision about how much water to allow ourselves had to be made blindfolded, because we had no idea of our ranking in the race and how big an impact the time penalties were going to have on our final position. We had to agree on how to ration it, but for that to happen, we needed to be talking again.

It was time to break the habit of a lifetime and apologize first. We were in this together and too close to the finish to argue about things that we couldn't control. Ben was coming out for his shift, so I steeled myself and took the plunge.

'Mate, I really am sorry. That was the wrong thing to say. I'm just gutted that we've got to dig into the ballast again after working so hard, and I guess I wanted to blame someone else.'

'It's OK,' said Ben. 'I'm sorry for over-reacting but it's too much to take. Every time we solve a problem, something else goes wrong.'

'At least nothing else can go wrong. Virtually everything is broken now,' I said, trying to lighten the mood.

'Hmmph.' Ben's response told me that I had a bit more work to do.

'We have got a decision to make about the water though,' I began again, tentatively.

'Yeah?' came the cagey response.

'Yeah. How much are we going to drink? Every time we crack open a bottle we receive a bigger penalty.' I tried to say this without sounding like I was leading the decision towards severe water rationing.

'I don't care where we come, I just want to get there as quickly as possible, but I'm not going to put myself through Christmas all over again,' he said, simply. I couldn't argue with his logic and at least he was being consistent with his attitude to racing.

'It's difficult because we don't know our position and what effect the penalties will have, but I'm with you on being thirsty again,' I said. 'How about trying to keep it down to five litres a day each? If we're desperate for more then we'll take it, but let's push as hard as possible to get to Antigua first,' I suggested.

'That sounds OK,' Ben said, in a way that managed to make him sound both relieved and worried at the same time.

I opened the hatch containing the ballast, saying cheerily, 'Right then, let's tuck in!' But as I broke the seal I was gutted at the thought that we were throwing away first place. Having no option and being incredibly thirsty was the only thing that made the situation just about bearable.

When I had read the event rules six months earlier, I remember thinking that it was stupid to have penalties for drinking the water you've pulled along all that way. The excessive punishment meant that people placed themselves at risk by not drinking water in an attempt to avoid a penalty – just as we had done at Christmas. I could see Woodvale's point that the ballast was vital for safety, since it would help the boat re-right if it capsized (as it had ours). Woodvale were clearly worried that the race might not be allowed to take place again if boats capsized and had to be rescued by other shipping – though ironically, more boats capsized and were rescued in this race than in any previous running of the course, despite the strict ballast penalties.

To my mind, a better solution would have been to lay some lead above the keel. It could be attached to the bottom of the boat, making it more effective in helping the boat re-right, and because of the density of lead it would take up less space and there would still be room for some emergency water – which could be then drunk without incurring a time penalty. It was your water; you'd carried it 3,000 miles and you should be allowed to drink it when you wanted.

Unfortunately that wasn't the case, of course, and we were going to have to live with the consequences. My goal now – as it had always been – was simply to get to Antigua first. No time penalty could take away the pleasure from being the first boat across, and with Ben's affirmation that he wanted to get there as quickly as possible, at last we had the same goal.

Before we left La Gomera, Ben and I had made a point of speaking about conflict resolution on board. According to previous competitors in the race, one of the biggest problems of life on board was the simmering arguments and long uncomfortable silences that could sometimes last for weeks. Ben and I had promised not to hold a grudge for whatever was said in the heat of the moment, or with the outcome of an argument. Once it was over, it would be forgotten. It was something that we had done successfully up until now, and although this had been our biggest argument so far, I was determined to keep to our promise.

I also had a more pressing problem of my own. My bum was becoming more painful with every shift, making rowing almost impossible. Considering we'd spent twelve hours a day rowing for over six weeks now, I thought our bums had held up pretty well; but losing our clothes and soap in the capsize had meant a significant drop in hygiene levels and it had affected my posterior in a very negative way. It was bad during the day, but massively worse at night, with nothing to look at, no music and just my limited imagination to take my mind away from the pain. I had to do something about it at first light, because I was spending as much time fiddling with my seat pad – in a fruitless attempt to get comfy – as I was rowing.

As soon as the sun came up, I tried to get a good look at the affected area, but working with a two-inch hand mirror (which was on board for emergency signalling) and the confines of the cabin, even a member of Cirque du Soleil would have struggled to get into a position to have a proper view. There was only one option: Ben was going to have to help me out. We'd shared so much already; what was a quick examination between friends? I went outside to break the good news to him.

'Buddy, can you do me a favour?' I asked

'OK,' came the slightly sceptical reply.

'It's nothing bad – well, it's nothing too bad. Can you take a look at my bum? It's giving me some serious gyp,' I said, trying to make it sound as casual as asking him to pass the snack bag.

'Do I have to?' he replied.

'Unless you want to row for twenty-four hours a day, then yeah; I can't get a good view with that tiny mirror and I need to do something as I'm spending half my shift rearranging my padding and that's not getting us anywhere.'

'OK.' He sounded resigned to his fate. I placed my feet either side of the footwell and dropped my shorts. My bum was now at Ben's eyeline about two feet away from his rowing position. I fully expected to hear retching, or at the very least a dramatic intake of breath when he first caught sight of my posterior, but was pleasantly surprised by his reaction.

'It's not too bad,' he said. 'There are quite a few spots, but nothing that looks too angry.'

'What about here?' I said, pointing to the two most painful areas: the skin above my sitting bones, which took most of my weight when I was rowing. The previous night it had felt like somebody was sticking needles in my bum whenever they touched the seat.

'Oh yeah, there are a couple of slightly larger spots there,' he admitted, rather too quickly and enthusiastically for my liking.

'Slightly larger!' I exclaimed. 'My ass feels like a map of the Himalayas – are you sure there aren't any boils?' Previously, Ben had said he didn't want to have to lance any boils. I'd countered that at least that was preferable to being a 'lancee'. His reluctance to perform minor surgery meant I wasn't totally convinced that he hadn't downplayed the state of my ass so as not to have to get the lancing needle out.

'No, honestly,' he protested, a little too vigorously. 'I'll have a look tomorrow if you want and we can see if it's getting better.'

It was my turn for the sceptical 'OK'. I wasn't convinced.

BEN

As I examined James's backside for him I was alarmed to realize quite how seriously it was damaged. But my anxiety for his health was complicated by my frustration at him for pushing himself quite so hard. I felt that, to some extent, James had brought his collapse on himself. The relentless drive to find more strength meant that he had burnt out. He had pushed his body to its absolute limit and it had nothing left to give him. I wanted to say this is why we needed to pace ourselves, but as I examined the pustulous boils on James's posterior I realized it was too late for that. I was also exhausted and digging deep to find the strength to continue. We had both started to go downhill at the same time but it had hit James harder and faster.

To see James go from an Olympic gold-winning medallist rowing two hours at full pelt day after day to an old man, unable to sit for more than five minutes until he jumped screaming from his seat was so distressing. He'd sit, row for thirty seconds, stand again, rail, shout and try to sit before leaping up again moments later. Over these last few days I offered to over-row to give James more of a break, but the only time he accepted my offer to row for him was on the final day. It was kind of heartbreaking because I really really cared for him but also a shock. It's comparable to seeing your father cry – it's not something you ever expect to witness. I didn't think James could feel pain, and it was an invisible pain that I couldn't really understand. When he told me he was worried about his health I was concerned that if I told him how bad his bum looked it would give him a terrible psychological knock.

JAMES

I spent my downtime making two doughnut-shaped pads from what was left of my seat cushion to tape to my bum. The boils would sit inside the ring, allowing me to sit down without the boils making contact with the seat. Ben may have avoided the dubious honour of lancing them, but it was only a temporary reprieve; instead he had the pleasure of taping my 'doughnuts' in place.

BEN

James was the only man on the ocean armed with a spreadsheet. He was the Olympian who had shaved oars and rowed four-hour shifts to protect me from the sun. And now, whilst I still pictured him shaving down anti-foul paint and checking out the competition, he was sitting in front of me cutting polo-mint shapes out of foam to fit around the weeping sores. I didn't know whether to laugh or cry.

JAMES

Not surprisingly, Ben didn't jump at the chance to fit my 'cushions', but he performed his task diligently and for the first time in a few days I didn't wince as I sat down and started rowing. I'd even have described the new arrangement as comfortable until a wave broke over the side of the boat, soaking me and the tape holding the doughnuts in place. As soon as they slipped out of position, the pain returned.

With the failure of my 'doughnuts' there was one option left. Every boat had a comprehensive first-aid kit ranging from plasters and bandages through to a variety of antibiotics and painkillers. I've always tried to avoid taking painkillers when I've had an injury. There's a danger that they might mask the pain to such a degree that I will push myself too hard and make the injury worse. The only time that I considered it acceptable was if I absolutely had to race and needed something to block out the pain, allowing me to perform and worry about the injury after the competition. So far Ben and I had both avoided taking painkillers, but if I was going to be able to row the last few hundred miles I had to be able to sit down. It was time to crack them open.

We had three different strengths of painkiller on board, and I decided the situation called for the strongest. The packaging had become wet however, so it was impossible to see the recommended dosage; all that was visible was the word 'strong' written on the box by Chiara, Ben's future sister-in-law (a doctor). I opened the packet and swallowed a couple of capsules.

BEN

We were both suffering by this point in the race. James's boils looked infected and I had a fungal infection that had left the lower half of my body covered in mould. We decided it was time to crack into the medical supplies and so I prescribed us both a course of antibiotics. I'm not sure that having a doctor for a future sister-in-law counts as full medical training but we were miles from anywhere with no means of establishing correct dosage. The painkillers had guidance written on the side of each packet in big letters. Each box was marked strong, very strong, or very very strong. In the absence of any medical or first aid books, which had all been lost in the capsize, we guessed quantities, with James administering himself two Tramidol painkillers an hour. We would later learn that the correct course is one every four hours, and that no more than four should be taken in a twenty-four-hour period…

JAMES

My next shift was almost bearable; two capsules later and it was better still, but I was incredibly tired. I hadn't slept well the night before because of the pain, and thought it was just the lack of sleep catching up on me. I came off my shift at 4 a.m. desperate for a pee, despite wanting nothing more than to dive into the cabin. I knew if I didn't go now I'd only have to wake up to go in a bit. I sat in the bow rowing position, put the bucket between my legs and prepared for action. The next thing I heard was Ben saying, 'You OK back there?'

'Huh?' I grunted and looked at my watch: 5 a.m. I'd fallen asleep for an hour with my dick in the bucket and hadn't even managed to go to the toilet! It was an unbelievably uncomfortable position to fall asleep in, and if I hadn't done it I would have thought it impossible.

The painkillers had worked magnificently but the side-effects were clear. If I could fall asleep while having a pee it could also happen while I was rowing and that could be fatal. I didn't want to feel like I was rowing with a red-hot poker shoved up my ass again, though, so I decided that every time I took the ultra-strong painkillers, I'd also take some Pro Plus caffeine tablets to help me stay awake. I'm not sure a doctor would have recommended such a cocktail, but with a lack of floating GPs in the Atlantic, I had no option; all I wanted was to be able to row and to get this boat to Antigua as soon as possible.

BEN

I appeared for my session and realized immediately that James was not quite himself. The enormous quantities of painkillers were seriously damaging his mental health. He was popping so much morphine he was crazed. This became glaringly obvious when he stumbled out halfway through my shift. I regularly interrupted James's shifts by getting up early, convinced that it was my turn to row when I actually had another hour to rest. So when James first appeared I assumed that he had woken up thinking the same thing. Admittedly this should have alerted me to a problem instantly – James never appeared early for his shifts – but it wasn't until he spoke that I realized just how badly the drugs were affecting him:

'Am I at Freddie Flintoff's testimonial?' he queried.

It was time to chop back his dosage.

Monday, 16 January 2006
JAMES

My self-prescription worked to a certain extent in that I was now just drowsy at the oars, rather than having to force myself to stay awake, but suddenly, I was snapped out of my daydreams as I heard a loud 'crack' and felt the seat beneath me give way. Adrenaline shot through my body, my heart rate soared and I could feel myself start to panic. We were down to one seat, with no spares and at least 300 miles to go. Ben and I wouldn't be able to row together, so if the wind turned against us (and with no sea anchor to stop us drifting backwards), we would be at the mercy of the weather. What if the last seat broke? Rowing without a sliding seat was going to slow our progress enormously, and did we have enough water if that happened? If by some miracle we were still leading, we now had no chance of maintaining that position.

I took the seat from the bow rowing position and carried on, determined to put on a cheery face and to think of a solution by the time Ben came out for his shift.

'Morning, dude,' Ben chirped as he appeared from the cabin.

'Morning, buddy. Do you want the good news or the bad news?' I asked cheerily, but evidently not cheerily enough; the slump in his shoulders told me he was bracing himself for the worst.

'What's happened now?' he groaned.

'We're down to one seat,' I replied, trying to sound positive, but he knew we were out of spares. 'It's not a total disaster; every other seat has lasted at least 700 miles, so it should last.' He wasn't convinced so I tried again to reassure him. 'Don't worry, I'll rig something up so that we can still keep rowing even if that seat breaks.'

'Huh,' he grunted, turning to concentrate on rehydrating a muesli. I tried not to take that as a slur on my DIY skills.

Having sat in the bows for a few minutes, I realized that with what we had left on board there was no way of mending the seat. The only thing I could do was to set up a fixed rowing position. I removed the undercarriage of the seat that held the wheels in place and unscrewed the slide beds in which the wheels ran up and down. I then drilled through the seat and screwed it directly on to the struts that had previously supported the slide beds. Instead of sliding up and down and being able to use big leg muscles to accelerate the boat, we would now have to propel the boat with our back muscles by leaning forwards and backwards. Our progress would be much slower, but I was confident it would get us there.

I told Ben to stop rowing and had a go in the new position; it worked OK, but when I rocked forwards and backwards my weight shifted on my bum and even through the haze of painkillers it was excruciating. I tried not to show it though, and just about managed to row enough strokes to convince Ben that if the last seat broke we'd be OK. It was lucky he couldn't see just how much I was grimacing through my little demonstration.

We had to make the most of the sliding seat while we still had it. I figured it wouldn't last too long before it snapped, so we should make the most of every last stroke in order to be as close to Antigua as possible when it broke. There was only one thing for it: we were going to have to pull harder.

Ben shouldn't have had a problem with this. Weeks ago we'd agreed that if the race was still close with 300 miles to go, then we would row more and rest less; surely that hadn't slipped his mind? Because of the broken seat we could no longer row two-up, so we had to make the most of each shift and work harder. Admittedly we didn't know how close the race was, but it had certainly been close the last time we'd had functioning communications, and as far as I was concerned it was better to assume it was still close and race hard to the finish. I was aware of my promise to Ben of getting him to Antigua in one piece, but all I wanted was for him to row harder – not to kill himself.

I put a lot of effort into my next shift and was pleased with the resulting increase in the boat's speed. When we swapped shifts, I decided to tell Ben that it was time to start cranking the boat for home. Ever since he'd complained about not knowing how much fluid to drink, or how to listen to what his body was telling him because he wasn't an athlete, I'd made sure I explained why I wanted us to do something and how to go about it. Today was no exception.

He came out on deck, made up some Lucozade Sport and got ready for his shift. 'OK,' I said, 'It's time for us to up the effort today. We're into the last few days, so let's try to work at a level where it's difficult to hold a conversation – not gasping for air, but panting a bit.' He said nothing and shook his head.

'Do you understand? Is that OK?' I asked.

'OK!' He growled.

BEN

For weeks we had rowed as hard as our arms allowed. We still had nearly 500 miles to go, and had been making the best part of 100 miles a day, by far the biggest distances of the race.

Since the capsize, we had been completely cut off from the rest of the world, and therefore unable to find out our position in the fleet. We were racing blind but I felt sure we were still in a strong position. The boat was significantly lightened of food and gas, and the wind and sea were on our stern, propelling us towards Antigua. I had been making a steady 4 knots on my shift, often increasing to 5.

The capsize had been the nadir of our trip but it was an event that had bonded us and life on board was as good as anyone could have hoped on a damp, smelly boat that was missing half its gear. In some senses, it was pleasingly simple – a life of subsistence. We were able to use only the last tenth of the boat, rather like ourselves.

The boat had started off as a complete stranger. I remember visiting it in Devon and it was all sharp edges and purely built for its purpose. It was even uglier on La Gomera, where the cabin had seemed totally inhospitable – the only semblance of domesticity was provided by Tamara's pockets sewn carefully along one side – and yet the more time we spent with her the more we understood her. After the capsize *Spirit* had become another member of our team: when she had righted herself she had saved our lives. I think nostalgically of her because she was an integral part of the journey and she reflected the state we were in. Life wasn't luxurious but we had overcome huge obstacles and the boat was holding out just as James and I were.

'Morning,' I smiled as I wedged myself through the hatch.

James was so engrossed in his rowing that he failed to even notice me emerge. Sweat streamed down his face, while huge, rope-like veins bulged on his arms and chest. He looked almost in pain, I thought, rowing like a man possessed.

'Morning,' I repeated.

'Today –' announced James in between strokes,

'I don't –' he continued,

'Want you, urgghh –'

'To be, phwww –'

'Able to, urggghf –'

'Say more, pwhhur–'

'Than two, urgggh –'

'Words at, pwhurrr –'

'A time, urggghh.'

And a very good morning to you too, I thought. What a wally.

James went on to explain that according to sporting science, if the body was working at a point where we were working hard but not going to exhaust ourselves we should only be able to utter two words at a time. After all we'd been through, after 2,500 miles of rowing, storms, dehydration and a life-threatening capsize, I'd woken up in boot camp.

JAMES

I went back into the cabin and left Ben to it. I could see that he was still shaking his head, but to be fair he was getting stuck into the rowing. I lay down for a nap on the sweaty mattress, dreaming of a proper bed with a sheet.

I came out of the cabin to get a drink and saw that Ben still wasn't happy. I decided I wasn't going to sit there while he sulked like a child just because I'd suggested we both work harder. After all, I hadn't asked him to do something I wasn't going to do myself.

'What's the matter?' I asked.

'I can't do this,' he pouted.

'What do you mean "can't do it", you're doing really well. What's the problem? We're only working a bit harder than yesterday,' I responded as calmly as possible.

'I come outside and get told that you want me to row and not be able to talk and that we have to be panting all the time!' he shouted.

'That's not what I said. But yeah, it's time to start working harder now,' I said defiantly. I wasn't going to back down over this.

'You want me to row hard, do you? You want to see me go mad, do you?' he shouted, then started rowing harder and harder, yelling, 'Is that hard enough for you? Is that hard enough for you?'

Then he fell off the seat.

'Don't be so immature, you're behaving like a spoilt brat,' I growled. I was determined to remain calm in response to his outburst. This either wound him up even more or he'd already gone past the point of no return, because he carried on ranting.

'I'm going mad, I can't do this, you've driven me to this, I don't care where we come in, I don't want to get there first. I lied when I said I did. I've hated being on this boat with you!'

'That's a shame because I've really enjoyed your company,' I said. 'It's the only thing that's got me through.' I got up and went into the cabin.

BEN

This was our biggest row and although I was furious with James for his total insensitivity I was more affected by my own reaction. In my anger I was trying to demonstrate how hard I would have to row in order not to be able to speak. In the course of my fit I wanted to show how crazy I was – screaming, 'Am I going crazy? Is this crazy enough for you?'

I had transformed from the controlled man I know myself to be to a ranting screaming madman. As I yelled at James I slammed the oars and began attacking the boat with all the strength I had. I was trying as hard as I could to break our last working seat, jumping up and down on it. I was completely out of control – and it terrified me.

JAMES

With some space for reflection, I had to concede that I hadn't discussed with Ben the thought process behind my plan to push on, nor reminded him that we had agreed a few weeks ago that we would try to increase our speed with 300 miles to go to the finish. Even so, there was no need for him to throw his toys out of the pram like that. A lot of what he'd said was heat-of-the-moment stuff, but it wasn't nice to hear; I had genuinely enjoyed Ben's company. He had seen sides of me that not even my closest friends have witnessed, and vice-versa. I was determined not to let this tarnish our memories of the journey or ruin our relationship, but I also wanted him to know that he couldn't behave like that.

Despite the rantings, Ben had put in a cracking shift and as I went past I said, 'Good work.'

'Thanks,' he replied before going straight into the cabin. He seemed calm enough but looked as though he didn't really know what to say.

Ben had regained some composure by the time he was back out on deck. He began to boil the kettle for lunch. 'Chilli con carne or spiced rice?' he asked. As we'd yet to rehydrate a chilli so it tasted like anything other than powder, I opted for the rice.

'I'm starting to lose it,' he said. 'I'm really worried. That wasn't me, I never behave like that.' He sounded genuinely concerned about his mental state. He wasn't the only one.

I decided humour was the best approach. 'Don't worry,' I said, 'I seem to have that effect on most people – ask Bev.' He smiled at that.

'I'm sorry I said I didn't care whether we won or not,' said Ben. 'It was the one thing I knew would hurt you.'

'Thanks very much,' I said jokingly. ' I thought you'd broken the seat for a minute then.'

'I know, I felt so stupid and that made me even madder.' He paused and added, 'I have enjoyed it, well parts of it, but I really don't know what's happening to me.'

'Don't worry, we're both exhausted. I should have explained myself better before, but let's just work as hard as we can and get there, eh?' I said, trying my best to be diplomatic.

Although our chat improved the mood on board, I couldn't help noticing that the atmosphere didn't return to normal as it had after previous arguments. I hadn't taken anything Ben had said personally and wasn't going to get in a sulk, but I didn't feel much like talking either. The sun was about to set and a quiet night of rowing might do us both the world of good.

Having managed to find a balance between taking enough painkillers so that I could sit down, but not so many that I'd fall asleep, I dived into the cabin with the last chocolate dessert and was looking forward to enjoying it before drifting off to sleep. Just as my head hit the pillow, a voice came through the VHF radio:

'*Spirit of EDF*, *Spirit of EDF*, *Spirit of EDF* this is *Atlantic 4*, this is *Atlantic 4* do you copy, over.' The first thing that went through my head was: 'Man, the radio still works!' followed closely by, 'It's only got a range of five miles, so they must be close,' then 'Hang on, that's *Atlantic 4*, the last time we heard anything, they were seventy miles ahead of us; we can't have caught them up, there's only two of us!' All this ran through my mind before my hand even reached the radio.

'*Atlantic 4, Atlantic 4* this is *Spirit of EDF*, we read you, over.'

'Hey, guys, it's George here, fancy a rumble do you? Over.'

'Hey, George, it's James, what do you mean? Over.' Ben had stopped rowing, opened the cabin hatch and was listening like a puppy.

'You've been taking about twenty miles a day off us for the last week and we just got your position from *Sula* [the second support yacht] and saw you were nearby, over.'

'Shit, we've got no idea what's happening. We capsized about 500 miles ago and lost the sat phone, GPS and water maker. We've only just found out that the radio works, over.'

'We had no idea. Are you guys OK? Over.' George asked.

'Yeah, OK now, we were both shaken up. Ben was rowing and got the worst of it but we got going pretty quickly after and have just been racing to get off this bloody boat, over.'

'You're not kidding, you're 150 miles ahead of *C2* with 220 miles left, over.'

What? Had I just heard George right?

'Say that again, we're 150 miles ahead? Over?' I asked.

'Correct, over.' George repeated the magic words. I let out a whoop and even Ben smiled.

'George, can you do me a favour and call my wife and say we're OK and will be in Antigua in a couple of days, over.' I gave him Bev's mobile number.

'OK will do, I'll radio back in a minute, out.'

Any hangover of the argument between Ben and me had disappeared; I felt amazing, we were much closer to Antigua than we thought and so far ahead there was no way we could be caught. We were going to win. I grabbed Ben round the back of the head as he was leaning into the cabin and said, 'Well done mate, well done mate.'

'*Spirit of EDF, Spirit of EDF, Spirit of EDF* this is *Atlantic 4*, this is *Atlantic 4* do you copy, over?' Did we ever.

'George, it's James.' All radio etiquette gone.

'James, I've spoken to Bev. Both your families are in Antigua, in fact they're just finishing dinner in a restaurant, over.' Bloody hell, they didn't waste much time. Ben was smiling like a Cheshire cat. Not only were we going to come in first, but our families were going to be there to welcome us.

'George, thanks for doing that; the beers are on us when we get there.'

'No problem, have a good night, out'

All of my fatigue and pain had dissipated during the course of the conversation. I still had an hour to go until my shift and I lay down and tried to sleep, but it was no use. I could visualize us arriving in Antigua and for the first time I was really looking forward to it. Eventually I might have been satisfied with just crossing the Atlantic, but to me it would never be the same knowing that someone else had made it before us. We weren't explorers rowing across uncharted waters, so finishing first was the next best thing. I couldn't wait. We were going to win; all the times we'd pushed hard and all the luxuries we had gone without to make the boat lighter had been worth it.

BEN

'*Spirit of EDF Energy*, this is *Atlantic 4*, do you copy, over?' crackled the radio.

James leapt from the bunk, and I threw down the oars. It was the first contact we'd had in nearly ten days and we both huddled around the small radio unit.

'We copy,' blurted James.

'Good to hear from you, this is George; we sent you a cheeky text a few days ago when you overtook us and were worried we'd upset you when we didn't hear back, over.'

It felt great to talk to someone again. We told him about the capsize and that we had lost our satellite phone and been out of contact ever since, and it sounded like *Atlantic 4* had been struggling too. They had almost run out of food and water and were down to strict rationing. According to George, they had been told that we were just a few miles away from them and they had decided to check we were OK.

'So, we're ahead of you?' ventured James. I could predict where this was going. 'Who else is ahead of us, over?' he added.

There was a long pause. 'Er, no-one – you're 150 miles ahead of the next pair, C2.'

We both fell silent as broad smiles stretched across our faces. It was the first smile I'd seen on James's face for weeks. His eyes sparkled as he sighed with relief and an enormous weight suddenly seemed to lift off his shoulders. He was a different man.

'Can you do us a favour and make some calls for us, over?' we asked. George kindly agreed and we gave him Beverley's and Marina's numbers. 'Shall I tell them about the capsize?' he asked. James and I looked at each other, 'Yes' we answered in unison.

I was nervous. I was convinced that my obituary had been written, and had been dogged by nightmares of Marina in mourning. Our loved ones had no way of knowing how we were, and our only hope had been that the Argos tracking beacon was still transmitting our position, showing everyone back home that the boat continued to move.

There was a long pause while George dialled the numbers.

'*Spirit of EDF*', this is George, over.' We waited with bated breath. 'I've just spoken to Beverley, she was eating with Marina and both your parents,' he continued. 'They're all in Antigua. They've been there for three days already waiting for you, they were expecting you today.'

Blimey, I thought, as I marvelled at all this information.

'It didn't take much to get them out to Antigua did it?' smiled James.

'Oh and one other thing,' said George, 'Beverley has put in a request that you don't come in during the middle of the night.' James rolled his eyes; according to his spreadsheets we were due in at around two o'clock in the morning, and the chances of us slowing our progress were about as likely as James settling for second place.

'And Marina passed a message that she loves you and that you're to row harder and make sure you beat the four-man crew.'

Marina was referring to *Atlantic 4* – our nearest competition – and hadn't cottoned on to the fact that this boat was also the vessel she was

251

on the phone to. George will have loved that, I thought, as I turned my attention to the home stretch.

Chapter Eleven

The Finish

Wednesday, 18 January 2006, 10 p.m.

1 *Atlantic 4* (four-man boat), 2,886 miles

2 **EDF, 2,879 miles**

3 *Team C2*, 2,768 miles

4 *Bout de Vie*, 2,523 miles

5 *Scandlines*, 2,296 miles

6 *Row 4 Cancer*, 2,285 miles

JAMES

Conditions didn't feel that different, but the miles were clicking past much slower. Perhaps the difference was psychological? After all, we'd won the race and it was just a case of completing the last few miles. Confident now that we weren't going to get overtaken, I began instead to think about arriving and seeing my family.

It felt similar to some races I've done in the past, in that the most painful finishes were often not those that were neck and neck all the way to the line, but rather the ones where I knew at halfway that I was going to win. With your lungs screaming, legs burning and throat rasping, a close race takes your mind off the pain, but when you think the race is won it is impossible not to start counting down to the finish line. That's when the metres start ticking past slowly.

I kept trying to tell myself that anything could happen in the last 200 miles and that the race wasn't won yet. We should have known better than anyone that it only takes a second for your whole world to turn upside down, literally, but my mind was saying, 'Who are you trying to kid? It's in the bag.'

I had found the last few days to be a real struggle, and I tried to focus solely on taking each shift at a time as a way of knocking the miles off. The nights were harder still, though; we were down to our last three chocolate bars and with at least a couple more nights on board, we decided to ration ourselves to half a bar a night, so that we would have a 'pick-me-up' in case we got a sugar low. I was finding it increasingly hard to concentrate as a result of the pain in my bum and the industrial-strength painkillers and visibility wasn't good, with the clouds masking the stars and only a sliver of moon offering any light.

I thought I could see something on the horizon behind us. It looked like a ship's mast, but I knew that they normally had lights on the top. I stopped rowing, stood up, leant on the cabin and had a good long look behind. The constant movement of the waves made it difficult to see anything. I must have been imagining it. I got back on the oars but fifteen minutes later there it was again, still behind us but further to the south this time. It was definitely a mast with no light; it was too far away to see the yacht itself, but surely its lights would come into view soon?

It was definitely heading our way and I could just make out the body of the yacht. It had no lights at all, and it was starting to freak me out. I ducked into the cabin and grabbed the VHF radio.

'Sailing boat, sailing boat, sailing boat this is an Atlantic rowing boat, Atlantic rowing boat, do you read me, over?' No response, so I called up again. Nothing. I decided to wake Ben up.

'Mate, can you come out here? Something strange is going on,' I said.

'OK,' he said, 'what time is it?'

'You're on in twenty minutes anyway, buddy,' I said; the actual time of the day was irrelevant. 'This is going to sound weird, but I think a yacht is following us.'

'It's probably *Sula* coming to check up on us,' he reasoned.

'That's what I thought, but there are no lights on and I tried the radio but nothing. Can you see the mast?' I pointed behind and to the north, where the yacht had tacked so that it was closer still.

'Let's watch it and see what happens, it could just be a yacht saving power,' Ben mumbled through his chocolate ration.

'Its movements haven't been random, it's been tacking directly behind us. Could be pirates,' I suggested. Ben's snort of laughter made me think he didn't take it that seriously.

'What, you think Johnny Depp's after us?' he chuckled, very pleased at his *Pirates of the Caribbean* gag.

I was deadly serious though; there are plenty of big yachts with wealthy people on board floating round the Caribbean at this time of year, and they aren't exactly well protected. Mind you, my theory fell down pretty easily, as I couldn't explain why they would be coming after a tiny rowing boat like ours, unless they wanted a couple of chocolate bars and a mouldy pair of Lycra shorts.

While I'd been explaining my conspiracy theory to the chocolate-munching sceptic behind me the yacht had got closer still, and we were now both convinced it was following us. 'Call them on the radio again,' I told Ben. Once more receiving no response, he went to the bows and grabbed a white parachute flare from the pockets on deck. We were just debating whether to fire it when a searchlight started to sweep the sea: it was definitely looking for us. I was both terrified and intrigued; I wanted to believe it was the safety boat, but couldn't understand why its lights weren't on and why it was refusing to respond to the VHF. When we last had full communications *Sula* was in Antigua, and if they had had an electrical problem it would have been sorted out then. A safety boat with no radio wasn't much use.

Suddenly, the searchlight blasted us right in the eyes, they'd seen us now, so there was no point in firing the flare unless we were going to use it as a weapon. We could hear voices coming from the boat, but couldn't even make out what language it was, let alone hear what they were saying.

The yacht was virtually on top of us now. 'Ben, what colour is *Sula's* hull?' I asked.

'I can't remember,' he replied. Either way, we were about to find out. There were four or five people on deck, and they didn't look much like pirates – but then, what do pirates wear these days?

There were more shouts from the yacht: 'It's us. *Sula*.'

'Thank god,' I thought, but then I got angry and shouted, 'What are you doing? Why aren't your lights on? You scared the shit out of us.'

'We've got a fuse problem. Are you guys OK?'

Fuse problem? It obviously didn't affect their radar or GPS, just the lights. Ben told them about our capsize but I didn't feel like making polite conversation. I was convinced they had snuck up on us on purpose, because we'd been going as fast as *Atlantic 4,* who had twice as many people. Maybe they thought we were cheating?

Small talk over, they said goodbye and turned south, and I left Ben to start his next shift. I ducked into the cabin only to hear over the VHF, ten minutes later, '*Atlantic 4, Atlantic 4, Atlantic 4* this is *Sula*, this is *Sula* do you copy, over?'

Right away, I called up Sula: '*Sula, Sula, Sula* this is *Spirit of EDF*, *Spirit of EDF*, over.'

'Go ahead *Spirit of EDF*, over.'

'You got your electrics working then, over.'

'Er yeah, it was just a fuse, over.'

'Give *Atlantic 4* our best, out.'

I stuck my head out of the cabin to talk to Ben. 'Why did they sneak up on us?' I asked.

Ben tried to console me by reminding me that previous competitors in the race had said they became paranoid.

'I'm not paranoid. I'm really pissed off!' I replied.

As it happens, my pirate theory wasn't so far off the mark after all. We found out later that another boat in the race had experienced it at first hand. *Move Ahead* crewed by Bobby Prentice and Colin Briggs was a boat we'd bonded with before the start because they were having as many problems as us. Ours had largely been due to a lack of preparation, but their main challenge had been a hull that was full of holes that were proving impossible to seal, meaning that the boat filled with water as soon as it put to sea. They only just made it to the start line and suffered problems from the outset: during the first storm their sea anchor got ripped from the boat, taking the rudder with it and leaving them at the mercy of the wind, while the repairs on the leaks didn't hold, so they had to stop and bail out once a day. Their race ended when they suffered irreparable damage after capsizing, forcing them to switch on their EPIRB, abandon ship and deploy their life-raft. Over fifteen hours later they were picked up by a yacht, but they weren't allowed below deck and were given no food or water. Two hours later they were forced off the yacht and back into their life-raft, drifting in the open ocean until a tanker rescued them. The only explanation for the behaviour of the people on the yacht is that they were either pirates and wanted to see if Bobby and Colin had any valuables on them, or that they were drug smugglers who, having picked them up, realized it probably hadn't been the smartest move. Either way I felt vindicated for my fears.

My worries didn't stop with pirates. To complete the race, our boat had to cross a one-mile-long stretch of water just south of Antigua; if we didn't, we would be awarded a DNF (Did Not Finish). Even if we'd made it into Antigua's English Harbour (where the boats were to be moored), missing this tiny stretch of water would mean that all of our efforts so far would count for nothing in the official records of the race. I had been concerned about hitting this line almost since setting off from the Canaries; currents around the Caribbean islands are so strong that it is essential to get your approach right. The location of the finish had been switched from Barbados to Antigua after a number of crews in previous races had got to within sight of the island, only to be swept south with no chance of getting back. Having rowed 3,000 miles, they had to suffer the indignity of being towed into the finish.

If crews missed the finish line but rowed a few degrees west, they would be credited with crossing an ocean but not with having finished the race, a consolation prize I was determined to avoid. Our nautical chart showed the average wind strength in this part of the world and the directions it usually came from in December, January and February. The most frequently occurring winds were the north-easterly and easterly trade winds, although winds from the south-east were also fairly prominent, especially in the last 500 miles to Antigua.

By now we were heading almost directly west (268 degrees), but clearly the winds weren't going to blow consistently from the east, so we had to decide whether to stick to our bearing regardless of the wind direction. If we encountered an easterly, fantastic: it would push us directly on our course; a north-easterly or south-easterly would hit us from 45 degrees and make life harder and more uncomfortable, but we would at least stay on track. The alternative was to go with the wind: if we rode the north-easterly and got blown further south than we wanted, there was a good chance that a south-easterly would blow us northwards.

Riding the winds in this way would mean that we would do more miles, but the extra speed gained would, we thought, more than make up for it. The risk was clear, though: we might get blown too far in one direction, and if that happened then our only solution would be to drop anchor until the wind turned – except, of course, we didn't have a sea anchor any more. Gambling with the wind direction was going to be a big decision, but it was more like Russian Roulette than a flutter on the Grand National.

Ben was in favour of going with the winds, which surprised me because throughout our journey, they had hardly ever blown in the predicted direction. Ben had the final say on navigation, but hitting a one-mile-long finish line from a starting point 3,000 miles away would be difficult on a lake with no wind; on an ocean with strong currents, fast winds and poor GPS, it seemed to me to be well-nigh impossible.

Ben was amused by my scepticism, but I wasn't convinced that we'd end up anywhere near Antigua. We had last seen land some forty-seven days before, as the Canary Islands disappeared over the horizon. Since then we'd headed south-west for a few hundred miles and then turned west, sticking pretty much on that bearing for the last 2,000 miles. I struggled to believe that Antigua would appear on the horizon. Without land as a reference point, the only real indication that we were actually going anywhere was that the sun was setting later and later, which at least gave me hope that we hadn't been rowing in circles for two months only to arrive back in the Canaries.

Ben thought we didn't need to concentrate on the finish line until we got to within 50 miles, whereas I was adamant that it could be too late to do anything about it by then, if we found ourselves to be too far south. We agreed to plot our position every couple of hours on the chart using the hand-held GPS and in the meantime to keep trying the main GPS, which was beginning to show signs of life again, if only for a minute at a time.

Our course wasn't my only worry, however; for the first time in the race, I felt really weak and unable to work hard. Even when we'd run out of water or been surviving on significantly fewer calories than we were burning, I'd still managed to push myself and to row hard, and I was genuinely worried by sudden loss of strength. To top it all, my bum was also getting more and more sore; the time had come for Ben to examine it again.

I broke the good news to him and adopted the position. He informed me that it was 'looking much better'; I wasn't convinced – he might have been avoiding telling me the truth, knowing that it wouldn't be long before we'd be on land and have access to a doctor – but I hoped he was being honest. On land he admitted it was the former, but at least it gave me an opportunity to tell him, without feeling too guilty, that I'd been using his toothbrush since the capsize.

My bum wasn't the only area that was suffering; the blisters on my hands and feet now had yellow pus inside them and the numerous cuts on my hands, arms and legs from constantly being knocked about by the boat were becoming infected. I had cold sores on my lips, my tongue had a layer of scum on it and the lymph nodes in my groin were the size of grapes. All in all not a great look; my body was fighting a massive infection, but I was cold and tired and couldn't sleep. I couldn't understand why my body had fallen apart so quickly.

BEN

As we rowed into the final hundred miles of our journey the profound difference in our motivations became more and more apparent. For James winning had been everything and with twenty-four hours to go it was obvious that we were almost certainly going to win our class. The last few miles were simply about getting to Antigua and with that sole aim James's immense psychological power began to evaporate.

He was desperate to see his family and friends but, unlike me, it had never been the thing that kept him going in those dark sessions. As I stared, frightened at his increasingly rapid decline, I recollected a conversation we'd had a few weeks previously. Unusually for James he had enquired about what went on in my head:

'What do you think about when you're mid-session?' he had enquired.

'Oh, you know, Marina, our weekends together, trips to the seaside walking the dogs. I tend to relive memorable moments – my trips to the Amazon and travels in South America – and I plan future adventures. I get myself as far away from here as possible.'

I've always been able to travel huge distances in my mind – I'm a born daydreamer and that imaginative capacity is definitely something that's got me through tough times in the past, particularly on *Castaway*. But these dreams weren't solely distractions; plans for new adventures were what spurred me on to Antigua. My life to come with Marina was one shimmering vision I pulled my oars for every time I took my seat.

'Why, what do you think about? What drives you through the toughest hours?' I asked.

'Our speed, how better to take advantage of the winds, whether or not we're following the right course, how to improve our chances of winning, basically.'

That pretty much said it all.

As I watched James's body deteriorate, I couldn't help but think that the motivation that had propelled him to Antigua was about to be his downfall. He was terrifyingly weak with infections springing up all over and his mental health was also continuing to crumble. Assessing his parlous state I realized two things: my strength was relatively undepleted and my motivation was stronger than ever. We were close to Antigua and all my family and friends – the reason I had kept going. One look at James's face, drawn with pain, and I decided I was going to use those two factors to get me and James to the finish as fast as I possibly could.

JAMES

On our sea survival course we had been told that 'To the emergency services, you are only considered a survivor when you get home.' The theory is that the human body is incredibly tough (as we had found out) and will force itself to survive in situations that don't seem possible, but that when your eyes tell your brain that help has arrived, the body seems to stop looking after itself, expecting someone else to do it for you. Apparently, this is why so many people relapse when the emergency services finally reach them.

Maybe that's what had happened to me. I was so concerned about winning that when I heard from *Atlantic 4* that we were 150 miles in the lead with only 220 miles to go, my mind told my body that we'd won and that it was all over, allowing it to fall apart. The problem, of course, was that we *weren't* there; and if the weather turned against, we could be on the boat for anything up to another week.

Ben, on the other hand, was coping magnificently. Maybe because his goal had always been simply to get there. He hadn't achieved that yet, so his mind was urging his body to keep working whereas mine had given up the ghost.

I was determined to do my share, although it was getting harder and harder for me to last a full two hours so I asked Ben if we could take the shifts down to ninety minutes. Apart from feeling weak I was struggling to sit on the seat for that long, and to make things worse the wind had shifted and was starting to blow us south. We could not afford to let that happen. We were only forty miles away from Antigua and in danger of missing the finish line, so we were forced to row with the wind at 90 degrees to the boat.

Waves were hitting us side-on, frequently knocking us off the seat, and every time that happened the pain shot up in my bum, making me scream out loud. The pain was bad but a broken seat would be worse, and with the abuse it took every time one of us got knocked off I was convinced it had been broken. The final run-in looked like it was going to mirror the rest of the trip; as soon as we thought things were going our way, something would come along and ruin it.

The next forty miles weren't going to fly by since the wind direction looked set, but as long as it didn't pick up we should be able to hold or course. As Antigua slowly approached we had things to look forward to. We knew Alexis was going to hire a helicopter to get some aerial shots for the documentary and would want us to be a long way from land, so we were hoping to see him soon. Fifteen miles from Antigua we had to radio the coastguard informing them of our arrival and at some stage we would see land, although given the amount our speed had dropped in the last few hours, that wasn't going to happen in daylight.

BEN

'Dikadikadikadikadikadikadikadikadika,' came a low bass grumble, audible over the din of the wind.

A helicopter hoved into view, swept in low over the ocean and soared past us. I could just make out Alexis's familiar beard, and the camera strapped to his shoulder.

'Whoooooooohaaaaaaa!' he screamed as the helicopter flew past us at 150 mph. His smile lit up the sky. He was beaming with pride, giving us the thumbs up. It was exhilarating watching as the helicopter circled overhead filming us from the air. I was surprised to realize I felt tremendously proud.

For an hour Alexis stayed with our little boat as we beat against the increasingly powerful northerly wind. Waves broke over the side of the boat, drenching us with salty water, while the powerful downdraught from the helicopter rocked us precariously with each low sweep of the chopper.

And then, as quickly as it had come into view, the helicopter disappeared. It would take us the best part of a day to cover a distance they would cover in just a few minutes. Once again we were left alone to battle the ocean.

JAMES

The wind was getting stronger and it was becoming harder to stay on course; water was constantly coming over the side, soaking everything on deck, including the open sores on my bum, the stinging salt water making me wince with every wave. I put the oars down and sat there shaking my head. It was agony; I was going to have to get Ben to take over. I couldn't row, it was too painful. I'd cut back on the painkillers because they had made me so drowsy, but there was no alternative but to start taking them again if I was going to contribute. I told Ben that I needed a break, and he bounded out of the cabin like a puppy; being within touching distance of his goal had energized him. He started rowing with a determination and enthusiasm that I wished had been there the whole journey.

Inside the cabin, I chastised myself for stopping. I felt worse every time I glanced outside and saw Ben struggling into the wind. The GPS seemed to work if we held the power button pressed in; not practical, but at least it was possible to see our progress, speed and bearing. As nice as it was to see, the information wasn't that inspiring, however: our speed had dropped to 1 knot and as I had feared all along, we were heading too far south and were in danger of missing the finish line. I stuck my head out of the cabin.

'You OK?' I asked.

'No, not really. I'm struggling to hold the course,' Ben grunted. He was rowing with only his right oar in an attempt to keep the boat on the right heading. 'I think you're going to have to help out,' he panted. I nodded and went up to the bow position, where the broken seat was screwed down. I looked at it thinking, 'This is going to hurt,' but luckily I only needed to use one oar. I rowed with my right oar, rocking forwards and backwards to make up for the lack of a sliding seat, and pushed my left hand down on the edge of the seat so as to take the weight off my bum. It was just about bearable and it seemed to be working; up in the bows I had more leverage so I could keep the boat straight, allowing Ben to row with both oars and propel the boat forwards. We were facing a long night, but at least we were making progress – just.

Our families were expecting us to arrive around midnight. *Atlantic 4* had arrived at 10 p.m. and told us over the radio that they were concerned that we might be blown south of the island. We were south of their position the last time we had spoken, and according to George they had really struggled to get home with two fully working rowing positions and a reliable GPS.

In retrospect it wasn't the best thing to admit to a group of worried parents, friends and other halves, who between them managed to turn *Atlantic 4*'s concern into a panic that we were going to be blown south, miss Antigua and never be seen again. Fortunately, neither of the two four-man crews that were ahead of us had missed the finish line, otherwise the panic might have turned into hysteria. In the weeks that followed, of the twenty crews that finished the race, three – *Atlantic Warrior*, *Row4Life* and *Sedna Solo* – missed the finish line and weren't credited with a final race position.

Meanwhile, we'd reached fifteen miles to go; it was time to call the coastguard. Ben got on the radio while I kept the boat straight. 'Antigua coastguard, Antigua coastguard, Antigua coastguard this is *Spirit of EDF*, this is *Spirit of EDF*, do you copy, over?'

'*Spirit of EDF* this is Antigua Coastguard, go ahead, over.'

'We are fifteen miles out and heading for Cape Shirley Lighthouse, over.'

'OK, out.'

Ben looked a little put out by the short conversation; it was the first person unconnected to the race that we'd spoken to since the Russian voice on the tanker six weeks ago, and I think Ben was hoping for a 'Welcome to Antigua! You guys are amazing!' We had a lot of work to do before we hit the finish line, though – or to be more accurate, Ben had a lot of work ahead of him, with him rowing and me making sure we stayed on course. I opened the last chocolate bar and gave Ben most of it; after all he'd done most of the rowing over the last four hours.

There was still no sign of Antigua. By now I'd hoped to be able to see the lighthouse we were aiming at, but the big swell was making it difficult to get a good look at the horizon for enough time to focus properly. It *had* to come into view soon. The wind turned slightly and it was now possible for Ben to keep the boat straight without me. I was cold and shivering but determined to row another shift before we got there. Ben was happy to keep rowing, though, fuelled by his enthusiasm at being so close.

The cabin was in a real state; waves had crashed in when we opened the hatch to talk to the coastguard and it was nearly as damp in there as it was on deck. I lay back and tried to get some rest.

I wasn't sure how long I'd been asleep, but when I pressed the button on the GPS we only had nine miles to go. We were so close. I Vaselined my bum, pulled on my wet lycra shorts and headed outside, to be greeted by the twinkling lights of Antigua's airport. Never has a runway looked so beautiful and I gave Ben a slap on the back. He'd been rowing non-stop for over four hours and would have carried on if I hadn't literally manhandled him into the cabin.

BEN

For the first time, we saw the ethereal glitter of distant lights that promised land. Somehow I couldn't quite believe it was really Antigua. (James was convinced that it was in fact La Gomera and that we had just done one huge circle.)

It is difficult to explain how it feels to cross an ocean, as there are no landmarks to confirm your progress. For nearly fifty days we had stared out at the same vista, with little indication that we were moving anywhere except for subtle changes in the timing of sunrise and of course the hand-held GPS, which indicated that we were indeed moving in the correct direction.

JAMES

Whether it was the painkillers or the sight of land that took the edge off the pain I wasn't sure, but I was able to row. More lights kept appearing on land and out on the water as we started to encounter yachts around Antigua, and I flicked our running light on so that they could see us. The last thing I wanted was a collision so close to the finish. We were approaching what I thought looked like a tall buoy with a light on top. It was lurching side to side in the water but on closer inspection it seemed to be moving. I'd just identified it as the mast of a boat when I heard the muffled sound of a radio in the cabin.

BEN

'Attention unidentified yacht, do you copy?' I yelled above the wind.

'Echo, Delta, Foxtrot. This is *Bacaloa*.'

How did they know who we were?

'We have some special people aboard, over,' he continued.

'Ben,' crackled the familiar voice; it was Marina, I recognized it instantly.

'MARINA!' I screamed, 'MARINA!'

'We can see you, we can see you!' she yelled excitedly. I could just make out some figures on the dark deck.

'We?' I asked. 'Who's with you?'

'Well, just a few people, there's your father, sister, Chiara, James's parents, Jake, Charles…' she reeled off the long list of names.

All my hairs stood on end as it began to sink in that they were all there, so close, there on that invisible deck. I looked at James for reassurance that I wasn't dreaming. His eyes were swimming in a hallucinogenic cocktail of painkillers.

JAMES

'Are you both OK? Is there anything we can get you?' Marina asked Ben.

'I'm fine but James isn't so good. He's got septic sores,' he replied, which was certainly a polite way of describing the state of my ass.

With the noise from the wind and the sea, 'septic sores' was misheard as 'septicaemia' over the radio, which made Bev and my family incredibly worried. To make matters worse, apparently our advance meeting party was also suffering from seasickness and a certain amount of shock from experiencing some of the conditions we'd been through during the last seven weeks. The skipper of the yacht wanted to get back before any more seared tuna was regurgitated over his deck and he didn't receive many complaints from his passengers as he headed back to English Harbour, leaving us to row the last few miles alone.

BEN

'Where's the lighthouse gone?'

The northerly wind had whipped the ocean into a bitter cauldron. Huge waves broke against our tiny boat, dousing us with each swipe and crashing against the rocky shore.

'Where's the fucking light gone?' I shouted over the din of the howling gale.

Through the inky gloom we could make out the silhouetted coastline, but the lighthouse we had been following for nearly twenty miles seemed to have vanished.

'They must have turned it off!' I bellowed into the wind.

'They can't have turned off a fucking lighthouse, check the GPS!' shouted James.

I flew through the hatch and peered into the familiar blue screen. According to the computer we were just a mile from the finish line, dead ahead. I peered back out into the darkness. Nothing. No lights. No harbour. No grand welcome party, just vast waves crashing on to the rocky foreshore. This wasn't the heroic finish we had been dreaming of. Where was the finish line?

'Are you sure we have the right coordinates?' shouted James, who was again forced to row one-handed to counteract the powerful northerly wind that threatened to blow us away from Antigua and in the direction of Guadeloupe. 'Fucking lighthouses don't just disappear!' shouted James before throwing down the oars in frustration.

By now we could clearly make out the mountainous white surf as it crashed against the bleak coastline. It was three o'clock in the morning and we had been rowing against the northerly wind more than twenty-four hours.

We rowed on into the gloom, as vast waves enveloped the boat. The shore was just a few hundred metres from us now, but the GPS told us it was another mile to the finish line. There were still no lights, no welcome party. If we came ashore here we'd be smashed up on the rocks. What the hell was going on?

'Antigua coastguard, Antigua coastguard!' I hollered into the VHF handset, 'this is *Spirit of EDF Energy*, we're lost!'

Somehow we had rowed 3,000 miles across the Atlantic Ocean, survived gales, a capsize and acute dehydration and now, just a hundred metres from the finish line, we were lost.

'This is Antigua and Barbuda coastguard,' came the reply, 'can we have your position?'

I blurted out our coordinates as our tiny boat edged ever nearer to the shore.

'You have to go around the peninsula,' came the reply. 'You can't row through it,' he added dryly.

Sheepishly and without a word, we turned the boat south and followed the foreshore around the craggy peninsula.

Through the darkness a small white light sped towards us. 'Whaaaaaaaaahooooo!' cried its crew excitedly as it screamed past us, before disappearing back into the gloom.

I continued to row, as James was taking a much-needed break. The speedboat appeared again. 'Come on!' they hollered. 'You're nearly there!'

Where? I wondered. For all we knew we were rowing in the English Channel; for forty-nine long days we had trusted our little blue screen, and never once questioned that we were heading in the right direction.

JAMES

We heard the roar of an engine and turned round to see the Woodvale RIB approaching.

'We must be really close to the finish line,' Ben shouted over the wind.

'I bloody hope so,' I said.

The RIB pulled alongside. 'One mile to go!' they shouted.

'Do you hear that mate, we're into the last mile, about half an hour left, that's all. I'm looking forward to a burger!' I jabbered excitedly.

What seemed like only a minute later an air horn blasted from the RIB and they all started cheering; we'd finished. It was the quickest mile and the biggest anticlimax to the finish of a race I've ever been involved in. We were still a mile away from land, it was four in the morning and there was nobody apart from the organizers there to see it. We shook hands, but it didn't feel right to celebrate until we set foot on Antiguan soil.

We entered English Harbour, threading our way through millions of pounds' worth of yachts to the berths set aside for the rowing boats. A group of people came into view, huddled together on the dock. They were all standing so still, I wasn't sure if they were there to welcome us or not; but then why else would so many people be standing on a dockside at 4 a.m.? Ben stopped rowing as we glided towards the dock and faces started to become recognizable: Mum, Dad, Bev… Where was Croyde? Was he here? There still wasn't any cheering and I wondered whether it was because we weren't recognizable, since we hadn't shaved since we left and had lost a lot of weight. I fended the boat off with an oar and stepped on to land, my legs immediately giving way beneath me. Someone grabbed my arm to steady me and a champagne cork popped in the background. As cameras flashed the small crowd cheered. Where was Bev?

My wife came out of the crowd, whoever was holding my arm let go and I staggered towards her. She was crying and saying, 'Are you OK? Are you OK?'

'I'm sorry. I'm sorry,' was all I could say, and instead gave her a kiss.

'Daddy, Daddy!' I recognized the voice but not the person who'd said it, he'd changed so much. I tried to give him a big kiss, to which Croyde said 'Spiky! Spiky!' and I turned to look for Mum and Dad, all the time shaking hands that were thrust in front of me.

There was one person I'd yet to greet on land: Ben. We'd both been completely absorbed by seeing our loved ones, but I wanted to thank him for an amazing journey. We were the first pair to reach Antigua. We embraced and congratulated each other, but considering the emotions we'd shared over our 3,000-mile voyage, the gesture felt almost formal. As much as I wanted to see my family, it would have been nice to have had a few minutes by ourselves on land to celebrate the moment together. There are things I wanted to say then that won't sound the same now. There was only one moment to say them and we missed it. I wanted to tell him that I couldn't have done it with a better partner. I wanted to tell him that I'm more proud of crossing the Atlantic than anything else I've ever done. And I wanted to tell him that next time, he'd better not forget the bloody sheet.

BEN

We sat there in stunned silence, our tiny boat bobbing about in the fierce swell.

'We've done it, dude,' I smiled, 'we've fucking done it.'

For the first time in days, a smile crept on to James's face.

The speedboat pulled alongside, and half a dozen unfamiliar faces leant over and embraced us. We had crossed the finish line but English Harbour was still another mile away, and the coastguard wanted to tug us in.

It was four in the morning and the harbour was stony silent as we edged past dozens of yachts, our tiny boat dwarfed by their masts. As I rowed towards the deserted jetty, I could hear my mother's voice and we were swathed in bright light. I could make out the silhouettes of dozens of people, and for the first time in forty-nine days I couldn't feel the wind in my face.

Dazzled, James leapt ashore and immediately collapsed on his weakened legs. Camera bulbs flashed, blinding me with each blink. Why was it so quiet?

'Ben!' I heard my mother call again, as I staggered from our little boat. My legs were like jelly, my head was swimming. I had dreamt of this day. I had longed for it and prayed for it, and at last I was here.

My mother embraced me, as the crowd gathered round. Why was everyone crying? Even people I didn't know had tears in their eyes.

I watched James as he embraced Croyde and Beverley, tears streaming from his sunken eyes. Away from the boat, I was suddenly struck by how different he looked. He just didn't look like James; I recognized the wispy beard and the square jaw, but he looked so small.

Marina appeared from the crowd, her blonde hair shining, her beautiful eyes brimming with happiness. How I had longed for this moment. I had dreamt of her, hallucinated about her. I had longed to hold her, smell her, breathe her.

I buried my head in her neck, tears streaming down my face. Was I still dreaming?

I wandered around in a daze, I held Marina tight, I rested my forehead against her face and closed my eyes, it was all too much. What had we done?

Where was James? I needed to talk to him, I needed to thank him.

'James!' I called, like a child lost in a crowd. This was the longest we'd been apart in seven weeks. He'd become part of the furniture.

'Thanks, dude,' I said as we hugged. 'You saved my life,' I added.

'We saved each other's lives,' he smiled.

Epilogue

BEN

It was 4.40 a.m., we were in Antigua and as far as I was concerned I had just landed on Mars. I starred goggle-eyed out of the window as we sped passed tiny wooden shacks and banana trees. My knuckles turned white as I gripped the seat with fear. For two long months we had crawled along at just a few miles per hour, and now we were bouncing across the Caribbean island at 80 mph. I wondered whether I was actually dozing in the cabin, about to be woken by James's 'Ten minutes till you're on, buddy.'

I buried my head into Marina's neck and breathed in deeply.

'Welcome to Antigua,' beamed the concierge as he opened the door.

James stepped from the taxi. 'I'm off, I'm off,' he hollered as his body lurched towards the hotel's lily pond. Beverley saved him just in time from a swim with the goldfish.

'Whoooa,' I cried as I collapsed in a pile. My legs had given way under me. James and I zigzagged over the wooden bridge, swaying wildly. James's eyes were wide and haunted. He looked crazed. I wondered whether I looked the same.

'Are you hungry?' asked Bev. 'You can have a hamburger if you want.'

James and I looked at each other and smiled. We had both longed for a burger and chips.

I didn't want this moment to end.

'Goodnight, James,' I smiled as Bev led him to her room. 'Night, buddy,' he replied, his eyes still bulging. This was the first time we would be apart in two months. It felt strange, seeing James disappear with his wife. Marina supported me as we walked down the long sandy path to our room. I loved her more than words could describe.

It was strange sleeping next to Marina again. I felt slightly ashamed at the fungus that had taken over most of my body, including my groin. We lay, side by side, together again in the unfamiliar surroundings of our palatial room. I rowed all night, convinced that the air-conditioner was the sound of the wind. Marina couldn't sleep for my arm twitching.

James was sitting at a table alone as I stumbled into breakfast. It was bright, and I was mesmerized by the sound of the waves crashing against the sandy beach, a noise we hadn't heard during our crossing. The table was littered with plates and bowls. 'I've been through the entire menu,' smiled James. 'And now I'm starting again' he chuckled.

The next day a small boat came to pick Marina and me up from the beach of our hotel. Marina looked beautiful in a white linen dress. She glowed, I thought, as we sped along Antigua's rugged coastline. It was peculiar to be back on a boat, and even more so to be speeding at 30 knots, nearly ten times our average rowing speed.

The boat pulled into the small bay of a tiny, deserted island. We waded ashore and lay a blanket on to the sands. The boat disappeared and I was alone with Marina.

'Will you marry me?' I smiled as I dropped to one knee.

I was nervous. We had never discussed marriage, and I wasn't sure she was ready for such commitment.

'Will you be my wife,' I added as Marina dropped to her knees too.

'YES,' she said, kissing me, 'YES, YES, YES.'

I fished into my pocket. There had been no time to buy a ring. James and I had discussed my proposal on the crossing and James had suggested one of the large orange plastic hoops from the oars. 'Offer it as a wedding bracelet,' he had suggested helpfully. While I was touched by his thoughtfulness, I resolved to make her a ring out of the tiny Spanish pennant, the one that had plagued our every waking and sleeping moment. It had become an unlikely symbol of our epic adventure: I had cut the thin piece of rope from the tiny flag and knotted it into a delicate rope ring.

I fished it from my pocket and slid it on to her finger.

'It's perfect,' she shone, 'just perfect.'

The hotel had packed a specially requested picnic hamper, filled with some of the things I had longed for on the ocean. I dipped in for two mugs, unscrewed the lid of the Thermos flask and poured us two steaming cups of Earl Grey tea.

'To the Atlantic,' I grinned as we clinked our mugs.

JAMES
Wednesday, 8 March 2006

I turned the page in my diary and was greeted by a black cross. March the 8th – why did I mark that date? I stared at it blankly, racking my brain for a few minutes. Surely it couldn't be… I counted the days backwards and after forty-nine (the length of our voyage) reached 19 January. The day we arrived in Antigua.

I remembered putting the cross in my diary a few days after we landed to try to make me appreciate how long our trip would have seemed if I'd been at home. Forgetting the cross summed up just how different life on land was. On the boat I'd have known exactly when and why I'd made such a mark, but back home even on a 'dull' day so many different things happen.

I looked back over the forty-nine days I'd been on dry land and for every day that I could remember there were two or three that I had no recollection of. The memories of all those days at sea seem to be etched on my brain, enhanced by smells, feelings, my relationship with Ben at that time, our position, boat speed and the weather conditions.

In the days since my return I'd made some significant decisions about the future direction of my life. It's impossible to say how much these decisions were influenced by the trip across the Atlantic, but the major reason for my taking part in the race was to have some time away to allow me to think about what I was going to do in the future and, more specifically, whether I wanted to compete at the Beijing Olympics. Before the race I was 70:30 in favour of carrying on, by halfway across I knew it was 'no'.

Speaking to Ben in the cabin and listening to the variety of things he had got up to in the last five years had made me long to have some different experiences. I have been incredibly lucky to have been a full-time athlete. I have raced at World Championships and Olympic Games. I have achieved my dreams. The highs were fantastic, but there were also lows, the sacrifices made were enormous.

I was convinced when I agreed to take part in the race that I could cope with the regime of training seven days a week and the lack of variety because I'd done it before and the Olympic flame still burned within me. But what could satisfy me in the way the Olympics had? It wasn't hours of soul searching on the Atlantic that made my decision for me; it wasn't even as some people have suggested that I'd just had enough of rowing by the time I'd reached the Caribbean. I knew it was time to stop when I was lying in the cabin unable to sleep for a second night, beating myself up because I thought we were slipping behind in the race and that I couldn't do anything about it. We were fifty miles in the lead at that point. Before we had set off I'd promised myself not to get too caught up in the race and to enjoy the experience and yet there I was, unable to sleep and driving myself mad. I knew I was competitive but I didn't realize how strong that impulse was. In the cabin that night it became obvious that I didn't miss rowing or even the Olympics, I just missed being competitive.

That may sound like semantics but to me it was like finding a way of dealing with the problem that every athlete faces when they stop competing: how do they replace that competition in their lives? I didn't miss rowing, I missed being competitive, so I realized I could stop rowing and would be happy as long as some part of my life was spent doing things that really challenged me.

I've tried to avoid using the cliché of the race being 'a life-changing experience' – that would be too strong to be true. But there is no doubt that I found out a lot about myself – especially the effect I have on people around me. I realized my straightforward (some would say uncompromising) attitude which I thought made me easy to get on with actually has a dramatic effect on people close to me, especially if they are looking for reassurance and support rather than the most honest answer I can give them. I also now understand how difficult I must be to live with and, having spent nearly two months away from Bev, how lucky I am to be married to her. When I came off the boat she had a doctor ready to check I was all right and spent the first week of my being back on land rubbing cream on to my blistered ass. If ever there was a test for true love that was it.

When I told Jürgen, my coach, about my decision to quit the Olympic team, he pretended to be disappointed for a few minutes and then asked, 'How hard was it?'

'What, deciding to stop?'

'No, the row?'

For a moment I thought he really cared about my decision-making process. I should have known better.

'I wish I'd done it before I was a serious athlete. I thought I knew what it was like to be exhausted and what the body could take but it can absorb so much more. You weren't really training us that hard after all.' He just raised his eyebrows. Later that day I got a text message from Steve Williams, a crewmate from the Athens Olympics who's in training for Beijing. It simply read 'Bastard!' I think his training might have just got harder.

The question I've been asked most since I've been back is: 'Are you still talking to Ben?' Others who've done the race together have never spoken again. Well the answer is 'yes'. During seven weeks at sea I got to know somebody I wouldn't have spent time with otherwise. That we managed to mould ourselves into a successful team is testament to the bond that formed between us.

I hadn't seen Ben that much since the race. He'd been busy climbing mountains, trekking through the rain forest and mucking about with polar bears in the Arctic for the BBC. So we agreed met up for a barbecue at Henley during the regatta. It was the first time we'd been there since our first outing as a pair. That first training session in the autumn of 2005 had been cold and uninviting. Leaves had littered the fields. Just a few rowers and my old rowing coach, Jürgen, had turned up to laugh at us. In the intervening ten months Henley, like our relationship, had changed beyond all recognition. The fields were now covered with marquees and grandstands, there were tens of thousands of spectators, hundreds of rowers, and enough Pimms to swim in.

We watched a couple of races and concluded that despite our Atlantic row we didn't stand a chance in boats that narrow. We turned and wandered back to the barbecue.

'James, have you got a minute?' Ben asked.

'Yeah, what's up?'

'I'd really like you to be my best man. We went through so much together it would mean a lot.'

'Mate, I'd love to.' That didn't really capture the feeling of what it meant to be asked. I was incredibly touched. It wasn't just that he'd asked me to be his best man. It was the realization that the crossing was as important to him as it was to me.